P9-AQM-813

THE VOICE OF PROSE

FINKELSTEIN
MEMORIAL LIBRARY
SPRING VALLEY, N. Y.

Boris Pasternak

THE VOICE OF PROSE

VOLUME ONE

edited by
CHRISTOPHER BARNES

Grove Press, Inc., New York

870304

English language translation ©Christopher Barnes 1986

All rights reserved.

No part of this book may be reproduced, stored in a retrieval system, or transmitted in any form, by any means, including mechanical, electronic, photocopying, recording or otherwise, without prior written permission of the publisher.

First published in 1986 by Polygon Books, Edinburgh

First Grove Press Edition 1986
First Printing 1986
ISBN: 0-394-55604-6
Library of Congress Catalog Card Number: 86-45238

First Evergreen Edition 1986
First Printing 1986
ISBN: 0-394-62285-5
Library of Congress Catalog Card Number: 86-45238

Library of Congress Cataloging-in-Publication Data

Pasternak, Boris Leonidovich, 1890-1960.
    The voice of prose.

    1. Pasternak, Boris Leonidovich, 1890-1960—
Translations, English. 2. Pasternak, Boris Leonidovich,
1890-1960—Biography. 3. Authors, Russian—20th
century—Biography. I. Title.
PG3476.P27A22 1986   891.71'42 [B]   86-45238
ISBN 0-394-55604-6
ISBN 0-394-62285-5 (pbk.)

Printed in the United States of America

Grove Press, Inc., 196 West Houston Street
New York, N.Y. 10014

5   4   3   2   1

In memory of Dr. Nikolay Andreyev

COPYRIGHT ACKNOWLEDGEMENTS

The translation of "Three Dramatic Fragments" first appeared in ENCOUNTER magazine in July 1970, and is here reprinted by kind permission of the editors.

"Dramatic Dialogue" © Nicolas Slater (translator). "Letters from Tula" and parts of "The Quintessence" and the Introduction appear by permission of Messrs Holt Rinehart and Winston (formerly Praeger Publishers) © 1977.

Max Hayward's translation of "Without Love" was first published in *Dissonant Voices in Soviet Literature*, by Max Hayward and Patricia Blake. Copyright © 1961 by Partisan Review. Reprinted by permission of Pantheon Books, a Division of Random House, Inc., New York. British copyright © by George Allen & Unwin Ltd., Hemel Hempstead.

The Russian text of "Suboctave Story" first appeared complete as "Istoriya odnoi kontroktavy" in *Slavica Hierosolymitana*, No 1, 1977, published by the Magnes Press, The Hebrew University of Jerusalem, Israel. The Magnes Press and the Pasternak Trust are thanked for permission to publish the present translation.

Manuscript variants from "Some Propositions" were first published by Professor Lazar Fleishman, who is thanked for permission to translate them here.

CONTENTS

PREFACE

Until three years ago no separate edition of Pasternak's prose had been printed in the Soviet Union since before the Second World War, and his reputation in his native land has continued to rest mainly on his verse and translations of foreign poets and dramatists. In other countries of the Western world, on the other hand, his prose fiction has enjoyed greater prominence. The novel of Pasternak's later years, *Doctor Zhivago*, remains almost constantly in print, and in recent years there have also been sensitive English translations of selected verse and publications of his correspondence, as well as important monographic studies by Henry Gifford, Ronald Hingley, Lazar Fleishman and Guy de Mallac. Paradoxically, though, apart from the novel, almost none of Pasternak's fiction, articles and essays has been readily available to English readers for many years. The present two-volume edition is designed to help fill this gap.

This edition is in fact the most complete English-language collection of Pasternak's prose so far to appear. The only significant omissions are the novel *Doctor Zhivago*, easily accessible under separate cover, and the half-finished dramatic trilogy *The Blind Beauty*, which appeared with Collins & Harvill in 1969. Other shorter items not included are more marginal to Pasternak's achievement and are less likely to be appreciated by the general English reader. Several early prose fragments, Futurist polemics and essays, reviews and articles on some European writers such as Kleist and Baratashvili, or Russian authors little-known in Britain such as Aseyev or Kruchenykh, may indeed be worth translating, but their presentation seems to me to involve a rather different and more specialised type of publication than the present one.

But despite all these omissions, the size of Pasternak's prose output is impressive enough to confound a frequently expressed view of him as primarily a poet. It is true that his prose writings are sometimes, and with reason, described as the "prose of a poet". Yet it would be quite wrong to think of Pasternak as a poet who simply happened by chance to compose a certain amount of prose. In fact, for lengthy periods of his career he worked concurrently in both prose and verse genres, which in

1

effect complemented one another. And while his prose often displayed themes and devices found also in his dense and more complex poetry, it was often only in prose that some of his most important artistic statements were possible.

The distribution of writings in these two volumes is mainly chronological, and also for this reason to a large extent thematic. The contents of volume one might be described in rough and ready fashion as "aesthetic prose" (i.e. describing or illustrating themes and problems of art and the artistic personality), as distinct from the second volume's "historical prose" (i.e. works not necessarily on historical topics, but evidencing an awareness of history, which inevitably impinged on the author's existence in post-Revolutionary years). The present volume thus contains mainly works written before or during the year 1918. The one exception is the earlier of Pasternak's two autobiographies, "Safe Conduct", first published complete in 1931. Because of its date, this work in some senses already belongs to, and partially describes, a period of Pasternak's life that was already deeply grazed by history – even some pre-Revolutionary episodes, such as the evocation of tyranny in Venice's past, are illuminated by recent Russian historical experience and conceal Aesopic parallels with Bolshevik rule. Nevertheless, "Safe Conduct" is notable mainly as a unique record of Pasternak's youth and early manhood, a period when the foundations of his artistic personality were laid in his musical pursuits and intoxication with Scriabin, his studies of philosophy in Moscow and Marburg, his discovery of Rilke and exposure to Russian Symbolist culture and the avant-garde movements of the 1910s. Moreover, "Safe Conduct" contains frequent excursions into the nature of creativity and describes experiences and approaches to literature that correspond more closely to the verse Pasternak wrote up to 1918 and to the prose of the same period included here, than to what he was writing in the later 1920s and 1930s. In more senses than one, therefore, Pasternak's first autobiography was a retrospective work.

Another slight anomaly in this first volume are the "Dramatic Fragments" of 1917. Their genre, first of all, is different from the other autobiographical or fictional prose items. Two of the three are also in blank verse and not in prose, and all three fragments raise directly or indirectly the "non-aesthetic" and topical theme of the Russian Revolution. In this thematic respect the "Dramatic Fragments" coincide with the prose fragment "Without Love". Yet all these works present a view of revolution, and thus of Russia's contemporary history, which complements the artistic personality and philosophy expressed in other

2

works of this volume. And they are recognisably different from what emerges in some later, more historically conscious writings included in volume two. The reason for departing from our own prose genre prescription in the case of the "Dramatic Fragments" is the importance of these unjustly neglected works for understanding Pasternak's reaction to what was going on around him in the summer months of 1917 and their relevance to other prose works written close in time. In addition, they also provide a brief glimpse of his *poetic* creativity about which so much is said, without illustration, in other parts of this book.

Four of the pieces in this first volume, as well as some in the second, consist partly or wholly of writing which has not before been translated into English. "Safe Conduct" in the version presented here contains passages which were omitted for ideological reasons in the original 1931 publication. Characterisations of the Bolshevik regime (Part Two, § 11), of the old Venetian public security and penal system (Part Two, § 17), and of the tsarist *ancien régime* (Part Three, § 1), as well as other shorter episodes, have here been restored and rendered in their original manuscript versions. "Suboctave Story" was never completed by Pasternak, but sufficient of it survives to make it publishable; the contents of one missing chapter can be reconstructed, and a readable and intriguing text can be pieced together from the other variant readings left by the author. The dramatic "Dialogue" appears here translated for the first time; we have not included articles of Pasternak's Futurist period, "The Wassermann Test" and "The Black Goblet": their archly convoluted polemical style makes them accessible only with difficulty to a modern English reader, although some of the more important ideas they contain have been outlined in the Introduction. Much more striking than these juvenilia, however, is an article printed here under the title "The Quintessence". This represents the complete, manuscript version of an abbreviated text which Pasternak published under the title "Some Propositions". (A fairly clear idea of the authorially sanctioned "Propositions" can be gained by mentally ignoring the final two sections of the text printed in this volume.) The inclusion of such incomplete or suppressed versions of Pasternak's works seems justified not only on scholarly grounds, but also because it provides an interesting glimpse into the backstage "laboratory" of his art. (It is only regrettable that for lack of space it has proved impossible to include also the early manuscript variants of "Zhenya Luvers' Childhood". To insist on including certain rejected episodes in the main text would have unduly marred one of Pasternak's finest pieces of finished writing, while their

3

accommodation in an appendix would have necessitated a fussy and detailed apparatus.)

The present translations of Pasternak's fiction and other prose works are probably only a pale and partial reflection of the often splendid originals. However, they can fairly claim, I believe, to be more accurate than several earlier translations of the same works. But, like all translations, they represent a compromise between various conflicting and irreconcilable elements. In his originals Pasternak often achieved a convolute density of expression, which is accessible to Russian with its inflected endings, verbal aspects and lack of articles, but is not at all congenial or germane to English syntactic habits. Moreover the earlier prose writings contained in this first volume were like Pasternak's early verse: a consciously brilliant display of imagic and verbal pyrotechnics in which the author showed a kinship with contemporary writers of "ornamental prose" in deliberately taking the literary language beyond traditional notions of what was possible or natural. Later on Pasternak rejected most of this early work. In the "Autobiographical Essay" (see volume two) he described his literary hearing as "marred by whirligigs and the fracturing of everything normal", and he confessed that "everything said in a normal manner rebounded off me". After several unsatisfactory attempts at translating Pasternak's early prose into equally mannered English, I have reluctantly concluded that such renderings of his earlier style produce a turgidity and awkwardness that appears to originate with the translator rather than the author. Much more than Pasternak's Russian, therefore, the versions in this book err towards what *can* be said "in a normal manner" in the target language, and while the imagery has been preserved so far as possible, several synctactic whirligigs have been unwound. Perhaps what has been lost in this transference might be preserved in other translators' approaches, and the present versions are thus offered as only one of several possible renderings.

These two volumes of prose are intended primarily for a general reader with little or no knowledge of the Russian language, literary tradition and background. The introduction in each volume is designed to provide some information on Pasternak's life and times (in addition to what can be gleaned from "Safe Conduct" or the "Autobiographical Essay"), to place his prose writings in context and to offer some ideas about their interpretation. Where the texts at certain points require more detailed information in order to be properly understood, this is given in the notes at the end of the book – a numeral in the text refers to these annotations. The notes themselves are by no means exhaustive. They concern mainly Russian figures and phenomena and presume an intelligent reader's familiarity with most of the remaining Western European cultural references.

The transliteration of proper names from Russian in this edition follows no absolutely rigid system. The spellings adopted are a compromise between traditional, though non-English, versions (e.g. Tchaikovsky), the demand for some consistent approach, and the need for a phonetic rendering to assist non-specialist readers. In cases where Russian surnames derive from an obviously German, French or other antecedent (e.g. Glière, Gay), these names have sometimes been restored to their original pre-Russian spelling.

I am grateful to Mr David Shankland of Polygon Books for the opportunity to present these translations as part of the new Polygon Russian series, to Miss Anna Antilli for her patient editorial work, and to my wife for her interest, critical reading and typing skills. At various times, Julius Telesin, Father Michael Fortounatto and Tatyana Chambers have also given generous advice on the understanding and translation of numerous difficult passages, and I wish here to record my thanks to them. I am specially grateful to Dr Nicolas Pasternak-Slater for allowing us to include his translation of the dramatic "Dialogue". It stands here not only in its own right as a first-rate and readable rendering of his uncle's Russian original, but also as a link with the Pasternak family as a whole, to whom I have an unrepayable debt of gratitude for many years of interest, assistance, encouragement and friendship. The appearance of Max Hayward's version of "Without Love" is also partly a symbolic and grateful token of recognition for his encouragement several years ago to translate Pasternak's prose works; apart from his collaborative efforts in *Doctor Zhivago* and *The Blind Beauty*, this is the only work by Pasternak which he translated. Finally, the dedication of this edition of Pasternak's translated prose to the memory of Dr Nikolay Andreyev records one further debt of many years' standing to an unforgettable and much beloved teacher and friend.

St Andrews   Christopher Barnes
May 1985

INTRODUCTION

Both from his own point of view and that of his readers, there were two obvious climactic points in Pasternak's career – an early fecundity and fame as the lyric poet of *My Sister Life* and *Themes and Variations* (both written for the most part in 1917–18 and published in 1922 and 1923), and his later, graver and more ambitious achievement as novelist-author of *Doctor Zhivago*, published in 1957. This sequence in itself suggests a gravitation from lyric miniatures to monumental prose narrative as Pasternak moved towards maturity. Yet, despite this shifting emphasis, he worked throughout his career on both poetry and prose with equal attention, viewing them as related aspects of the same basic creative process. As he wrote in 1918, "poetry and prose are two polarities, indivisible one from another". Later on, too, at the First Congress of Soviet Writers in 1934, he again underlined the essential oneness of poetry and prose:

> What is poetry, comrades, if its birth is such as we have witnessed here? Poetry is prose. Prose, not in the sense of someone's complete prose works, but prose itself, the voice of prose, prose in action, not narration. Poetry is the language of organic fact – that is, fact which has live consequences. . . .

Writing about Pasternak's short prose in the 1930s, Roman Jakobson described it as "the characteristic prose of the poet in a great poetic epoch". In stating this he was not pointing out faults or virtues so much as indicating a certain quality or accent in Pasternak's prose style which is not normally considered native to the genre. Perhaps it is symptomatic that the central character of the early short stories "The Apelles Mark" and "Letters from Tula" is a poet. And the close and permanent symbiosis of verse and prose is confirmed in *Doctor Zhivago*, where the two idioms are shown to combine: Zhivago's life as a sustained piece of objectified biography in prose, with the creative essence of his personality distilled in verses that form the concluding chapter of the novel. In fact, some form of poetic, or poetically inclined, *alter ego* appears in most of Pasternak's prose and serves to illuminate and explore a vital aspect of the author's own personality. His vision is thus rarely that of a detached, 'realist', or omniscient observer, but rather that of a poet who in landscapes, characters and situations invariably discovers a function of his own self.

Pasternak's early identification of a poetic centre of gravity for all his writing, regardless of form or genre, reflected the artistic priorities of Symbolist culture, which he imbibed as a youth and student, and of the Futurists with whom he made his literary debut. The underlying theories of both these movements variously emphasised the role of imagery and trope as part of a renewal of literary language which pointed obviously towards poetic rather than prosaic expression. Also, as Pasternak said in "Safe Conduct", the very lateness of his literary debut after a youth in which verbal expression was sacrificed to the wordless communication of music was in itself a guarantee of eccentricity and linguistic novelty, and this too developed qualities in his prose which are more usually associated with poetry.

Pasternak's emergence in literature took place under the aegis of Futuristic innovation, but he was never by temperament an avant-gardiste, iconoclast or mindless rejector of inherited values. His childhood was spent in a Muscovite artistic intelligentsia household. His father was a celebrated painter and friend of Tolstoy, his mother was a concert pianist and former protégée of Rubinstein, and their home was regularly visited by artists and intellectuals. From his infancy, therefore, communion with artistic genius was for Boris Pasternak not something confined to museum, library or concert-hall, but a living and shaping presence in everyday life. A further factor that rescued him from the frivolous excesses of Futurism was, again, his relatively late emergence in literature. The decision to follow this profession was evidently taken at the age of twenty-two, while he was studying in Marburg in 1912. By this time the foundations of character and taste were already firmly established.

Pasternak's first polemical sally in 1914 in "The Wassermann Test" was more than an empty piece of Futurist spear-rattling. Some of it reflected an ephemeral conflict with Burlyuk's Cubo-Futurist group (a manifestation of "false Futurism", characterised by its mediocre, self-opinionated spokesman, Shershenevich). But out of the contrast of his own position with Shershenevich Pasternak succeeded in formulating some of the ideas that remained central to his own concept of creativity: genuine art, he argued, was not written consciously or mechanically. True poetry arose from the unconscious and its metaphor might often defy attempts to explain or understand it. The basis of Pasternak's poetic imagery was thus not a rationally explainable metaphor generated by obvious similarity or contrast, but an altogether more random association based on coincidence and contiguity. Later on Pasternak's "Safe Conduct" talked in similar terms about the "interchangeability of images", and basing himself on this, Roman Jakobson spoke of metonymy (as distinct from metaphor) as being the general characteristic of Pasternak's perception and expression. This quality is as discernible in his early prose as in his verse. In "Zhenya Luvers' Childhood", for example, the lamps in a room are "warm, zealous and faithful", reflecting the relief felt on a human plane at a family reconciliation; and in "Safe Conduct" the jingle of cowbells is itself "sucked by gadflies" as the music's own hide moves in sudden twitches. Examples of such imagery in Pasternak's prose can be cited ad infinitum.

The posturing and style of Pasternak's early polemics inevitably hinted at a certain romantic flamboyance and personality cult on his own part. But this was a shortlived tribute to Futurist group behaviour and Pasternak himself later specifically rejected the romantic label as smacking of an unwarranted form of exhibitionism. Yet there is nevertheless an aspect of romantic aesthetics in the emphasis on a ubiquitous poetic presence that observes and establishes metonymic links with *nature morte* and landscapes, and in later works such as "Safe Conduct" which stress the role of subjectivity and the unconscious – or even in "The Quintessence", where inspiration is described as a form of possession, and the poet as a medium rather than an active agent. Thus, if Pasternak is a romantic, he is so in the manner of Keats rather than of Byron (he translated both poets into Russian – the former with specially fine understanding), and he could share a Keatsian claim to an empathy with all creation, resulting in a quite "unpoetical" loss of personality.

The Cubo-Futurists, however, perpetuated a modified version of the Symbolist generation's neo-romantic myth-making. As Pasternak explained in Part Three of "Safe Conduct", this involved an unnatural self-dramatisation by the poet both in his writings and in his life, and it presupposed a contrast between the poet's passionate and coruscating personality and the dull philistinism of the general public. Pasternak's acceptance of this behaviour pattern was brief and he quickly suppressed it in himself as something alien to him. The romantic approach, prevalent among other innovator contemporaries, was epitomised by the life and art of Mayakovsky. Pasternak's strongest early statement against this brand of romanticism was made in "The Quintessence" (1918) which he published in 1922 under the title "Some Propositions", and later on he more than once confirmed the article as a statement of permanent conviction with him. Without naming Mayakovsky specifically, Pasternak inveighs against the theatricality of much contemporary poetry, a quality which recent war and revolution had helped intensify. Yet even earlier than 1918 a number of Pasternak's other prose writings had explored and countered the "grand manner" of romanticism, and two of his stories did so with reference to some traditional nineteenth-century Romantic material.

Though not lacking humour, Pasternak emerges in "Safe Conduct" and elsewhere as at least a solemnly self-aware artist. In view of this, his first complete short story, "The Apelles Mark", written in 1915, shows a perhaps surprising lightness of touch. It also strongly demonstrates the author's familiarity with German literature – the opening, for instance, is strongly reminiscent of Heinrich von Kleist's "The Marchioness of O". But the story is more than a fanciful pastiche; it has satirical and polemical implications. Relinquimini, whose very name suggests that he is destined for abandonment, previously appeared in several of Pasternak's unpublished semi-autobiographical prose sketches. In "The Apelles Mark" his exaggerated romantic posturing is made to look stupid when his rival, the Westphalian poet Heinrich Heine, answers his challenge to a literary contest by transferring it from the realm of literature to that of real life and seduces Relinquimini's mistress. Heine's sortie to Ferrara and his merry exploits there are thus in fact a serious probing of the frontiers between literary invention and reality. Heine rapidly identifies the rival's literary heroine as his mistress Camilla Ardenze and thus identifies the reality behind the romantic illusion. The banal truth that "all the world's a stage" is thus established, all people are actors, not just Relinquimini, and the value of the latter's pretentious performance is thus denied. It is also no coincidence that Heine is the name of a nineteenth-century German poet who regularly used irony to expose the naïveté of Romantic poetic statement. Paradoxically, his apparent frivolity is a sign of seriousness and of a down-to-earth realism which contrasts totally with Relinquimini's ponderous make-believe. Moreover, Heine is successfully recognised by Camilla as a true poet. And although he had artfully planned how his visit to Camilla might end, all artifice is erased in the genuine passion which they finally awaken in one another. Thus Heine on the author's behalf traces his Apelles Mark.

"Suboctave Story" was written some eighteen months after "Apelles Mark" and was left as a half-finished manuscript which was only rediscovered and printed after the author's death. It too shows signs of Pasternak's reading of the German Romantics and in particular contains echoes of E. T. A. Hoffmann's tales on musical themes, and of Kleist's "Saint Cecilia, or The Power of Music". The story tells of a nineteenth-century provincial town organist in Germany who surrenders to inspiration during an improvised fantasia and unwittingly causes his son's death by crushing him in the instrument's coupler mechanism (a highly unlikely occurrence, particularly in those days of hand-blown bellows and tracker action!). Almost immediately the guilt-ridden musician flees the town. Several years later, though, he makes a mysterious return and applies for reinstatement. But the local worthies on the council are outraged at the suggestion, and for a second time and finally the hapless organist is ushered out of town. There are several motifs here that recall earlier Romantic models. The most obvious one is the impiety and guilt which earth-bound bourgeois morality attributes to the artist-outsider. But more important and relevant to Pasternak in this presentation is the idea of the artist who appears to wield elemental forces, yet is in fact himself wielded by them and is the mere fulcrum for their operation. The ability of artistic involvement to shape or destroy and to exercise power over life and death was to become apparent in an almost unfathomable, legendary manner in Pasternak's later life. But even the early "Suboctave Story" has some interesting autobiographical aspects. It obviously reflects numerous German impressions from Pasternak's student days in Marburg and also from an earlier visit to Berlin in 1906 with his parents, when he and his brother made frequent pilgrimages to hear organ music in the Gedächtniskirche. Also of interest is the fact that in winter 1916–17, when the story was written, Pasternak was suffering acute anguish and nostalgia for the musician's life which he had given up soon after meeting Scriabin in early 1909 (see Part One of "Safe Conduct"). Some of this feeling no doubt lies behind the story's inspiration.

The image of the poet as an actor recurred regularly in Pasternak's work, and with it the concomitant problem of literature involving the artist in either a staged fiction or else the serious "untheatrical drama" of real life. "Letters from Tula" (1918) deals with the topic in relation to a poet and a performing actor and makes a paradoxical reversal of their expected roles. The setting this time is contemporary Russia. Tormented by a powerful amorous passion, the young poet sees the vulgarity of his attempts to express it mirrored in the behaviour of a rowdy troupe of film actors. He is overcome with disgust. But the shooting of some film sequences in Tula has been witnessed also by an elderly retired actor. He too is perturbed by what he sees, but unlike the poet he is able to express and artistically consummate his feelings. Returning home, he employs a masterly stage technique to play out a little scene for himself in his lodgings and in this way he brings back to life a part of his own past. The successful artist is thus shown to be the one who does not strive to articulate passion by posing to a public or a lover. The old actor's art is equally genuine back at home, away from the stage. He needs no platform posture, and his art is "real". He needs only to achieve "complete physical silence within his soul", sublimating passion and allowing accumulated impression and living experience to speak through him.

The idea of the artist as medium rather than agent is shown once again in "Letters from Tula" to be of central importance for Pasternak's art. It also manifestly transcends mere aesthetics and becomes a moral issue for the artist's conscience – hence the significance of Tolstoyan references in the story. The same idea is expressed again in "The Quintessence", written nearly at the same time. In the third of these "propositions" there is, characteristically, hardly a mention of the artist in the first person singular. A book, we are told, has a life of its own, its own memories and experiences, and the artist is there only to assist these in finding verbal expression. Later on "Safe Conduct" too reiterates this principle in insisting that "In art man falls silent and the image speaks out". And like his early prose stories, Pasternak's lyric verse provided ample evidence of this, showing a lyrical personality yielding up its voice to surrounding image and metaphor which speak on its behalf and metonymically engulf it.

Russia has enriched world literature with some unique evocations of childhood. One thinks, in particular, of the well-known accounts by Tolstoy, Gorky or Bunin, but the list can be extended and must certainly contain Pasternak's masterly "Zhenya Luvers' Childhood". This was written during the Russian Civil War as part of a full-length novel. But the novel was never finally completed and was eventually destroyed before publication, apart from this one section which was printed separately in 1922 and stands alone as a complete story. In one of her poems Anna Akhmatova describes Pasternak as "endowed with a sort of eternal childhood", and the studied naïveté of his artistic approach – allowing "Sister Life" to write itself – corresponds closely to the childlike vision recreated in this story. "The childhood of some people takes place in towns that do not at all resemble everything that is said about them by those forming their population," Pasternak wrote in an early review article. He was not, of course, the first to discover the disparity between language and immediate experience. Many Russian and Western poets, philosophers and philologists of the past had been aware of it. But it was experienced with especial acuteness and vigour by the Russian twentieth-century avant-garde, who displayed new techniques and even created "transmental" languages to convey this new awareness. At more or less the same time the Formalist critic Viktor Shklovsky described and explained how Tolstoy had used *ostraneniye* ("making strange") in the nineteenth century, and some new prose writers of the 1920s, including Olesha, Nabokov and Pasternak, began cultivating their own novel form of vision, showing the world as viewed through fresh and "innocent eyes".

As in "Safe Conduct", conventional biographical elements are only nominally present in "Zhenya Luvers' Childhood". The author hastens over the introductory formalities and plunges as quickly as possible into his young heroine's world of vivid, immediate sensations. These surround Zhenya as she experiences her first encounters with life, and it is in terms of these fresh, sometimes frightening, inchoate perceptions that such adult concepts as "cards", the factory at Motovilikha, the town, and "Asia" are first presented to the child's mind. By contrast, the world of grown-ups is one of dull and too readily articulated thoughts, conventions and prohibitions, which serve only to obscure the true essence of "living life". There are, as Pasternak explains, very few adults who "know and sense what it is that creates, fashions and binds their own fabric".

If the first part of Pasternak's account of Zhenya's childhood is concerned with language and cognition of the physical world, including her own physicality, the second part shows her growing moral awareness and her developing perception of other human beings. She learns the meaning of being a woman, the suffering involved in loving, the giving and receiving of compassion. But, as in the first part, all these are instilled into her in terms of freshly experienced sensation for which there is no name, and which differs completely therefore from a conventional adult moral system of abstract principles and rules. It is therefore only at the end of the story that Zhenya realises that what she has experienced is what the Ten Commandments had in mind, and only then is the essentially Christian message of the story made explicit.

As with most of his verse and prose, the characterisation, incidents and setting of this "Childhood" are strongly linked to Pasternak's own experience. The unforgettable descriptions of weather and nature are from the author's own memories of his time in the Urals and Kama region during the First World War. Zhenya's perceptions clearly coincide with those of her creator. Like him, she is presented as unusual in the sensitivity of her observations and thoughts. Exactly why Pasternak projects himself into a specifically female character is open to speculation – part of the answer may lie in later sections of that now lost novel. Clearly, though, there is an intentional contrast between her passive, feminine open-eyed awareness, acceptance and appreciation of what life brings her way and the rugged, unnoticing practicality of her boyishly active brother Seryozha. Evidently the character of Zhenya Luvers meant much to Pasternak, and not only because this was his first story to achieve widespread critical acclaim. Some of his writings in the 1930s, and even some features of Lara in *Doctor Zhivago*, can be identified as relating to a now grown-up Zhenya Luvers.

A natural extension of Pasternak's artistic personality were his attitudes on public issues. It is evident that in an art in which man was silent and where only the image spoke on his behalf there was little room for an author's conscious discussion or pronouncements on social and historical themes. That part of his generation with which he grew up he later described in "Safe Conduct" as apolitical. His family belonged to the liberal intelligentsia, and as Jews from Odessa, his parents were well aware of the discriminations and injustices rife in the Russian Empire. At the time of the 1905 Revolution Leonid Pasternak supported the liberal reforms, while Boris was an excited schoolboy witness of revolutionary incidents some of which were enacted literally on their doorstep at the Moscow School of Painting. It was then, as he later wrote in a poem, that he "fell in love with the storm".

Pasternak's first professional literary involvements, however, were again with men who had little use for pamphleteering and civic stances. In a polemical article of 1916 called "The Black Goblet", Pasternak described a view of art which was no more than "a peculiar homework assignment" and whose sole requirement was that it be "executed brilliantly", and he inveighed against other poets who had dared to confuse the mutually exclusive realms of Lyricism and History. No names were named, but the obvious targets for attack included the Symbolist Bryusov with his jingoistic war poetry, as well as Mayakovsky, who was already exploring social satirical themes in his verse and as a poet

14

of the revolution was shortly to fall entirely into the thrall of History. Once again, though, in a nominally set-piece article commissioned by Bobrov, the "Tsentrifuga" leader, Pasternak succeeded in making an important statement about the central essence of his own poetic art. The black goblet was then, as now, a common symbol on packages to discourage tilting or breakage, and the article with this title emerged as a form of "safe conduct" not so much for the artist as for the fragile, lightning-swift sensations stored in his consciousness. It was not, of course, an apology for "art for art's sake". Pasternak fully acknowledged the "flattering, responsible, exceedingly important and urgent assignment" that art constantly received from the age. His objection was to the deliberate "preparing of History", the abandonment of Lyricism in a too single-minded pursuit of some historical assignment. Moreover, Lyricism had its own demarcation and frontiers which were clearly sketched out in the verse and prose Pasternak wrote in the revolutionary years.

Pasternak's emotional response to the upheavals of February and October 1917 was similar to his experience in 1905. He and his art remained uninvolved in any articulated political statement. At the same time he sympathised with the forces of protest and responded to the events with the thrill of one who sees himself as the privileged witness of an elemental happening which is world-shaking in its consequences and which he himself is powerless to affect or alter. Pasternak's Zhivago also went through the same experience and in a memorable episode of the novel described the October events as a splendid act of surgery and a marvel of history. But the rapture to which Pasternak and his hero were prone when faced by an awe-inspiring spectacle was essentially that of the non-participant. Shortly after news of the February Revolution reached the Urals where he spent part of the war years, Pasternak set off to return to Moscow. The journey, which was partly by sleigh, he made together with Boris Zbarsky, a family friend and at that time a committed Socialist Revolutionary. The sleigh ride is described in Pasternak's "Auto-biographical Essay" (see volume two) and impressions of it also went into the prose fragment "Without Love" which he composed the following year. Zbarsky and the author in fact served as prototypes for the revolutionary Kovalevsky and the day-dreaming Goltsev in this short piece. The lyrically musing Goltsev is described, paradoxically, as being in close touch with reality – the reality of remembered experience – while conversely the political activist Kovalevsky is shown as living in a fantasy world of revolutionary schemes. Like the grim adults in Zhenya Luvers' childhood, he simply misses the point of what life is really about.

15

"Without Love" is only a fragment. A subtitle describes it as a "chapter from a tale". Like "Zhenya Luvers' Childhood", it was printed as part of some longer prose work which remained incomplete and was eventually forgotten. Its rediscovery after Pasternak's death in an obscure Socialist Revolutionary newspaper was significant, however. It demonstrated that a central theme of *Doctor Zhivago* – the relationship between the hero and Pasha Antipov – had already been formulated in 1918 in the characters of Goltsev and Kovalevsky. In addition to this some other details, such as the episode of the accident and characters called Galliula, Gimazetdin and Mekhanoshin, all reappeared four decades later in the novel.

In June and July of 1917, the high summer of the Revolution, in addition to some of the poetry of *My Sister Life* Pasternak also wrote some dramatic fragments. The time of their composition in itself makes them of interest to us. The genre, too, is unexpected for an artist whose talents and personality were the the antithesis of anything theatrical. Pasternak resorted to dramatic form on only two other occasions – in an unpublished play called *The Here and Now*, written during the Second World War and containing material that eventually went into *Zhivago*, and in *The Blind Beauty*, a historical trilogy on which he was still working at the time of his death in 1960. The "Dramatic Fragments" appeared in the first half of 1918 in the Socialist Revolutionary newspaper *Znamya truda* (*Banner of Labour*), where they toned well with other contributions from poets such as Bely, Blok, Esenin, Oreshin and others, with their fervent nationalism, religious imagery, and their elemental "Scythian" view of revolution, with winds and blizzards providing a regular atmospheric backdrop to the poetic landscape. (Pasternak himself later drew on precisely this imagery for the setting in which Yurii Zhivago first learns of the new Bolshevik decrees in 1917 as he stands under a gaslamp and excitedly reads his newspaper as snowflakes fall around him.) A note of this mystic messianic patriotism sounds in Pasternak's dramatic "Dialogue". The work is set in France, evidently in the early twentieth century. An absent-minded Russian intellectual has been arrested for the theft of a melon and for preaching dangerous seditious doctrines in a public place. The dialogue consists of his interrogation by a police official and of his attempts to justify his behaviour. This he does by explaining his mysterious, Russian philosophy of life. He describes the nature of his Russian-ness as an inspired ecstatic involvement with nature and men and with all life's various activities. Hence his lack of concern for material surroundings or for private possessions, whether his own or other people's. By contrast with the earth-bound, inert

16

rationality and dullness of life in France, for Russians life is described as a state of spiritual combustion, a peculiar national quality akin to genius itself in its total commitment and sacrifice to an all-consuming purpose. In effect, what the unnamed Russian character describes is an accurate picture of his countrymen in the grip of revolutionary euphoria such as Pasternak himself witnessed and experienced in 1917.

The other two fragments also have a French setting, this time in past history. The action of both takes place during the Terror of 1794, with the historical figures of Saint-Just and Robespierre as chief protagonists. Carlyle's history of the French Revolution had for many years been favourite reading of Pasternak's and it probably fired him with the idea for a novel on the same theme in February of 1917. Very little came of this scheme, though, and it was soon followed by the plan for a drama on the last days of Robespierre – an echo perhaps of the German dramatist Georg Büchner's play *Danton's Death*. Nevertheless, at a time when the literary and political press were full of historical analogies and parallels, Pasternak's two fragments (all that survive of the planned drama) were an unmistakable form of comment on recent Russian events.

Since he was a professional revolutionary, there might seem to be little common ground between Saint-Just and the lyric poet. Yet some surprising and intriguing parallels emerge in the first of the two "Dramatic Fragments". Speaking in virtual monologue with only occasional interpolations from Henriette, Saint-Just gives an existentialist's account of the human condition. He defines man as "the Creator's sword of Damocles", who cannot rest content with the mere fact of birth and living, but must justify himself creatively as a "guest of existence". For Saint-Just revolutionary action is thus a form of creative, quasi-artistic activity, a sublimation of his love for Henriette, and a "flash of ecstasy unleashed upon the years". But as with the Russian character in the dramatic "Dialogue", this creativity is bought only at the price of total surrender to the creative forces that have been invoked, and by renouncing all right to control his own fate. And when the artistic medium is revolution, all this amounts to a triumphant form of self-immolation.

The second "Dramatic Fragment" is a dialogue between Saint-Just and Robespierre on the eve of their surrender in the night of 9–10th thermidor. Both men await destruction by a historical process they themselves have brought about and neither is capable of steering events further. But while Saint-Just exults in an act of creative sublimation, Robespierre is in a fury of despair and frustration at the abatement of his

17

mental powers. For unlike the artistic and emotional Saint-Just, he is the "incorruptible", the cerebral revolutionary ascetic. He curses his inability to control events by an effort of the intellect and he vainly seeks refuge behind now useless "barricades of concepts" and in "fortresses of intellect and reason". In these two contrasting revolutionary types we therefore discover a further adumbration of the Zhivago-Antipov relationship which actually antedates the October Revolution as well as the composition of the story "Without Love". In view of the author's attitude to revolutionary commitment in this latter work it seems strange to be seeking an analogy between the creative personality and the man of revolution such as Saint-Just was. The explanation probably lies in the early date of the "Dramatic Fragments", for they were written before the October events and the Bolshevik aftermath which helped to crystallise and polarise Pasternak's views. Again, there seems to be a parallel situation in *Doctor Zhivago*, a work which in many respects reconstructs the changing feelings and opinions of its creator during this period.

Between the February and October Revolutions, Yurii Zhivago is described as pursued by two "circles" of thought which constantly entangle. They represent not an allegiance to the "bourgeois" February Revolution and an abhorrence of the proletarian uprising – nor even an ambivalent attitude to the old order and the changes wrought in February and October – so much as an awareness of two quite different psychologies of revolution. The first circle of thoughts is described as containing Zhivago's "thoughts of Tonya: their home and their former settled life" and also "his loyalty to the revolution and his admiration for it, the revolution in the sense in which it was accepted by the middle classes and in which it was understood by the students, followers of Blok in 1905". What we know of Pasternak's state of mind at the time coincides clearly with the spirit in which Zhivago greets and enthuses over the mounting wave of revolution in summer 1917, and also the initial Bolshevik uprising. But then he is pursued also by a "second circle" of thoughts, and this one is occupied, *inter alia*, by a totally different view of revolution – "not the one idealised in student fashion in 1905, but this new upheaval, born of the war, bloody, pitiless, elemental – a soldiers' revolution, led by its professionals, the Bolsheviks". The first circle of revolutionary enthusiasm was almost as shortlived as the February Revolution itself, but the full effects of the second were quick to make themselves felt and were long-lasting. If October had brought its initial bright enthusiasm, within a few weeks Zhivago's family were overcome by sombre disappointment. His father-in-law recalls:

"Do you remember that night in winter, in the middle of a snowstorm, when you brought me the paper with the first government decrees? You remember how unbelievably direct and uncompromising they were? It was that single-mindedness that appealed to us. But such things keep their original purity only in the minds of those who have conceived them, and then only on the day they are first published. But the day after, the casuistry of politics has turned them inside out."

The change of attitude depicted in *Doctor Zhivago* probably reflects with some accuracy the course and chronology of Pasternak's own disillusionment and more anguished awareness of history. Regret at the subversion of the revolution by politics was implicit perhaps in the "Dramatic Fragments" and "Without Love", and the following years brought an increasing realisation that an initial revolutionary spontaneity had been smothered by doctrinaire rigidity and terror. None of this put a stop to Pasternak's creativity. After an interruption during the Civil War, when sheer poverty and hardship forced him to undertake translating and other paid literary work, poetry and prose flowed again during the 1920s, and Pasternak's contribution to a general blossoming of the arts under early Soviet rule was an impressive and significant one. But the effects of a new cultural environment and of history in a more abrasive and intrusive form also inevitably found reflection in the writings of Pasternak and of several contemporaries. Several of the works contained in the second volume of this set help us to chart Pasternak's further evolution in a new age.

SAFE CONDUCT

(To the memory of Rainer Maria Rilke)

Part One

1

One hot summer's morning in the year 1900 an express train left Moscow's Kursk Station. Just before it started, someone in a black Tyrolean cape appeared outside the window. A tall woman was with him. Probably she was his mother or an elder sister. They talked with my father about something familiar to all three of them and which evoked the same warm response. But the woman exchanged occasional phrases in Russian with my mother, while the other stranger spoke only German. And although I knew the language perfectly well, I had never heard it spoken like that. For that reason, between two rings of the departure bell, that foreigner on the crowded platform seemed like a silhouette among solids, a fiction in the thick of reality.

During the journey, the couple reappeared in our compartment as we approached Tula. They said the express was not supposed to stop at Kozlovka Zaseka, and they were uncertain whether the chief guard would tell the driver in time to pull up at the Tolstoys. From the ensuing conversation I realised they were going to see Sofya Andreyevna,[1] since she used to travel to Moscow for symphony concerts and had recently been at our house. But the immeasurable significance of the letters "Ct. L.N.",[2] which played a concealed, brain-teasing and smoke-befugged role in our family, received no embodiment. It had been seen too early in infancy. His grey head, later revived in sketches by my father,[3] Repin[4] and others, was long ago transferred in my childish imagination to another old man whom I saw more often and probably later on – Nikolai Nikolayevich Gay.[5]

Then they bade farewell and returned to their own carriage. A little further on the hurtling embankment was gripped by our brakes. Birch trees flashed, and there was a snort and racket of colliding coupling-plates down the length of the track. With relief a cumulus sky tore itself free from a vortex of singing sand. Crouched low as in dancing the russkaya, an empty carriage and pair half-turned as they emerged from a grove and flitted up to meet the people alighting from the train. Like a gunshot came a momentary thrill of silence at that rail-halt which had no knowledge of us. But we were not to tarry there. Kerchiefs were waved as they bade us farewell, and we responded in turn. We could still see as the coachman helped them into their seats. He handed the lady a dust-rug and stood up in his red sleeves to adjust his sash and tuck the long flaps of his coat beneath him. They would be off at any moment. . . . But then we were caught up by a curve in the track and, slowly turning like the page of a book, the country halt disappeared from sight. Both the face and incident were forgotten – forgotten, so it might have seemed, for good.

2

Three years passed. Outside it was winter. The street lost a third of its length to the fur-coats and twilight. The cubes of carriages and street-lamps slipped by noiselessly. The inheritance of proprieties, already inter-rupted more than once, was brought to an end. They were washed away by a more powerful order of succession – that of personalities with faces.

I am not going to describe in detail what went before – how nature was revealed to the ten-year-old in a sensation reminiscent of Gumilyov's "Sixth Sense",[6] how botany appeared as his first passion in response to the fixed and five-petalled gaze of a plant, and how the names identified in the manual brought calm to those fragrant pupils, which rushed unquestioning to Linnaeus, from obscurity to glory.

I shall not describe how in spring of 1901 a troupe of Dahomeyan Amazons was put on display in the Zoological Garden, nor how my first awareness of woman was bound up with a sense of their naked ranks and serried suffering, a tropical parade to the sound of beating drums. Nor shall I describe how, earlier than I should, I became a captive of forms because I saw in them too early the form of captives. Nor will I describe how in summer of 1903 at Obolenskoye, where the Scriabins[7] were our neighbours, the young ward of some friends who lived across the Protva was almost drowned while bathing, how a student perished when he plunged in to help her, and how she later went mad after several suicide attempts from that same precipice. I shall not describe how later on when I broke my leg and escaped two future wars in a single evening and lay motionless in plaster, the same friends' house across the river went up in flames, and the shrill village fire alarm went crazy and shook in a fever. I shall not describe, either, how the slanting sky-glow drummed and tautened like a kite being launched before curling its splint framework in a roll and diving with a somersault into the flaking pastry layers of grey-crimson smoke.

Nor shall I describe how, as he galloped back that night from Maloyaroslavets with a doctor, my father turned grey at the sight of the glowing cloud that billowed up over the woodland road two versts away – he was convinced it was his three children and the woman he loved who were in the blaze, together with a hundred-pound hunk of plaster of paris that could not be lifted without fear of crippling me permanently.

I shall not describe any of this. The reader can do it for me. He is fond of stories with plots and horrors, and he regards history as an endlessly continuing tale. Whether he wishes it to have a sensible conclusion is impossible to tell. Only those places beyond which he has never ventured on his walks appeal to him. He is completely taken up with prefaces and introductions, whereas for me life has only revealed itself at the point where he is inclined to start summing up. Quite apart from the fact that it is the image of inevitable death which has driven home to me the internal articulated structure of history, in life itself I have only come wholly alive on those occasions when the wearisome stewing of ingredients is over, and when feeling dines on a completed dish and breaks free, decked and rigged out in its full expanse.

And so, outside it was winter. The street spent the whole day running errands, and the twilight docked a third of its length. Falling back in a whirl of snowflakes, the streetlamps themselves whirled in chase. On the way home from school the snow-covered name of Scriabin leapt down from a poster and landed on my back. I bore it home on the flap of my schoolbag and water ran from it on to the windowsill. And that adoration racked me more obviously and cruelly than any fever. On seeing him I turned pale and then my very pallor would immediately cause me to flush deeply. He spoke to me and I lost the power of reason. I would hear myself answer something quite off the point and everyone would laugh, although exactly what I answered I never heard. I knew he had guessed everything already. But he never once came to my assistance. That meant he was not sparing me, and this was precisely the unresponding, unrequited feeling that I craved for. Simply that alone. And the more hotly it blazed, the more it shielded me from the ravages wrought by his indescribable music.

Before his departure for Italy he called to say goodbye to us. He played – something beyond words – and he dined with us. He launched into philosophy, he talked good-naturedly and joked, yet to me he

23

seemed all the time as if tormented by boredom. Then came the time to say goodbye. Good wishes resounded, and my own fell like a clot of blood on to the common heap of farewell phrases. It was all said on the move, and the exclamations crowded in the doorway then gradually advanced into the hall. And there it was all said again with reiterated urgency – like a collar-hook that simply refused to slip into its narrow loop. Then the door banged and the key was turned twice in the lock. Walking past the grand-piano that still spoke of his playing with the radiant fretted loops of its music-stand, my mother sat down to look through the études he had left with us. Only the first sixteen bars had formed into a sentence full of astonished readiness that nothing on earth could reward, before I raced down the staircase without hat or coat and ran through the night along Myasnitskaya Street to try and bring him back or catch one more glimpse of him.

Everyone has experienced this. Tradition has appeared to all of us. To everyone it has promised a face, and in different ways it has kept its promise to everyone. All of us have become people only in the degree to which we have loved people and had occasion to love. Hiding behind the nickname of "environment", tradition has never been content with the compound image invented about it and has always dispatched to us one or another of its most decisive exceptions. So why have the majority of folk disappeared as a common crowd which is endurable yet merely tolerated? To personality with a face they have preferred faceless impersonality, and they are frightened of the sacrifices demanded of childhood by tradition. To love selflessly without reserve and with a force equal to the square of the distance – that is the task of our hearts while we are children.

3

Of course I never caught up with him, and indeed I hardly imagined that I would. We met again six years later, on his return from abroad. That period fell full upon the years of my youth. And everyone knows the boundlessness of youth. However many decades we accumulate later on, they are powerless to fill that hangar to which they return separately and in droves in a day and night search for memories, like trainer aircraft coming to refuel. In other words, these years in our life form a part that exceeds the whole – and Faust, who lived through those years twice, experienced something quite inconceivable and measurable only in terms of a mathematical paradox.

Scriabin arrived and immediately rehearsals began for *L'Extase*.[8] (How I would now like to change that title – so redolent of a tight soap wrapper – and exchange it for something more apposite!) Rehearsals took place in the mornings. The way there led through a gloom of molten pulp, along Furkasovsky Lane and Kuznetsky Bridge that lay drowned in icy kvass-steeped bread.[9] Along the sleepy road the pendulous tongues of bell-towers were plunged in mist. And each of them gave out one boom from a solitary bell. The remainder stood silent with all the abstinence of fasting copper. At the exit from Gazetny Lane, the Nikitskaya whipped eggs and cognac in the cross-road's sonorous pool. Iron-shod sleigh runners shrieked as they rode into puddles, and flint tapped beneath the canes of those going to the concert. At such hours the Conservatoire resembled a circus during the morning cleanout. The amphitheatre cages were empty. The stalls filled slowly. Like an animal driven back with staves into its winter area, the music kept slapping a paw up on to the wooden casing of the organ. Suddenly the public began arriving in a steady stream as though the city was being abandoned to the enemy. The music was let loose. Multicoloured, shattering to infinite fragments, multiplying like lightning, it leapt and teemed across the platform. It was set in tune and rushed with feverish haste towards concord. Then suddenly rising to a roar of unprecedented unity as a whirlwind raged in the bass, it would break off, die away entirely and flatten out along the footlights.

This was man's first settlement in those worlds discovered by Richard Wagner for fictitious beings and mastodons. And on this land was erected a quite unfictitious lyrical dwelling-house, equal in substance to the entire universe that had been ground up to make its bricks. The sun of Van Gogh glowed over the wattle fence of the symphony, and its windowsills were covered with the dusty archive of Chopin. Yet the residents did not poke around in the dust. With their whole being they fulfilled their forerunner's brightest behests.

I could not hear it without tears. It had engraved itself on my memory before it settled on the zincographic plates of the first proofs. There was nothing unexpected in this. Six years before I had felt the hand that wrote it press upon me with no less weight.

And what had all those years been but the transformations of a living imprint surrendered to the arbitrary dictates of growth? It is no surprise that in that symphony I encountered my own enviably fortunate contemporary. Its proximity could not fail to affect the people close to me, my studies, and the whole of daily life. And it affected them in the following way.

I loved music more than anything in the world – and Scriabin more than anyone in music. Not long before I made his acquaintance, my own first musical babblings had begun. By the time of his return I was the pupil of a certain composer still alive today.[10] The one thing I had yet to study was orchestration. All sorts of comments were made, but the important thing is that even had people said the opposite, I could still not have imagined any life outside music.

But I did not have perfect pitch. That is the name for an ability to recognise the pitch of any note played at random. The absence of this facility, bearing no relation to general musical ability yet possessed in full measure by my mother, gave me no peace. If music had been my true profession, as it seemed to be to an outside observer, I would not have been concerned about perfect pitch. I knew that some prominent contemporary composers did not have it, and it was thought that perhaps both Wagner and Tchaikovsky lacked it. But music for me was a cult – that is, the destructive point where all my most superstitious, self-abnegating elements focused. And so, every time that my will took free wing on some evening inspiration, the next morning I was quick to humiliate it by repeatedly recalling the defect I have mentioned.

Nevertheless, I had composed several serious works, and now I was to show them to my idol. The meeting that was arranged between us was quite natural in view of our family friendship. But I responded with my usual excess. In any circumstances such a step would have struck me as a piece of importunity, and in this case in my eyes it assumed the scale of sacrilege. On the appointed day, as I headed for Glazovsky Lane where Scriabin was temporarily lodging, I was taking to him not so much my compositions as my love which had long outgrown all expression, and my apologies for the imagined awkwardness which I knew I had involuntarily caused. The overcrowded number four crushed and jolted these feelings as it bore them inexorably towards their terrible goal. Along the brown Arbat it went, drawn knee-deep in water towards Smolensky by shaggy, sweating black horses and pedestrians.

4

I appreciated then how well schooled our facial muscles are. With my throat tight from nervous excitement and with a parched tongue, I could only mumble. And I washed my answers down with frequent gulps of tea in order not to choke or commit another solecism.

The skin twitched along my jawbone and forehead protrusions, I moved my brows, I nodded and I smiled. And each time that I touched the bridge of my nose and the wrinkles of this mimicry which tickled and irritated like a cobweb, a convulsively clasped handkerchief appeared in my hand and I used it repeatedly to wipe large beads of sweat from my brow. Behind my head springtime was caught up by the curtains and came vapouring from everywhere in the lane. In front of me my hosts strove with exaggerated volubility to draw me out of my embarrassment, and between them the tea breathed in the cups, the samovar hissed pierced by an arrow of steam, and a watery, manure-misted sunlight billowed. The smoke from a cigar butt was fibrous like a tortoiseshell comb as it stretched from the ash-tray towards the light, and upon reaching it it was sated and crawled away sideways as though across a swath of woollen fabric. I do not know why, but the swirl of dazzled air, steaming waffles, smoking sugar, and silver that burned like paper increased my alarm unbearably. It subsided only when I crossed the room and found myself at the grand piano.

I played the first piece still gripped by agitation, the second – with it almost under control, and the third – surrendering to the urgency of something new and unforeseen. Quite by chance my glance fell on the man listening to me.

Following the progress of the performance, he first raised his head and then his eyebrows. Finally, rising to his feet with a radiant expression and accompanying the shifts of melody with elusive changes in his own smile, he floated towards me along its rhythmic perspective. He liked it all. I hurried to finish. He immediately began assuring me that it was stupid to speak of musical ability when here there was something incomparably greater, and that I had it in me to say something of my own in music. Referring to some fleeting passages he had just heard, he sat down at the piano in order to repeat one which had specially attracted him. It was a complicated phrase and I did not expect him to reproduce it exactly. But another unexpected thing happened: he repeated it in a different key, and the defect which had so tormented me all these years splashed out from beneath his hands as his very own.

And again preferring the vagaries of guesswork to the eloquence of fact, I gave a shudder and made a private wager. If he countered my admission with "Why, Borya, but I don't have it either", then all was well. That meant it was not I who was imposing myself on music, but that music itself was to be my destiny. But if his answer contained talk of Wagner and Tchaikovsky, piano-tuners and the like. . . . But I was already moving close to the alarming subject and, interrupted in mid-sentence, there I was gulping down his reply. "Perfect pitch? After all that I've told you? What about Wagner? And Tchaikovsky? What about the hundreds of tuners that have the gift? . . ."

We walked up and down the room. He would lay a hand on my shoulder or keep taking my arm. He talked about the harm of improvising and about when, why and how one should compose. As models of the simplicity for which one should always strive he quoted his own new sonatas, notorious for their intricacy, while instances of a reprehensible complexity were cited from the most banal song literature. I was unabashed by the paradox of this comparison. I agreed that lack of personality was more complex than personality itself, that thoughtless prolixity appeared accessible because it was devoid of content, and that because we were corrupted by clichéd inanity we took it as formal pretentiousness when after long unfamiliarity we actually encountered something unprecedentedly rich in content. Without my noticing, he went on to offer more precise instructions. He inquired about my education and when he heard I had chosen the Faculty of Law because it was easy, he immediately advised me to transfer to the Philosophy Department in the faculty of History and Philology, which I did the following day. Meanwhile, as he talked, I thought about what had happened. I did not break my bargain with fate. I recalled the sorry outcome of my wager. Yet did this chance happening unseat my god from his throne? No, not at all. It raised him from one height to an even loftier one. Why had he denied me that simple reply that I so longed for? That was his secret. At some later point, when it would be too late, he would grant me the omitted confession. How had he overcome his own youthful doubts? That too was his secret, and that was what raised him to his new height. However, it was already dark in the room. Streetlamps were burning in the lane. It was time to leave.

As I said goodbye I did not know how to thank him. Something welled up within me. Something was tearing and straining to break free. Something was weeping. And something exulted.

There was a breath of houses and of distance in the first stream of chill down on the street. The uproar rose skywards, carried up from the cobbles by the common consent of a Moscow night. I remembered my parents and the questions they were impatiently waiting to ply me with. However I told it, my account could convey only the happiest of meanings. It was only here, as I succumbed to the logic of my forthcoming tale, that I faced the happy events of that day as a fact. And in this guise they did not belong to me. They only became a reality in the form intended for other people. However much the news I was bearing to those at home excited me, I felt uneasy at heart. But the awareness that this sorrow was something I could not pour out into anyone else's ears and that, like my future, it would remain below in the street along with the whole of my Moscow – mine at this hour as never before – this awareness became more and more like joy. I walked through the lanes, crossing the road more often than I needed to. Completely without my awareness, a world was melting and breaking up within me which only the day before had seemed native and permanent. I walked on, quickening my pace at every turning. That night I did not know that already I was breaking with music.

Greece had an excellent understanding of the ages of man. She was careful not to confuse them. She was able to think of childhood as a separate independent entity, like an identifying nucleus of integration. How great her ability was can be seen in the myth of Ganymede and in a host of similar ones. The same views entered into her conception of the demigod and hero. She believed that a certain element of risk and tragedy must be gathered sufficiently early in a handful, demonstrable and surveyable in a single instant. Certain parts of a building, including the basic arch of fatality, had to be laid all together at the very outset to ensure its eventual fine proportion. And finally, death itself had to be experienced in some memorable likeness.

That is why in its art of genius, forever unexpected and enthralling as a fairy tale, antiquity never knew romanticism. Educated to a rigour that has never since been repeated, and to superhumanity of feat and task, it had no knowledge of the superhuman as a personal aberration. It was insured against that because it prescribed entirely for childhood a complete dose of the world's extraordinariness. And when, having taken it, man stepped with giant stride into a gigantic reality, both his stride and his surroundings were deemed just ordinary.

5

One evening soon after, I was setting off to a meeting of "Serdarda", an intoxicated company of some dozen poets, musicians and artists. As I did so I recalled that I had promised to Yulian Anisimov,[11] who had previously recited some excellent translations of Dehmel, that I would

29

take him another German poet whom I preferred to all his contemporaries. And again, as often before, the poetic collection *Mir zu Feier*[12] appeared in my hands at a most difficult hour for me. Away it went with me through the slush to the wooden houses of Razgulyai,[13] to a damp latticement of antiquity, heredity and youthful promise, in order to be driven crazy by rooks in the attic under the poplars and then return home with a new friendship – that is, with a feeling for one more open door in a town where at that time there were only few. However, it is time for me to tell how I came across that collection of verse. Six years earlier, in the December twilight that I have twice tried to describe already, together with the silent street which was waylaid everywhere by mysterious grimacing snowflakes I also shuffled around on my knees helping mama to tidy father's bookshelves. Wiped down with a duster and roughly stacked, their printed entrails were being returned in regular rows to the disembowelled shelving. Suddenly from one of the piles – a specially unsteady and recalcitrant one – there fell a little book in a faded grey cover. By the merest chance I happened not to push it back but picked it up off the floor and later took it to my room. A long time went by and I came to love that book, together with a second one which shortly joined it and was inscribed to my father by the same hand. But even more time elapsed before one day I realised that their author, Rainer Maria Rilke, must be that same German whom one summer long ago we had left behind on our journey on the circling section of a forgotten woodland rail halt.

I ran to my father to check and he confirmed my guess, unable to grasp why it should so excite me.

I am not writing my biography. I turn to it when someone else's requires me to. Together with its main character I believe that only the hero merits an actual account of his life, whereas the story of a poet is utterly inconceivable in such form. It would have to be assembled from inessentials that would bear witness to the concessions he made to pity and coercion. Of his own accord, the poet imparts to the whole of his life such a steep incidence that it cannot exist in the vertical axis of biography where we expect to encounter it. It cannot be found under his own name and has to be sought under someone else's, in the biographical column of his followers. And the more a productive individuality is shut in on itself, the more its story is – in a quite literal sense – collective. It is made up of everything that happens to his readers and of which he himself is unaware. I am not presenting my recollections in memory of Rilke. On the contrary, I myself received them as a gift from him.

30

6

Although my story may have led one to expect it, I have not asked the question as to what music is and what it is that leads to it. I have not done so, not only because on waking one night at the age of two I found the entire horizon bathed in it for more than fifteen years ahead, so that I had no occasion to experience its problematics, but also because it now ceases to have a bearing on our theme. However, I cannot avoid the same question in its overall relation to art, art as a whole – in other words, in relation to poetry. I shall give neither a theoretical nor a sufficiently general answer, but much of what I am going to relate will be a reply that I can offer for myself and for the poet in me.

The sun used to rise from behind the Post Office, and slipping down Kiselny Lane it would set on the Neglinka. Having gilded our part of the house, it used to move after lunch into the dining-room and kitchen. The apartment was an officially provided one and its rooms were converted classrooms. I studied at the University. I read Hegel and Kant. The times were such that at each meeting with friends an abyss would yawn and one or another of us would emerge with some newly manifested revelation.

Often we would rouse one another at dead of night. And the pretext always seemed an urgent one. The person wakened was ashamed of his sleep as though it were some weakness that had accidentally been discovered. And to the fright of our unfortunate domestics, every one of whom were regarded as nonentities, we would set off immediately for Sokolniki and the Yaroslavl railway crossing as if we were just going into the next room. I was friendly with a girl from a wealthy family. It was clear to everyone that I loved her. She took part in these outings only in the abstract, on the lips of more wakeful and adaptable ones. I used to give a few twopenny-halfpenny lessons so as not to take money from my father. In the summer, when our family went away, I used to remain in town and supported myself. And my illusion of independence was achieved by such moderation in eating that on top of everything else I had hunger to contend with, which finally turned night into day in the deserted apartment. Literature was already becoming interwoven with music, to which I was merely postponing a final farewell. I could not fail to discover the profundity and splendour of Bely[14] and Blok.[15] Their influence combined peculiarly with a force that transcended mere ignorance. Fifteen years of abstinence from words, which had been sacrificed

THE VOICE OF PROSE

to sound, doomed me to originality just as another injury might condemn one to acrobatics. Together with some of my friends I had connections with "Musaget".[16] From others I learned of the existence of Marburg – and Kant and Hegel were replaced by Cohen,[17] Natorp[18] and Plato.

I am deliberately characterising my life in those years in a random fashion. I could add to these features or else replace them by others. But the ones I have cited are sufficient for my purpose. Using them in a rough fashion like a surveyor's sketch, to designate what reality meant for me, I immediately ask myself whereabouts and by what token poetry was born of that reality. And I do not need to ponder the answer for long. It is the only feeling which memory has retained in all its freshness.

It was born from the interruptions in these ranks and orders, from their diversity of movement, from the more sluggish falling behind and piling up in the rear on memory's deep horizon.

It was love that sped most impetuously of all. Sometimes it appeared at the head of nature and would overtake the sun. But since this occurred very rarely, one could say that something moved forward that was constantly superior and almost always vied with love, something which when it had gilded one side of the house set to work bronzing the other, something which washed weather away with weather and turned the heavy capstan of the seasons. And trailing in the rear at various removes, the remaining orders followed after. Often I heard the shrill of an anguish that began somewhere outside myself. Catching me from behind, it inspired fright and pity. It originated in a dissevered daily life, and it either threatened to clamp brakes on reality or else implored to be fixed to the living air which meanwhile had moved far ahead. And the thing called inspiration consisted in this backward focused gaze. In view of their distant regress it was the more dropsied, uncreative parts of existence that appealed for a special vividness. Inanimate objects acted even more powerfully – these were the models for still life, that branch of art most beloved of painters. Accumulating in the farthest reaches of the living universe and in a state of immobility, they conveyed the fullest idea of its moving whole, like any apparently contrasting extreme. Their distribution marked a frontier beyond which surprise and sympathy had no function. It was there that science was at work, seeking out the atomic foundations of reality.

But there was no second universe whence one could have lifted reality from the first, taking it by the apex, as though by the hair. Hence the manipulation for which it appealed required one to take a representation

32

of it as in algebra, whose measurements are similarly uniplanar and confined. However, this representation always struck me as being a way out of a difficulty and not as an aim in itself. The aim I always saw as being to transfer the thing represented from a cold set of axes on to hot ones, to launch what had been lived through so that it would pursue and catch up with life. My reasoning at that time did not differ sharply from what I think at present. We represent people in order then to cast a cloak of weather about them – weather, or, what amounts to the same thing, nature – and in order to cloak it in our passion. We drag everyday life into prose for the sake of poetry. We draw prose into poetry for the sake of music. This in the widest sense of the word is what I called art, something which was set by the clock of the living race that chimes with each generation.

That is why my awareness of the city never corresponded to the place in it where my life went on. A spiritual thrust always hurled it back into the depths of the perspective just described. There clouds puffed and promenaded, and their throng was pushed aside by the mingled smoke of countless stoves that hung across the sky. There collapsing houses with porches plunged in snow stood in lines as though along an embankment. There the fragile squalor of vegetating drudgery was fingered by gentle, drunken pluckings of guitars, and stately ladies flushed and hardboiled from the bottle emerged with their swaying husbands into the nightly wave of horse-cabs, as though coming from the feverish hilarity of wash-tubs to the birchwood coolness of the bathhouse ante-room. There they took poison and were burnt by fire, they threw acid at their rivals, they drove out in satin to weddings and pawned off their furs. There winks were exchanged by the lacquered smirks of a way of life that was cracking apart, and my pupils who were all repeating the year, their faces painted bright as saffron by stupidity, settled in their seats as they set out their textbooks and waited for the lesson to start. There, too, the grubbily bespattered grey-green university's echo boomed and subsided in a hundred lecture rooms.

With spectacle glasses slipping over those of pocket watches, the professors raised their heads to address the galleries and ceiling vaults. The heads of students detached themselves from jackets and hung on long cords, paired up to the green lampshades.

During these visits to the town, where I came each day as from another, my heartbeat invariably increased. Had I shown myself then to a doctor, he would have presumed I had malaria. But these bouts of chronic impatience would not have responded to quinine treatment.

33

This strange perspiration was caused by the stubborn crudity of these worlds and by their swollen obviousness which nothing within them expended for their own benefit. They lived and moved as though adopting poses. Mentally uniting them in a form of colony, an aerial antenna of total predestiny rose from among them. And my fever attacks came right at the foot of this imaginary rod. They were generated by the currents sent by this mast to the opposite pole. Conversing with the distant mast of genius, they summoned some new Balzac from that region to their own small hamlet. But it was enough to move a short way from that fatal rod for an immediate calm to be restored.

Thus, for instance, no fever gripped me at Savin's lectures because here was a professor who was not true to any type. He lectured with genuine talent that increased as his actual subject grew. Time took no offence at him. It did not tear free from his assertions, it did not leap for the air-vents or make a headlong rush for the doors. It did not blow the smoke back into the flues or fall off the roof and clutch at the hook of the tramcar trailer as it whirled away into the snowstorm. No, as it engrossed itself in the English Middle Ages or Robespierre's Convention, it drew us after it, and together with us – everything we could imagine living outside the high university windows which extended right to the cornices.

I also remained healthy in the cheap furnished lodgings where I was one of several students who supervised the studies of a group of adult pupils. No one there had any shining talent. And it was sufficient that since they were not expecting to inherit any legacy, both the teachers and the taught joined together in a common effort to stir themselves from the motionless spot where life was about to nail them. Like their teachers, including some who had stayed on at university, they were untypical of their professions. Minor clerks and employees, workers, servants and postmen, they came here in order that they might one day become something different.

I was not gripped by fever in their active midst. And in a rare state of peace with myself, I often used to leave there and turn off into the next lane, where whole companies of florists lived in one of the courtyard wings of the Zlatoustinsky Monastery. It was here that the lads would stock up with the complete flora of the Riviera before hawking their wares on the Petrovka. Peasant wholesalers would order them from Nice, and the treasures could be bought there on the spot for a song. I was specially attracted there after the academic half-year break. Discovering one evening that lessons had already long been in progress without lamp-light, the bright March twilight would frequent those grubby lodgings more and more. And eventually it was not even left behind at the entrance when the lessons were over. Without its usual kerchief of a winter night the street seemed to rise from beneath the ground at the exit with some dry fairytale on its barely stirring lips. The spring air shuffled with gusty abruptness over the vigorous roadway. The outlines of the lane seemed to have a live skin stretched over them and trembled with a chill shiver, waiting for the first star, whose appearance was painfully delayed by an insatiable and wonderfully leisurely sky.

The stenching gallery was stacked to the ceiling with empty wicker hampers bearing foreign stamps stuck on under the sonorous Italian frankmarks. In answer to the felted grunt of the door a buxom, billowing cloud of steam rolled out as though to relieve itself and it already contained a hint of something inexpressibly exciting. Opposite the entrance, in the depths of the gradually lowering chamber, youthful hawkers crowded at the fortress window, and after receiving and checking their wares they stuffed them into their baskets. At a broad table in the same room the sons of the proprietor were slitting open fresh parcels that had just been delivered from the Customs. Folded back in two like a book, the orange lining exposed the fresh heart of the cane basket. The clustered ganglions of chill violets were removed all of a piece like the dark blue layers of sun-dried Malaga. And they filled that room resembling a janitor's lodge with such a stupefying aroma that even the pillars of early evening twilight and the shadows on the floor seemed as though they were cut out of dark lilac turf.

But the real miracles were still in store. The proprietor went over to the far end of the courtyard, unlocked one of the doors of a stone store-shed and lifted the trapdoor of the cellar by its ring. And at that instant the tale of Ali Baba and the forty thieves came true in all its dazzling brilliance. Down in the bottom of the dry cellar four turnip-shaped Molniya lamps flared and sputtered like the sun. And vying with the lamps, hot sheafs of peonies, yellow chamomiles, tulips and anemones sorted by colour and species ran riot in enormous tubs. They breathed and were agitated, as though competing with one another. The dusty fragrance of mimosas was washed away by an unexpectedly powerful, rushing wave of lightly scented anise, watery and threaded through with liquid needles. It was the bright perfume of narcissus, like some liquor infusion diluted to whiteness. But here too this entire storm of jealousy was defeated by the black cockades of violets. Secretive, half-crazed, like pupils without eye-whites, their very aloofness was hypnotic. Their sweet, uncoughing breath from the bottom of the cellar

35

filled the wide frame of the trapdoor. They stuffed one's chest with a certain woody pleurisy. The smell recalled something, yet only then to slip away duping one's awareness. In response to this scent the spring months might well have invented the idea of the Earth inducing their return each year, and the sources of Greek belief in Demeter were also somewhere near at hand.

7

At that time and much later too I regarded my efforts at writing verse as an unfortunate weakness and I had no expectation that anything good would come of them. But there was one man, Sergei Durylin, who even then supported me by his approval. This could be explained by his unique sensitivity. But from the rest of my friends, who had already seen me almost find my feet as a musician, I carefully concealed these tokens of a new immaturity. On the other hand I was studying philosophy with wholehearted enthusiasm and imagined that the seeds of some future application lay somewhere in this area. The range of subjects that were lectured on to our group was as far from the ideal as the actual method of instruction. It was a strange mixture of superannuated metaphysics and unfledged enlightenmentism. And in order to reconcile them, both these trends had been stripped of the last remnants of meaning which they might still have possessed taken separately. The history of philosophy thus turned into belletristic dogmatism, while psychology degenerated into a mass of frivolous, journalistic inanity.

Young lecturers like Shpet, Samsonov and Kubitsky were unable to alter the state of things. But the senior professors too were not altogether to blame. They were tied down by the requirement already making itself felt to lecture in a popular, nursery-school manner. Without those involved being clearly aware of it, the campaign to eradicate illiteracy was already then beginning. Students who had any basic grounding thus endeavoured to work independently and became more and more reliant on the University's first-rate library. Sympathies were divided between three different names. The majority were Bergson enthusiasts. Adherents of the Göttingen Husserlian school found support from Shpet. The followers of the Marburg school had no leadership and, left to themselves, were united by the accidental ramifications of a personal tradition handed down from Sergei Nikolayevich Trubetskoi.[19]

A remarkable phenomenon in this circle was young Samarin. A direct descendant of the best in Russia's past and with connections through various degrees of kinship with the history of that actual building on the corner of Nikitskaya,[20] he would appear about twice a term at a meeting of some seminar or other like a son who has already received his inheritance turning up at his parents' home just when everyone is gathering for dinner. The person reading his paper would break off and wait while the lanky eccentric who was embarrassed by the hush he had caused and was himself prolonging by his search for a seat, clambered over the crackling boards to the farthest bench of the plank amphitheatre. But discussion of the paper would only just be getting under way when all the banging and creaking that had just been hauled with such effort to a place under the ceiling came back down again in a revived and unrecognisable form. At the speaker's very first stumble, Samarin would seize on it and launch into some extemporisation on Hegel or Cohen, rolling it like a ball down over the ledges and ridges of a great pile of boxes. He would grow excited and swallow his words. And he spoke with natural loudness and on one steady note which he sustained from childhood to the grave, which knew neither shout nor whisper, and which together with his constant rounded uvulars always instantly betrayed his breeding. I later lost sight of him, but I could not help recalling him when I reread Tolstoy and came across him again in the person of Nekhlyudov.[21]

8

Although the summer coffee house on Tverskoi Boulevard had no name of its own, everybody called it the Café Grec. It stayed open throughout the winter, when its designation became a strange conundrum. Quite by chance and without prior arrangement, Loks,[22] Samarin and myself once met in that bare pavilion. We were the only visitors there, not just on that evening, but maybe for the whole of the past season. The weather was just turning warm and there was a breath of spring in the air. Samarin had appeared and hardly had time to sit down and join us before starting to philosophise. Arming himself with a dry biscuit, he used it like a choirmaster's tuning-fork to beat out the logical divisions of his argument. A piece of Hegelian infinity stretched out across the pavilion, made up of successive statements and negations. Probably I mentioned the theme I had chosen for a doctoral thesis, and he quickly leapt from Leibniz and from mathematical infinity to the dialectical variety. Then suddenly he started talking about Marburg. This was the first account I heard not of the Marburg school but of the town itself. I was eventually convinced there was no other way to talk of its antiquity and poetry. But just then his enamoured description with the ventilator fan chattering in the background was a novelty to me. Then, all of a sudden, he recollected he had only looked in for a moment and had not come to drink coffee. He startled and roused the proprietor dozing in a corner over his newspaper, and on hearing the telephone was out of order, tumbled out of that icy bird-house even more noisily than he had entered. Soon after that we also got up to go. The weather had changed. The wind had risen and scalded us with February sleet. It settled on the ground in regular skeins like figures of eight. There was something maritime in its furious looping – that was the way they stowed nets and hawsers, slinging one waving layer upon another. As we walked, Loks several times started on his favourite theme of Stendhal. But I kept silent, aided considerably by the snowstorm. I could not forget what I had heard, and I was sorry about that little town which I thought I would never set eyes on, any more than I would ever glimpse my own ears.

That was in February. But one morning in April mother announced that from her earnings and household economies she had saved up two hundred roubles which she was giving me, and she advised me to travel abroad. I cannot describe either my joy or the total unexpectedness of this gift, or how undeserved it was. To save such a sum she had had to endure not a little of her pupils' strummings on the piano. But I had not the strength to refuse. And there was no need to choose which route to take. At that time European universities were regularly informed about one another. I began rushing round the various offices that very day, and along with a small number of other documents I brought away from Mokhovaya Street one particular treasure. It was a detailed list, printed two weeks before in Marburg, giving the lecture courses on offer in the summer semester of 1912. Pencil in hand I studied the prospectus and never parted with it as I walked around or stood waiting at the various counter grills. My engrossment smelt of happiness a mile off, and as I unwittingly infected various secretaries and clerks with it, I actually expedited what was already a fairly simple procedure.

My programme was of course a Spartan one. Third-class travel – and if necessary even fourth-class while abroad – the slowest trains, a room in some village outside town, and a diet of bread and wurst with tea to drink. Mother's self-sacrifice obliged me to a tenfold avarice. On her money I ought also to get to Italy. In addition, I knew that a considerable amount would be swallowed by the university enrolment fee and payment for individual seminars and courses. But even had I ten times more money, as things stood then, I would never have departed from this programme. I do not know how I would have disposed of the surplus, but at that time nothing on earth would have shifted me to the second class or persuaded me to leave behind one crumb on a restaurant table-cloth. It was only in the postwar years that I developed a tolerance of comforts and a need to be comfortable. Those years have placed such constraints on a world that once banished all decoration and indulgence from my room, that for a while my entire character could not help but change also.

9

The snow at home was still melting and pieces of sky swam into the water from beneath the frozen crust like a transfer sliding from its tracing-paper mount. But all over Poland the apple trees blossomed warmly and from morn till night the country swept past, moving from west to east in a state of summer sleeplessness, like some Romance part of a Slavonic scheme.

Berlin seemed to me a city of raw youths who just the day before had been presented with swords and helmets, canes and pipes, real bicycles and frockcoats like adults. And I had caught them on their first outing. They were not yet used to the change, and each of them tried to look important with his new acquisitions of the day before. On one of the finest streets Natorp's handbook on logic called to me from the window of a bookshop and I went in to buy it, aware that next day I was to see its author in real life. In my forty-eight hour journey I had already spent one sleepless night on German territory. Now I was in store for a second.

Folding-down bunks in third-class compartments have only been introduced here in Russia. But abroad the penalty for cheap travel has to be paid at night, nodding four in a row on a deeply worn bench seat divided by armrests. Although on this occasion both benches in the compartment were at my disposal, I had no time for sleep. Only rarely and at long intervals individual passengers, mostly students, came in and travelled one or two stops before leaving with a silent bow and vanishing in the obscurity of the warm night. At each change sleeping towns rolled in beneath the platform roofing. For the first time the Middle Ages immemorial were revealed to me. Like any original object their authenticity was fresh and terrible. Clanging familiar names like naked steel, the journey took them one by one from descriptions I had read, as though from the historian's dusty scabbard.

In its flight towards them the train stretched the chain-mail marvel of its ten riveted coaches. The leather joints of the corridor connections billowed and sagged like a blacksmith's bellows. Beer shone clearly in clean glasses, splotched by the station lights. Along platforms of stone and on broad, stone-like rollers empty luggage trolleys glided away into the distance. The torsos of short-snouted locomotives sweated under the vaults of colossal passenger platforms. They seemed as if reared to such height by the low play of their wheels which at full wind had suddenly come grinding to a halt.

From all sides six-century forebears reached down to the desolate concrete. Quartered by a framework of oblique beams, the walls unfurled their sleepy murals. And on them were crowded pageboys, knights, maidens and red-bearded ogres. And the criss-cross laths of woodwork were repeated as an ornament on the barred visors of helmets, the slashes of ballooned sleeves, and the cross-lacing of bodices. The houses came almost up to the lower window of my carriage. Utterly amazed, I rested on its broad upper edge and entranced myself by repeating a short whispered exclamation of rapture that is nowadays out of fashion. But it was still dark, and the leaping paws of wild vines barely showed black against the stucco work. However, when I was hit again by the hurricane with its echoed trace of coal and dew and roses, I was suddenly showered with a handful of sparks from the rapturously rushing light and I quickly raised the window and fell to reflecting on the next day's unforeseeable events. I must say something, though, about where I was going to and why.

Created by the genius of Hermann Cohen and prepared for by his predecessor in the chair, Friedrich Albert Lange, who is known in this country for his *History of Materialism*, the Marburg school of philosophy had two special features that won me over. First of all it was original. It dug everything over down to the foundations and it built upon clear ground. It did not share the lazy routine of all the "isms" one can think of, which always cling to their profitable tenth-hand omniscience, are always ignorant, and are for some reason or another always afraid of a review conducted in the free air of our ancient culture. The Marburg school did not suffer from any terminological inertia and it turned back to primary sources, that is, to the authentic signatures left by thought in the history of science. If current philosophy talks about what one writer or another thinks, and current psychology – about how the average man thinks, and if formal logic teaches us how we should think at the baker's in order to get the right change, then the Marburg school was interested in how science has thought in its twenty-five centuries of continuous authorship at the blazing source and origin of the world's discoveries. In such a disposition, authorised as it were by history itself, philosophy grew young and wise beyond recognition, and from a problematic discipline it turned into the primordial discipline about problems, which indeed it ought to be.

A second feature of the Marburg school derived directly from the first and consisted in its discriminating and exacting approach to the legacy of history. Quite foreign to this school was any of that repulsive condescension to the past which views it as a sort of almshouse where a handful of old men in chlamyses and sandals, or periwigs and camisoles, churn out some impenetrable trumped-up nonsense which is excusable only by the whimsies of the Corinthian order, the Gothic, the Baroque or some other architectural style. Homogeneity in the structure of science was as much a rule for the Marburg school as the anatomical identity of historical man. In Marburg they knew history to perfection and never tired of hauling treasure after treasure from the archives of the Italian Renaissance, French and Scottish rationalism and other little-studied schools. In Marburg they looked at history through both Hegelian eyes – that is, in a brilliantly generalised fashion, but at the same time within the exact limits of commonsense plausibility. Thus, for instance, the school did not talk about the various stages of the World Spirit, but – let us say – about the postal correspondence of the Bernoulli family. Yet it still knew that if any thought of however remote a time is caught on the spot and in action, then it must be completely accessible to our logical comment. Otherwise it loses its direct interest for us and passes into the province of the archeologist or the historian of costume, custom, literature, socio-political trends, and so forth.

Both these features of its independence and historicism say nothing of the actual content of Cohen's system (and I have never meant, nor would I undertake, to talk about its essence). However, both features do explain its attractiveness. They speak of its originality, of the vital place it occupies in living tradition for one part of our contemporary awareness.

And as one particle of that awareness, I was rushing towards its centre of attraction. The train crossed the Harz. Leaping from the woods on a smoky morning, millenarian Goslar flashed past like a mediaeval coal-digger. Later on Göttingen also swept by. The names of the towns became louder and louder. And as the train rushed on in full flight it hurled most of them aside from its path without stooping. On the map I could find the names of those spinning-tops as they whirled away. Ancient details rose up around some of them and were drawn into their vortex like stellar satellites and rings. Sometimes the horizon broadened as in "The Terrible Vengeance",[23] and smoking simultaneously in several orbits, the earth of separate townships and castles began exciting me like the night sky itself.

10

For two years preceding my journey the word Marburg had been forever on my lips. In every school history textbook there was mention of the town in its chapters on the Reformation. "Posrednik" publishers had even brought out a little book for children about Elisabeth of Hungary, who was buried there in the early thirteenth century. Any biography of Giordano Bruno named Marburg in a list of towns where he lectured on his fatal journey from London back to his native land. And yet, unlikely as it may seem, in Moscow I never once guessed that the Marburg of these references was identical with the one for whose sake I had chewed away at tables of derivatives and differentials and leapt from Maclaurin to Maxwell, who finally proved beyond me. I had to pick up my suitcase and walk past a knight-errants' inn and an old posting station in order for the identity to strike me.

I stood there gasping with my head thrown back. Above me reared a vertiginous hillside on which the stone models of the University, Rathaus and an eight-centuries-old castle stood in three tiers. After ten paces I ceased to realise where I was. I recalled having left behind my ties with the rest of the world in a railway carriage, and now, like the latter's coathooks, luggage nets and ashtrays, there was no way of recovering them. The clouds hung idly over a clock-tower. The place seemed familiar to them. But they too explained nothing. It was apparent that like the custodians of this nest they never went away. A midday silence reigned. It consorted with the silence of the plain stretched out below. They both seemed to sum up the total of my bewilderment. The upper one exchanged oppressive wafts of lilac with the one below. Birds

chirruped expectantly. I hardly noticed any people. The immobile contours of the roofs were curious to see how all of this would end.

The streets clung to the declivity like Gothic dwarfs. They were set out
one below another and the cellars of one looked into the attics of its
neighbour. The defiles between them were stacked with marvels of box
architecture. The storeys broadened out upwards and rested on project-
ing beams, and with roofs almost touching they stretched out their arms
towards one another above the roadway. There were no pavements,
and in some streets two people could not have passed.

Suddenly I realised that before Lomonosov[24] spent five years trudging
these roadways, there must have been a day when he entered this town
for the first time, bearing a letter to Leibniz's pupil Christian von Wolff
and still knowing no one. It is not enough to say that the town had not
changed since that day. One has to realise that in those days too it might
have been just as unexpectedly small and ancient. It was a shaking
experience to realise that a turn of the head was a precise repetition of
another man's bodily movement in an age so terribly remote. Just as it
did in Lomonosov's day, the town scattered at one's feet the teeming
grey-blue of its slate roofs and resembled a flock of pigeons descending
to their replenished feeding tray and bewitched in animated flight. I
quaked as I celebrated the bicentenary of another man's neck muscles.
But as I came to, I noticed that stage scenery had become a reality, and I
set off in search of the cheap hotel to which Samarin had directed me.

Part Two

1

I rented a room on the outskirts of town. The house was one of a final
row standing along the Giessen road. At that point the chestnut trees
flanking it seemed to move shoulder to shoulder on command and
wheeled away to the right, still in formation. The roadway cast a final
backward look at the sullen hill and its ancient township, then disappeared beyond the forest.

My room had a squalid little balcony with a view on to the neighbour's kitchen garden. The carriage of an old Marburg horse tram stood there, removed from its bogies and converted into a henhouse.

The room was being let by an old woman, the widow of some civil servant. She lived there together with her daughter on a meagre widow's pension. Mother and daughter were alike as two peas in a pod. As always with women suffering from goitre, they kept catching my gaze directed furtively at their collars. At such instants I kept imagining children's balloons tied tightly at one end and gathered in a bleb. Maybe they could guess my thoughts.

One felt like placing a palm to their throats and releasing a little air from those eyes of theirs through which an ancient Prussian pietism gazed out into the world. Their type, however, was not characteristic of this part of Germany. A different type was dominant here – the Central German – and even Nature was affected by first suspicions of a South and West, and of the existence of France and Switzerland. So, faced with the conjectures of her green foliage at the window, it seemed appropriate to be leafing through French volumes of Leibniz and Descartes.

Beyond the fields that advanced up to the ingenious poultry house, the village of Ockershausen could be glimpsed. It was a long cantonment of long barns, with long waggons and hefty *percherons*. Another road stretched out from there along the horizon, and as it entered the town it was christened the Barfüsserstrasse. In the Middle Ages "Barfüsser", or "barefoots", had been the name for Franciscan friars.

It was probably along this road that winter approached each year. As one looked in that direction from the balcony, one could imagine plenty of things that matched: Hans Sachs;[25] the Thirty Years War; the dull and somnolent nature of a historical disaster measured not in hours but decades; winters, winters, and more winters, and then, after a century desolate as an ogre's yawn, the first appearance of new settlements under nomad skies – somewhere in the wild remoteness of the Harz, with names black as burnt-out ruins, like Elend, Sorge,[26] and others similar.

Behind the house, to one side, flowed the River Lahn with its crumpled bushes and reflections. Beyond it stretched the railway track. In the kitchen in the evenings the dull wheeze of the spirit-lamp was invaded by the automatic bells' accelerated jingle as the railway barrier descended of its own accord. Then a man in uniform loomed up in the darkness at the crossing and rapidly sprinkled water from his can to lay the dust. And at the same instant a train rushed past, leaping convulsively up and down and in every direction at once. The sheaves of its drumming light fell in the landlady's saucepans. And always the milk would get burnt on to the pan.

A star or two slithered down into the fluvial oil of the Lahn. In Ockershausen the cattle had just been driven home and were bellowing. Marburg on its hill flared operatically – if the brothers Grimm ever came back here, as they had a hundred years before to study law with the famous lawyer Savigny, they would leave here once again as collectors of fairytales.

Making sure I had the front-door key with me, I would set off into town. The regular citizenry were asleep already. The only people I encountered were students. They all looked as if they were part of Wagner's *Meistersinger*. In daylight the houses seemed like a stage set, and now they pressed together even closer. The streetlamps suspended from wall to wall above the roadway had nowhere to disport themselves. Their light crashed down with full force on to the sounds, drenching the ring of receding footsteps and salvoes of loud German speech with fleur-de-lys highlights. It was as though even electricity knew the legend of this place.

Long, long ago, half a thousand years before Lomonosov, when the new and perfectly ordinary year on this earth was that of twelve hundred and thirty, down these slopes from Marburg castle had come a living historical person, Elisabeth of Hungary.

The time is so remote that if imagination can stretch that far a blizzard will arise there quite spontaneously. It will arise from the effect of excessive cooling – according to the law of the conquered unattainable. Night will close in, the hills will be clothed in forest, wild beasts will inhabit them, and human habits and customs will be covered in a crust of ice. The future saint (she was canonised three years after death) had a tyrant as her confessor; that is to say he was a man who lacked imagination. This sober pragmatist saw that the torments imposed by confession induced a state of exaltation in her. So he looked for tortures that would be a genuine pain to her and forbade her to help the sick and poor. At this point legend takes over from history. Evidently this all proved beyond her strength, and in order to purge away the sin of disobedience a snowy blizzard would shroud her on her way down to the town, turning the bread into flowers during her nighttime passages to and fro.

Thus nature sometimes has to depart from its laws when a convinced zealot insists too harshly on the fulfilment of his own. It does not matter that the voice of natural law is here invested in the form of miracle. In a

45

religious age that is a criterion of authenticity. We also have ours, yet nature will continue as our defence against casuistry.

As it neared the University, the street became more and more crooked and narrow in its downhill flight. In one of the façades that were baked like potato in the centuries' cinders there was a glass door. It opened into a corridor leading out to one of the sheer northern slopes. There there was a terrace set out with tables and bathed in electric light. The terrace hung above the lowlands that had once caused the countess such disquiet. Since then the town had established itself along the route of her nocturnal visits and had set in the form it had assumed by the middle of the sixteenth century. But the lowlands that had tormented her peace of mind and forced her to flout religious ordinance . . . the lowlands that were set astir as before by miracles strode away in perfect step with the times.

From the lowland a nocturnal dampness came wafting up. And down there iron clangoured sleepily and sidings roamed back and forth, running together and flowing apart. Something kept constantly and noisily rising and falling. The water thundering at the weir had picked up a steady, deafening note in the evening and sustained it right through till the morning. The oxen at the abattoir were accompanied in thirds by the piercing screech of the sawmill. Something constantly kept bursting and glowing, emitting steam and overturning. Something kept fidgeting and shrouding itself in tinted smoke.

The café was patronised mainly by philosophers. Other folk had their own cafés. On the terrace sat G-v[27] and L-z[28] and some Germans who went on to receive chairs in their own country and abroad. Among the English girls and the Danes and Japanese and all the others who had gathered here from every corner of the globe to hear Cohen lecture, a familiar and excitedly singsong voice could already be heard. It was an advocate from Barcelona, a pupil of Stammler. He had played a part in the recent Spanish revolution and was furthering his education here for a second year. Just now he was declaiming Verlaine to his friends.

I knew many people here already and was not shy of anyone. And already my tongue had entangled me in two promises and I was anxiously preparing myself for the time when I had to read a paper on Leibniz for Hartmann,[29] and on one of the parts of the *Critique of Practical Reason*[30] for the head of the Marburg school. An image of the latter had formed in my mind long ago, though it emerged as awfully inadequate on first acquaintance. Now, however, it had become part of me. That is to say, it had begun a spontaneous existence within me, changing according to whether it sank to the bottom of my selfless enthusiasm or else floated to the surface. At such times, with a novice's delirious ambition I wondered whether I would ever be noticed by him and invited to one of his Sunday dinners. That was something which immediately raised one in local opinion, because it signified the start of a new philosophical career.

By his example I had already verified how a great inner world became dramatised in its projection by a great man. I already knew how the shock-headed old man in spectacles would lift his head and step back as he talked about the Greek concept of immortality, flourishing a hand towards the Marburg fire-station as he interpreted the image of the Elysian fields. I already knew how on some other occasion he would make a stealthy approach to pre-Kantian metaphysics and coo away in a show of paying court to it, before suddenly uttering a rasp and giving it a frightful scolding with quotations from Hume. I also knew that after a bout of coughing and a prolonged pause he would then drawl in a weary and peaceable voice: "Und nun, meine Herren. . . ." And this would mean that that particular age had received its reprimand, the performance was over, and we could now move on to the subject of the course.

Meanwhile, hardly anyone was left on the terrace. The electric lamps were being switched off. It was discovered to be already morning. Looking down over the railing, we convinced ourselves that the low-lands of the night had vanished without trace. And the panorama that replaced them knew nothing of its nocturnal predecessor.

2

At about that time the V- sisters[31] arrived in Marburg. They came of a wealthy family. While a schoolboy in Moscow I had already been friendly with the elder sister and had given her occasional lessons in some subject or other. Or rather, her family had paid me to converse with her on a series of topics that were quite unpredictable.

But in spring of 1908 the period when we both finished our schooling coincided, and while preparing for my own examinations I also undertook to coach the elder V- daughter for hers.

The majority of my examination questions embraced areas I had thoughtlessly omitted at the time when they were gone over in class. And now there were not enough nights to work them up. But on odd occasions, regardless of the hour and usually at daybreak, I would run round to V- to work at subjects that were always at variance with my own, since naturally the order of exams at different schools never coincided. This confusion complicated my position still further. But I failed to notice. My feelings for V- were not new – I had known of them since the age of fourteen.

She was a lovely and delightful girl, excellently brought up, and spoilt since infancy by an old French nurse who doted on her. The old woman realised better than I did that the geometry I was bringing to her precious darling at such unearthly hours was more Abélardian than Euclidian. And she cheerfully underlined her sagacity by constantly attending our lessons. I was secretly grateful for her intrusion. In her presence my feelings could remain inviolate. I neither judged them nor was I judged by them. I was eighteen years old. And in any case, by character and upbringing I lacked the ability or courage to give free rein to my feelings.

It was the time of year when paint was dissolved with hot water in small pots and when gardens piled high with all the cleared snow were left alone to bask idly in the sunshine. They were filled to the brim with quiet, bright water. And outside their borders, beyond the fences, the gardeners, rooks and belfries stood drawn up along the horizon and exchanged two or three words a day in loud remarks for all the town to hear. A damp, woolly grey sky rubbed up against the ventilator window. It was full of a night that still lingered. For hours and hours it kept silent, then all of a sudden it bowled the rounded rumble of a cart-wheel into the room. And now it was safely home, it broke off so suddenly, as though all this was a game of "tig-stick"[32] and the cart had no other concern but to come up from the road and in at the window. And even more puzzling was the lazy stillness whose springs poured into the hole which the sound had carved out. . . .

I do not know why all this was imprinted on me as the image of a school blackboard which had not been rubbed clean of chalk. If only we had been stopped just then after the board had been wiped down till it shone with a moist gleam, and if instead of theorems about equal pyramids we had had a copperplate, emphatic exposition of what lay in store for both of us . . . how stupefied we would have been!

But where does this idea come from, and why has it occurred to me just now?

Because spring was there, completing its rough-sketched scheme for the eviction of the year's cold half, and all around lakes and puddles lay like unhung mirrors face upwards on the ground and told how the crazily capacious earth had been cleaned and the premises made ready for another lease. Because the first person who so wished might then embrace and experience anew all the life that existed on this earth. Because I loved V-.

Because the mere perceptibility of the present is already the future. And the future of man is love.

3

But there exists on this earth a so-called noble attitude towards women. I shall say a few words about it. There is a boundless circle of phenomena which in adolescence lead to suicides. There is a circle of mistakes made by the infant imagination, childish perversions, youthful fastings, a circle of Kreuzer Sonatas and of sonatas written against such sonatas. I too have been in that circle and tarried there for shamefully long. But what exactly is it?

It savages one to shreds and nothing ever comes of it but harm. And yet we shall never be free of it. All those who enter history as human beings will always pass through it, because these sonatas which are a prelude to the only complete moral freedom are written not by Tolstoys and Wedekinds[33] but by nature itself – through the medium of their hands. And only their mutual contradiction is an expression of the fullness of nature's design.

Basing matter on resistance, and separating fact from fancy by a dam called love, nature concerns herself with the world's stability and with its entirety. This is the focal point of nature's obsession and of her morbid exaggerations. Here one can truly say that at every step she turns a fly into an elephant, makes a mountain out of a molehill.

But, begging your pardon, nature really does produce elephants! It is said to be her main occupation. Or is that just a phrase? And what about the history of species? And the history of human names? In fact it is precisely here that she manufactures them, in those sections of living evolution that are held back by flood-gates, at the dams where her disturbed imagination runs free!

In that case could it not be said that it is in childhood that we exaggerate and that our imagination is disordered, *because* at that time we are flies and nature makes elephants of us?

Holding to the philosophy that only *the almost impossible* is real, she had made feeling extremely difficult for every living thing. She has made it harder in one way for the animal, and in another for the plant. And the manner of difficulty she has created for us expresses her astonishingly high opinion of man. She has made it harder for us not through some mechanical trickery, but by something which she believes has absolute power for us. She has made it harder through the sense of our own fly-like banality which grips each of us more strongly the further we advance away from being flies. This idea is expounded with genius by Hans Andersen in "The Ugly Duckling".

Any literature about sex, like the word "sex" itself, smacks of an intolerable banality, and in this lies its purpose. It is precisely and solely in its repugnance that it is of use to nature, because her contact with us is based precisely on this fear of banality, and nothing other than the banal could add to her means of control.

Whatever material our thoughts may provide in this connection, the *fate* of this material is in her hands. And with the help of the instinct she has assigned to us from her totality, nature always disposes of this material in such a way that all the efforts of teachers designed to make natural things easier in fact invariably render them harder – and *that is just how it should be!*

And it should be so in order that feeling itself has something to conquer – a perplexity of one sort or another. And it does not matter what nastiness or nonsense makes up this barrier. The motion that leads to conception is the purest thing in the universe. And this purity alone, triumphant so often down the ages, would suffice for everything else by contrast to reek of utter filth.

And then there is art. Art is concerned not with man, but with the image of man. And as it turns out, the image of man is greater than man. It can only be engendered by movement – and not by every movement. It can be generated only in the transition from fly into elephant.

What does an honest man do when he speaks *only* the truth? Time passes by as he speaks, and in that time life moves on. His truth lags behind and is deceptive. But should a man everywhere and always speak in such manner?

Now in art his mouth is gagged. In art man falls silent and the image speaks out. And it emerges that only the image keeps pace with the progress of nature.

In Russian "fabrication" has more the meaning of "spinning a yarn" rather than "deceiving".[34] And it is in this sense that art "fabricates". Its image embraces life and looks for no spectator. Its truths are not depictive ones but are capable of endless development.

And as it tells down the centuries about love, only art is *not* at the disposal of instinct in order to increase the obstacles in the path of feeling. Having cleared the barrier of some new spiritual development, a generation preserves the lyric truth and does not discard it. So that from a far distance one can imagine lyrical truth as the form in which humanity is gradually built up from generations.

All this is something unusual. It is all breathtakingly difficult.

It is taste that teaches morality, but taste is taught by some power or force.

4

The sisters were spending the summer in Belgium. Someone told them I was in Marburg. So when they were summoned to a family gathering in Berlin they decided to visit me on the way.

They stayed at the best hotel in town, which was in the oldest quarter. And the three days I spent in their continuous company were as unlike my every day life as holidays are unlike workdays. I constantly told them about this and that and I was intoxicated by their laughter and by the signs of understanding from people that happened to be near. I took them to places. The two of them were seen with me at lectures in the university. And so came the day of their departure.

The evening before, as he laid the table for supper, the waiter said to me: "Das ist wohl Ihr Henkersmahl, nicht wahr?" Which is to say: "Enjoy your last meal, because tomorrow you're for the gallows, aren't you?"

In the morning when I entered their hotel, I bumped into the younger of the two sisters in the corridor. She glanced at me and, realising something, stepped back without a greeting and locked herself in her room. I went on to see her elder sister, and in awful agitation I told her things could not go on like this and that I wanted her to decide my fate. Apart from my insistence there was nothing new in any of this. She rose from her chair and retreated from the manifest agitation that seemed to advance upon her. But when she reached the wall she suddenly realised that there was an immediate way of putting an end to all this . . . and she refused me. Soon there were noises out in the corridor. They were dragging a trunk out from the room next door. Then there was a knock at our door. I quickly pulled myself together. It was time to go to the station, which was five minutes' walk away.

51

There, the ability to say goodbye completely left me. Just as I grasped that I had only taken leave of the younger sister and not even begun with the elder, the express from Frankfurt loomed up and glided down the platform. Almost in the same movement it quickly took on its passengers and moved off again. I sprinted along beside the train and at the end of the platform took a run and jumped on to the carriage step. The heavy door had not yet been slammed. The furious guard barred my way and at the same time seized me by the shoulder lest I be so shamed at his reprimands as to go and sacrifice my life. My two lady companions came running out of their compartment and began thrusting banknotes at the guard in order to rescue me and buy me a ticket. He relented, and I followed the sisters through into the carriage. We were speeding on to Berlin. Almost interrupted, the fairytale holiday now continued, enhanced by the fury of our speed and by a blissful headache after all that I had just been through.

I had jumped on board the moving train only in order to say farewell. But once again I forgot everything and remembered only when it was too late. I had still not come to myself before the day passed, evening approached, and the sonorously breathing roof of the Berlin station enclosed us and pressed us to the earth. The sisters were due to be met. It was not desirable for them to be seen with me in my present state of emotional upset. They persuaded me that our goodbyes had now been said and that only I had failed to notice. I melted into the crowd, which was gripped by the gaseous dinning of the station.

It was night. A foul drizzle was falling. I had nothing to do in Berlin. The next train in my direction left only the following morning. I could quite easily have waited for it at the station, but I could not bear to stay in human company.

My face kept twitching in spasms and tears constantly started to my eyes. My craving for one final and utterly devastating farewell remained unsatisfied. It was like the need for a great cadenza that shatters an ailing music to its foundation in order suddenly to remove it entirely with the single lunge of a final chord. But that relief was denied me.

It was night. A foul drizzle was falling. On the asphalt in front of the station it was as smoky as on the platform, where the hipped glass roofing bulged in its iron frame like a ball in a string-bag. The echoed patter of the streets resembled bursting carbon-dioxide bubbles, and everything was wrapped in the quiet ferment of falling rain. Since the occasion was unforeseen, I was still wearing what I had on as I left home and it meant that I had no hat, no belongings and no papers. At several

52

lodging-houses I was turned away on the spot with polite excuses about there being no vacancies. But at last I discovered a place where my travelling so light was no objection. It was a lodging-house of the lowliest sort. Once alone in the room, I sat down sideways on a chair by the window. A little table stood next to it. I slumped my head on it.

Why describe my posture in such detail? Because I stayed like that throughout the night. Just occasionally as though at someone's touch, I would raise my head and do something with the wall that slanted away under the darkened ceiling. As if with a footrule, I measured it from below with a fixed and sightless stare. Then I would start to sob again, and my face sank back into my hands.

I have described the position of my body with such accuracy because this had also been its position that morning on the step of the moving train and it had memorised the posture. It was the position of someone fallen from a lofty eminence which had long sustained and carried him but had then let him fall and rushed on noisily over his head, vanishing forever round turning.

At last I stood up. I looked around the room and flung open the window. The night was over. The rain hung in a foggy spray. It was hard to tell whether it was still falling or had stopped already. The room had been paid for in advance. Not a soul was there in the entrance-hall. I left without a word to anyone.

5

Only then was I struck by something which had probably started earlier. But it had been obscured all the time by the proximity of events and the ugliness of an adult person weeping.

I was surrounded by things transformed. Something never before experienced had invaded the substance of reality. The morning had recognised my face and appeared precisely in order to be with me and never leave me.

The mist dispersed, promising a hot day in store. Little by little the city began to move. Carts and bicycles, vans and trains began to slip in all directions. Above them human plans and desires snaked like invisible plumes. They moved and vapoured with the terseness of parable, familiar and fathomed without explanation. Birds, dogs, houses, trees and horses, men and tulips became shorter, more abrupt than I had known in child-hood. Life's laconic freshness was revealed to me. It crossed over the road, took me by the hand and led me along the pavement. Less than ever did I deserve that immense summer sky as brother. But as yet there was no talk of that. All was forgiven me for a time. In the future some day I must work to repay the morning for its faith in me. And everything around inspired a vertigo of trustfulness, like a law permitting no one to remain in debt for such a loan as this.

I had no trouble in buying a ticket and took my seat in the train. There was not long to wait before it left. And there I was bowling back to Marburg. This time, unlike the first, I was travelling by day with expenses paid and quite a different person. I was travelling in comfort on money I had borrowed from V-, and every now and then I had a mental picture of my room in Marburg.

Opposite me, smoking and with their backs towards the engine, sat a swaying row of passengers: a man in a pince-nez awaiting its chance to slip from his nose into the newspaper held directly beneath, an employee from the Forestry Commission with a game-bag over his shoulder and his shotgun in the bottom of the luggage net, and someone else, and someone else. They disturbed me no more than that mental image of my room in Marburg. They were hypnotised by the form of my silence. Occasionally I broke it deliberately to test its power over them. They understood. It was travelling with me. I was attached to its suite for the journey and wore its uniform – a popular one, and familiar to everyone from his own experience. Otherwise, of course, I would not have earned my neighbours' silent sympathy for aimiably ignoring them instead of conversing, and for the fact that without posturing I posed for the compartment rather than simply sitting there. In that compartment there was more affection and animal intuition than engine and cigar smoke. Old towns swept to meet us, and still from time to time I kept seeing a vision of my Marburg room. Why was that so?

About a fortnight before the sisters' visit, a trifling event had occurred which at the time had been of some importance to me. I had read papers in both my seminars and they had been a success and met with approval. I was prevailed upon to develop my arguments in greater detail and present them again at the end of the summer semester. I had seized on this idea and set to work with double fervour.

But an experienced observer might have told from this very ardour of mine that I would never make a scholar. I lived my academic studies more intensely than the subject itself required. I had rooted in me a certain vegetable thought habit. Its special peculiarity was that any secondary idea would unfold endlessly in my interpretation and begin demanding nourishment and attention. And whenever under its influence I referred to any books, I was drawn to them not by a selfless interest in knowledge, but by a search for literary references in support of my idea. And although my work was accomplished with the help of logic, imagination, paper and ink, I loved it most of all for the way that in the process of writing it acquired an increasingly thick incrustation of bookish quotations and comparisons. And since because of limited time I had to abandon writing things out at some point and instead left authors open at the required page, a moment arrived when the theme of my work took on substance and could be surveyed with the naked eye on entering the room. It trailed across the room in the likeness of a tree-fern whose leafy volutions rested on the table, couch and windowledge. To disturb them would have meant breaking the flow of my argument, while clearing them away completely was tantamount to burning a manuscript before any fair copy had been made. My landlady had been forbidden with utmost severity to lay a finger on them, and my room had not been tidied for some time. And during the journey, when I mentally pictured that room of mine, I actually saw my philosophy in the flesh and also its probable fate.

6

When I arrived I failed to recognise Marburg. The hill had grown taller and drawn in. The town was blackened and wizened.

The landlady opened the door for me. She looked me up and down from head to foot and asked that on future such occasions I should give either her or her daughter due notice in advance. I told her I was unable to warn them earlier because I had been compelled to make an urgent visit to Berlin without returning home. She gave me a still more mocking look. My sudden appearance from the far end of Germany without any luggage as though just back from an evening stroll did not at all match her way of thinking. She took it for a clumsy fabrication. Still shaking her head, she handed me two letters. One was in a sealed envelope, the other was a local postcard. The sealed message was from my Petersburg cousin who had unexpectedly turned up in Frankfurt. She announced that she was on her way to Switzerland and would be spending three days in Frankfurt. One third of the postcard was covered in neat, impersonal handwriting, but it was signed by another hand – one all too familiar from signatures at the foot of university announcements – Hermann Cohen. It was an invitation to dinner the following Sunday.

Roughly the following conversation in German took place between the landlady and myself: "What is today?" – "Saturday." – "I shall not be having tea. Oh, before I forget: I have to go to Frankfurt tomorrow. Please wake me in time for the first train." – "But, if I am not much mistaken, Herr Geheimrat. . . ." – "It's all right, there'll be time." – "But it's impossible. At Herr Geheimrat's they sit down at table at twelve noon, and you. . . ." But there was something unseemly about her concern. I shot the old woman an expressive glance and went to my room.

I sat down on the bed in a state of distraction, although it lasted barely more than a minute. After that I suppressed a wave of superfluous regrets and went down to the kitchen to fetch a brush and dustpan. Throwing off my jacket and rolling my sleeves up, I set to work dismantling the jointed plantlike growth. Half an hour later the room looked just as it did on the day I moved in. And not even the books borrowed from the library disturbed its orderly state: I tied them up neatly in four bundles so they would be ready to hand when I chanced to go to the library again, then I pushed them right under the bed with my foot. Just then the landlady knocked at my door. She came to tell me the exact time of tomorrow's train according to the timetable. At the sight of the change that had taken place she stopped short and with a sudden shake of her skirts, blouse and headpiece like a ruffed ball of plumage, she floated towards me in a benumbed state of quivering. She held out her hand and with wooden ceremony congratulated me on completing my difficult task. I did not want to disappoint her a second time. So I left her in her noble delusion.

Then I had a good wash, and as I dried myself I went out on to the balcony. Evening was drawing in. Wiping my neck with the towel, I looked into the distance at the road from Marburg to Ockershausen. I could now no longer recall having looked in that direction on the evening of my arrival. The end, the end! The end of philosophy! The end of any thought of it!

Like my companions in the rail compartment, philosophy too must come to terms with the fact that any love is a crossing over into some new faith.

7

It was a wonder I did not return home there and then. The value of the town lay in its school of philosophy. I had no further need of it. But it turned out to have another value.

There exist both the psychology of creativity and the problems of poetics. Yet in the whole of art the thing most immediately experienced is its actual origination. And on this subject there is no need for any guesswork.

We cease to recognise reality. It manifests itself in some new category. And this category appears to be its own inherent condition and not our own. Apart from this condition everything in the world has a name. Only it is new and is not yet named. We try to name it – and the result is art.

The clearest, most memorable and important thing in art is its actual emergence, and while recounting a great variety of things, the world's finest works of art in fact tell of their own birth. I first realised this in all its magnitude at the time I am describing.

Although as I discussed matters with V- nothing occurred to alter my situation, our discussion was accompanied by some unexpected elements resembling happiness. I was filled with despair and she consoled me. Yet her mere touch was such bliss that a wave of exultation swept away the distinct bitterness of what I had just heard and what could not be altered.

The events of the day were like a rapid, noisy rushing to and fro. All the time it was like taking a flying leap into darkness, only to come shooting out again without pause for breath. And without once stopping to look around, we paid some twenty visits that day to the overcrowded ship's hold that provided motive power for time's rowing galley. This was the adult world of which in my schoolboy's love for V- the schoolgirl I had been so furiously jealous ever since childhood.

Returning to Marburg I found myself parted not from the girl I had known six years, but from the woman I had glimpsed a few moments after she had refused me. My shoulders and arms no more belonged to me. Like someone else's limbs they begged me for the chains that shackle a man to the common cause. Because without fetters I could now no longer think of her. And I loved *her* only as a prisoner chained and fettered – I loved her only for the cold perspiration in which beauty serves out its sentence. Any thought of her instantly made me one with that cooperative chorus that fills earth with a forest of inspired and memorised movements and resembles battle, penal servitude, mediaeval hell and craftsmanship. I mean something which children do not know, and which I shall call a sense of *actual reality*.

At the start of *Safe Conduct* I said that at times love had outpaced the sun. I had in mind that manifest display of feeling which every morning

57

preempted everything around like the authenticity of a piece of news just now confirmed anew for the hundredth time. By comparison with it even sunrise assumed the character of an urban rumour that still had to be verified. In other words, I had in mind the conspicuous evidence of a force that outweighed even that of light.

If, given sufficient knowledge, ability and leisure, I had the idea of writing an aesthetics of creativity, I would build it on two concepts, those of force or energy, and of symbol. I would show that unlike science, which seizes on nature in the cross-section of a shaft of light, art is concerned with life at the moment when a beam of energy passes through it. I would take the concept of energy in that broadest of senses understood by theoretical physics, with the one difference that we would be concerned not with the principle of energy, but with its voice and presence. I would explain that in the context of self-awareness this force is referred to as "feeling".

When we imagine that *Tristan*, *Romeo and Juliet* and other memorable masterpieces contain a depiction of powerful passion, we are underestimating their content. Their theme is broader than this forceful theme. Theirs is the theme of power itself.

It is out of this theme that art is born. And it is more one-sided than people think. It cannot be arbitrarily directed where one wishes like a telescope. Focused on reality dislocated by feeling, art is a record of this dislocation and it copies it from nature. So how is nature displaced? Details gain in brilliance and lose their independence of meaning. Each can be replaced by another, and any one is precious. Any you choose is good as evidence of a condition that envelops the whole of displaced reality.

When the signs of this condition are transferred on to paper, life's own features become those of creativity. The latter strike the eye more forcibly than the former. They have been better studied, and there are terms for them. They are referred to as devices.

Art is realistic as an activity and symbolic as a fact. It is realistic because it has not itself invented metaphor, but has discovered it in nature and faithfully reproduced it. Figurative meaning also means nothing in isolation and refers to the general spirit of art as a whole, in just the same way as the parts of a dislocated reality mean nothing when taken singly.

And art is symbolic in the overall configuration of its drawing power. Its only symbol lies in the brilliance and arbitrariness of its imagery, which are characteristic of it as a whole. The interchangeability of images is the sign of a situation in which the parts of reality are mutually indifferent. Interchangeability of images – which means art itself – is energy's own symbol.

In fact, energy is the only thing that requires a language of material proofs. The remaining aspects of consciousness are durable without signs or tokens. From them there is a direct path to the visual analogy with light – to figures, precise concepts and ideas. But apart from the mobile language of images – that is, the language of accompanying features – there is no way of self-expression for energy, the fact of energy, a force lasting only for the moment of its appearance.

The direct speech of feeling is allegorical, and nothing can be used to replace it.*

8

I went to see my cousin in Frankfurt and also my own family who by that time had arrived in Bavaria. My brother came to visit me, and then my father. But I noticed none of this. I became thoroughly engrossed in writing poetry. Night and day and whenever chance offered, I wrote about the sea, about dawn, about rain in the south, and about coal in the Harz.

On one occasion I was particularly carried away. It was one of those nights that found it hard to reach the nearby fence and hung above the earth, dazed with exhaustion and with all its strength spent. There was not a breath of wind. The only sign of life was a black profile of the sky leaning feebly on the wattle fencing. And there was one other sign: the strong aroma of gilly-flowers and of tobacco in bloom, which was the earth's response to this enfeeblement. And what is beyond comparison with the sky on such a night? Large stars were like an evening party. The Milky Way – a great company. But the chalky streaks of those diagonal expanses were even more like a flowerbed at night. There were heliotropes and night-scented stocks. They were watered in the evening

*For fear of misunderstandings, let me remind the reader that I am not talking about the material content of art, nor about aspects of the substance that fills it, but about the meaning of its appearance, its place in life. Separate images in themselves are visual and rest on the analogy with light. The separate words of art, like all concepts, draw their life from cognition. But the speech of art as a whole, which cannot be quoted, consists in the movement of the allegory itself and it speaks symbolically of energy, or power.

and bent sideways. And flowers and stars were brought so close that it seemed as if the sky had come under the watering can, and now there was no way to disentangle stars from the white-flecked grass.

I was completely absorbed as I wrote, and a new sort of dust, different from before, covered my desk. The earlier, philosophical one was the accumulations of apostasy as I trembled for the wholeness of my labours. But the present dust I did not wipe away, for solidarity's sake – out of sympathy with gravel on the road to Giessen. And at the far end of the desk's oilcloth cover a tea-glass, long unrinsed, gleamed like a star in the heavens.

Suddenly I stood up soaked in sweat as everything absurdly dissolved away. I began pacing the room. "What swinish behaviour!" I thought. "Will he not still remain a genius for me? Am I breaking with *him*? It is over a fortnight since his postcard came and I began this despicable game of hide-and-seek with him. I must offer him an explanation. But how can I do that?"

I recalled how pedantic and severe he was. "Was ist Apperzeption?" he would ask some non-specialist candidate at the examination. And to a translation from the Latin that it meant "durchfassen" (to grasp through) his answer would ring out: "Nein, das heisst durchfallen, mein Herr" (No, sir, it means to fail your exam).

At his seminars the philosophical classics used to be read. He would interrupt in the middle of a reading and ask what the author was driving at. One was required to rap out the idea immediately with a single noun, in soldier fashion. It was not just vagueness that he could not tolerate, but also any approximation to the truth instead of the truth itself. He was hard of hearing in his right ear. And it was on that side of him that I sat to analyse a set passage from Kant. He allowed me to get started and lose myself in the discussion. Then, just when I least expected it, he confounded me with his usual "Was meint der Alte?" (What does the old man mean?)

I do not recall what it was. But imagine that on the multiplication table of ideas I was supposed to give the answer to five times five. "Twenty-five," I answered. He frowned and flapped a hand to one side. Then came a slight modification of my answer, which dissatisfied him because it was too tentative. And as he prodded the air, appealing for someone who knew, it is easy to imagine how my own answers kept varying and getting increasingly complex. Still, though, the talk was of two and a half tens, or of roughly half a hundred divided by two. But it was precisely the growing clumsiness of the answers that aggravated him.

Yet after his look of disgust no one ventured to repeat what I had first said. Then with a gesture that seemed to imply: "Help us out, you there in the back row," he swung round to the others. And all around there were cheery shouts of: sixty-two, ninety-eight, two hundred and fourteen. . . . He raised his hands and was hardly able to quell the storm of exultant nonsense. Then, turning towards me, he quietly and drily repeated to me my own first answer. A new storm arose in my defence. When he had grasped the situation, he surveyed me, patted my shoulder and asked where I was from and how many terms I had studied there. Then with a snort and a frown he asked me to continue, while he kept commenting: "Sehr echt, sehr richtig. Sie merken wohl? Ja, ja. Ach, ach, der Alte!" (Very true, absolutely right. Do you see that? Yes, yes. Oho, the splendid old fellow!) And there was plenty more of all this that I recalled.

But how was I to approach such a man? How could I tell him? "Verse?" he would drawl. "Verse!" Had he not studied enough of human mediocrity and its subterfuges? "Verse!"

9

Probably all this took place in July, because the lime-trees were still in blossom. The sun cut through the diamonds of their waxen flower clusters as though through a burning-glass and it scorched black circlets on the dusty leaves.

I had often walked past the parade ground. At midday the dust moved around on it like a pile-driver, and a dull shuddering clangour could be heard. Soldiers were being trained there and whenever they were drilling, schoolboys from the town and lads from the Wurstladen with trays on their shoulders would stand around in front of the parade ground and stare. Certainly it was something worth watching. Spread out all over the field were pairs of spherical dummies which leapt and pecked at one another like cockerels in sacks. The soldiers wore padded jackets and headpieces of steel netting. They were being trained to fence.

The spectacle meant nothing new to me. I had watched enough of it in the course of the summer. However on the day I have described, as I drew level with the training-ground on my way into town, I suddenly recalled that less than an hour before I had dreamed about this field. Having failed to decide what to do about Cohen during the night, I had gone to bed at dawn and slept all the morning and just before waking I had had the dream. It was a dream about a future war – a dream that was "adequate", as mathematicians say, and unavoidable.

It has often been observed that however much the regulations driven into army companies and squadrons may go on about war-time, in a period of peace the transition from premise to conclusion is beyond human grasp. Because the narrow streets of Marburg were impassable to a military unit, each day pale riflemen in faded uniform and up to their eyebrows in dust would march around the lower town. But the most that came to mind on seeing them were the stationery shops, where sheets of these same riflemen were sold together with gum-arabic as a gift offer with each dozen purchased.

In my dream, though, it was a different matter. Here impressions were not limited by the requirements of habit. Here colours were in motion and drew their own conclusions. I had a dream of a desolate field, and something suggested it was Marburg under siege. Pale, lanky Nettelbecks[35] filed past, pushing wheelbarrows. It was some dark hour of the day which never occurs in reality. The dream was one in Frederick the Great style, with earthworks and entrenchments. On the battery mounds one could just distinguish the outlines of men with telescopes. The silence enveloping them had a physical tangibility that never occurs in real life. It pulsed in the air like a crumbling blizzard of earth. And it was not a condition but an *event*, as though it was constantly being tossed up by shovels. It was the saddest dream I have ever had. Probably I wept in my sleep.

The affair with V- had settled deep within me. I had a healthy heart and it worked well. Working at night, it picked up the most accidental and worthless of the day's impressions. And now it seized on the training-ground, and this jolt was sufficient to start up the machinery of the drill-ground and in its circular path the actual dream quietly beat out a message: I am a vision of war.

I do not know why I set out for the town. But I did so with such a weight on my heart, as though even my head had been packed with earth for use as a sand-bag. It was the lunch break. At that hour none of my friends were at the university. The departmental reading-room was empty. Private houses abutted it on the lower side. The heat was merciless. Here and there at windowsills drowned corpses appeared with chewed-up collars all awry. Behind them was the vapouring half-darkness of front rooms, and from inside, pinched-looking female martyrs entered, and the fronts of their house-coats looked thoroughly boiled in laundry coppers. I turned towards home, deciding to take the upper road where there were several shady villas beneath the castle wall. Their gardens lay prostrate in the smithy-like heat and only the rose stalks bent proudly in the slow blue fire, as though taken fresh from the anvil. I longed for the little lane that descended steeply behind one of the villas. There I knew there was some shade. I decided to turn off into it and recover my breath. But apart from the stupor in which I prepared to settle down for a rest, imagine also my astonishment when I saw Professor Hermann Cohen there too! He had noticed me. My retreat was cut off.

My son is now in his seventh year. Whenever he has failed to understand some phrase in French and only guesses its meaning from the context in which it is said, he says: "I understood it not from the words, but *because*." "Because" full stop. Not because of *this* or *that*. He had understood simply "because".

I shall use this terminology of his. And the sort of mind used to *get somewhere*, as distinct from one that is simply ridden out for exercise, I shall describe as a *causal mind*. Cohen possessed just such a causal mind. Talking to him was quite frightening, and a walk with him was no joke. Strolling next to you with frequent pauses and leaning on a stick was the very soul of mathematical physics, which had assembled its basic propositions step by step, much like his present gait. Dressed in an ample frock-coat and floppy hat, this university professor was to some degree filled with the same precious essence which in times gone by was corked up in the heads of men like Galileo, Newton, Leibniz and Pascal.

He did not like to talk while walking and he only listened to the chatter of his companions, which was always disjointed because of Marburg's many stepped pavements. He would stride on, listening. Then he would suddenly stop and make some caustic pronouncement about what had just been said, after which he would use his stick to push off again from the pavement and continue the procession till the next aphoristic breathing space.

Our own conversation proceeded along the same lines. The mention of my solecism only compounded it. He led me to realise as much in quite murderous fashion, without saying a word and adding nothing to the mocking silence of his walking-stick propped on the stone. He asked about my plans, and he disapproved of them. In his opinion I should stay on to complete my doctorate and then, having passed it, return home to take the Russian state exams with the idea perhaps of coming back eventually to the West and settling there. I thanked him fervently for his hospitable offer. But my gratitude told him less than the attraction of returning to Moscow. In the way I presented it he correctly

63

detected some falsehood and absurdity, which offended him because in view of life's enigmatic brevity he could not abide enigmas that artificially shortened it further. Containing his irritation, he slowly made his way down from one flagstone to another, wondering whether this fellow would finally state his point after such obvious and wearisome platitudes.

But how could I tell him that I was throwing up philosophy once and for all? How could I say that I was going to graduate in Moscow like everybody else, just in order to have it behind me? And that I was not even thinking of coming back to Marburg? How could I tell that to a man whose farewell words on retiring were about fidelity to great philosophy? And those words of his were so delivered before the university that there was a flurry of pocket handkerchiefs along the benches where his numerous young female audience were sitting.

10

In early August my family moved from Bavaria to Italy and they invited me to join them down in Pisa. My money was exhausted and I had barely enough for the return to Moscow. On one evening of a sort I foresaw ahead of me in plenty, I was sitting in time-honoured fashion with G-v on the terrace and complaining about the sorry state of my finances. He mulled the whole question over. On various occasions he had had to live in genuine poverty, and it was at just such times that he had done plenty of globe-trotting. He had been in England and Italy and knew methods of surviving on journeys on almost nothing. His plan was that I should use the remaining money for a journey to Venice and Florence, and then go to my parents for a remedial feed-up and a fresh supply of cash for the return journey. And a subsidy might not even be necessary if I was miserly enough with the remaining money. He began putting figures down on paper and they really produced a very modest total.

The head waiter at the café was a friend of all of us. He knew everyone's inside story. At the height of the examinations, when my brother came to visit and hampered my work during the daytime, this weird eccentric discovered he had a rare talent for billiards and got him so fond of the game that early each morning he went off there to improve his play and left my room to me for the entire day.

The waiter took a lively part in the discussion of my Italian plans. Though constantly getting called away, he kept returning, and tapping G-v's estimate with his pencil, he found room for even more economies.

After one of his absences he came hurrying back with a fat reference book under his arm. Placing a tray on the table with three glasses of strawberry punch, he splayed the book and ran through the whole of it twice from cover to cover. Amid the whirling pages he found the one he wanted and then announced that I should leave that very night on the express which departed some time after three a.m. And as a token of this he proposed that we should drink a toast to my trip.

I did not need to hesitate for long. He was quite right, I thought, as I followed his reasoning. I already had my discharge from the university. My mark record was in order. It was now half past ten. It would be no great sin to wake up the landlady, and there was time and to spare for packing my belongings. It was decided. I was going.

He was as delighted as if he himself would be seeing Basel next day. "Listen," he said, licking his lips and collecting up the empty glasses, "Let's take a good look at one another. It's one of our customs. It might come in useful some day, you never know what the future holds in store." I answered with a laugh and assured him that it was quite unnecessary – I had done so long ago and would never forget him.

We said goodbye and G-v led the way out. The dull ring of nickel cutlery died away behind us – as it then seemed, forever.

A few hours later, G-v and I were in a stupor after endless talk and strolling round the town, which had quickly exhausted its small stock of streets. We walked down to the quarter adjoining the railway station. We were surrounded by mist and stood motionless in the midst of it like cattle at a watering place, and we smoked stolidly in a dull-witted silence that repeatedly extinguished our cigarettes.

Little by little day began dawning. Kitchen gardens were astringed with gooseflesh by the dew. Beds of satin seedlings burst forth from the gloom. And at this stage of dawning suddenly the whole town emerged complete and at its proper height. People were sleeping there, and there were churches, a university and castle. But they still merged with the grey sky like a wisp of cobweb on a damp mop. It even seemed as if the town had hardly made an appearance before starting to dissolve, like a trace of breath upon a pane, cut short at half a pace.

"Well, it's time to go," G-v said.

It was growing light. We walked quickly back and forth along the stone-built platform. Chunks of an approaching rumble came flying out of the fog and hit us in the faces like stones. The train rushed in. I embraced my friend, flung up my suitcase and jumped into the carriage. The flints in the concrete rolled back with a shout, a door clicked, and I pressed against the window. In an arc the train sheared away all I had experienced. Sooner than expected, the Lahn, the crossing and the highroad together with my recent home swept past, piling on top of one another. I wrenched at the window frame to lower it. It refused to budge. Then suddenly it crashed down on its own. I leaned out as far as I could. The coach swayed as it rounded a sweeping bend, and there was nothing to be seen. Farewell, philosophy! Farewell, my youth! Farewell to Germany!

11

Six years passed. Everything had been forgotten. War had dragged on and ended and revolution broken out; space, once the homeland of material, had grown sick with the gangrene of rearguard fiction and was consumed by the fading gaps of abstract non-existence; we were melted in a liquid tundra and our souls were beset by a lingering, tinkling, state-owned drizzle; water began consuming bone and there was no time left to measure it; having tasted independence we were forced to part with it and relapse long before old age into a new infancy at the imperious prompting of things; and I also lapsed into this state and settled in my family's house at their request to help maximise the use of living space. And one day, when all this had happened, the jingle of a telephone sounding out from another time crept through the snow out of the dark and into the low, single-storey twilight and rang in our apartment. "Who is speaking?" I asked. – "G-v," came the answer. It was so amazing that I was not even surprised. "Where are you?" I forced out the words, which again came from another time. He told me. Another absurdity. It turned out to be right next to us, across the yard. He was calling from a former hotel now taken over as a hostel by the People's Commissariat of Education. One minute later and I was sitting with him. His wife had not changed in the slightest. I had not met his children before.

But this was the unexpected thing. It turned out that all these years he had been living on this earth like everyone else, and although he had been abroad he had lived under a sky overcast by that same war for the liberation of small nations. I learned he had arrived recently from London, and that he was either in the party or else an ardent sympathiser. He had some official job, and with the government's removal to Moscow he had been automatically transferred with his section of the Commissariat staff.[36] And so he became our neighbour. That was the whole story.

But it was as an old Marburger that I ran to see him. Not, of course, in order to start life over again with his aid, beginning with that distant foggy dawn when we stood in the gloom like cattle at a ford, nor with the idea this time of living life just a little more carefully and avoiding war. Of course that was not my aim. But knowing in advance that such a reprise was out of the question, I ran to him to ascertain why this was the case in my life. I ran to him in order to glimpse the colour of my inescapable plight, to see its unjustly personal hue, because the commonly shared plight which I had fairly accepted along with everyone was devoid of colour and offered no escape. So I ran out to view that living absence of escape an awareness of which would in fact have amounted to escape. But there was nothing to look at. This man could not help me. He was harmed by the rising damp even more than myself.

Subsequently I had the good fortune to pay a further visit to Marburg. I spent two days there in February of 1923. I went there with my wife, but I had not the presence of mind to bring the two of them close to one another. In this I was guilty before them both. But for me too it was far from easy. I had seen Germany before the war. Now I was seeing it afterwards and was presented with a horrendous foreshortened image of what had taken place in the world. It was the period of occupation of the Ruhr. Germany was cold and hungry. She was deceived by nothing and deceived no one. In a quite uncharacteristic gesture she stretched out a hand for alms, and the whole country walked on crutches. To my surprise I found my landlady still alive. At the sight of me, she and her daughter threw up their hands in astonishment. When I appeared they both sat sewing exactly where they had sat eleven years before. My room was to let. They opened it up for me. I would not have recognised it but for the Ockershausen road which as before could still be seen from the window. And it was winter. The untidiness of the cold, empty room and the bare willows on the horizon were all unfamiliar to me. A landscape that had once brooded too much on the Thirty Years War had finished up by visiting upon itself a prophecy of war. As I departed I called at a confectioner's and had a large nut-cake sent to the two women.

And now à propos of Cohen: Cohen we could not see. Cohen had died.

12

And so came station after station after station. Like moths made of stone, they rushed by and fled to the rear of the train.

In Basel there was a sabbath stillness and one could hear scurrying swallows scrape the eaves with their wings. Beneath roof overhangs of black cherry tiles blazing walls rolled up like eyeballs, and the whole town seemed to stare or blink from under prominent eyelashes. And the same kiln fire that blazed from the wild vines of private houses burned also in the ceramic gold of the Primitives hanging in the cool, clean museum.

"Zwei francs, vierzig centimes." The peasant shopwoman in her canton costume enunciated with amazing clarity. But the confluence of two reservoirs of language was not here. It was further to the right, beyond the low overhanging roof, towards the south, across the hot broad federal azure, a steady uphill climb. It was somewhere below the St Gotthard so they said – somewhere in the depths of night.

And to think that I went and slept through such a place, exhausted as I was by the night vigils of a two-day journey! The one night in life when I should not have slept – it was almost like "Simon, sleepest thou?". May it be forgiven me. But there were still moments when I did awake and when I stood for a shamefully short time by the window. "For their eyes were heavy," and then. . . .

. . . And then all around was the din of a rural gathering of peaks met in motionless assembly. Aha, so while I was dozing and we had bored our way with repeated whistleblasts through the cold smoke of tunnel after tunnel, we had been surrounded by a breath of air three thousand metres loftier than the one to which we were born!

The dark was impenetrable, but the echo filled it with a sculpture of convex acoustics. The chasms conversed with unashamed loudness, like old wives' gossip at the earth's expense. And everywhere, but everywhere, was the carping prattle and gossip of trickling streams. It was easy to imagine them strung about the steep declivities and dangling down into the valley like twisted yarns. And plummeting slopes leapt on to the train from above and settled on the carriage roofs, kicking their legs and shouting, enjoying the free ride.

But sleep was overcoming me. On the threshold of the snows, beneath the blinded Oedipal eye-whites of the Alps, at our planet's demoniac perfect pinnacle, at the height of the self-enamoured kiss planted on her own shoulder by Michelangelo's Night . . . there I lapsed into an illicit slumber.

When I awoke, a clean Alpine morning gazed in at the windows. Our train had been halted by some obstacle or a landslide, and we were asked to change to another. We set off on foot along the mountain railtrack. The ribbon of the rails twisted away through disjointed panoramas, as though the track were constantly being thrust round a corner like stolen goods. My belongings were carried by a barefooted Italian boy, just like the ones on the chocolate wrapper. Somewhere nearby one could hear the music of his herd. The tinkling of the little bells fell in lazy swings and shakes. The music was sucked by gad-flies and its hide probably moved with sudden twitches. There was a sweet scent of chamomile and never an end to the constant aimless pouring and splashing of invisible water on every side.

The effects of too little sleep were soon to be felt. I was in Milan for half a day and recall nothing of it. I have a dim impression only of the cathedral. As I approached it through the city, it changed aspect all the time according to the crossroads where it successively revealed itself. Several times it loomed like a melting glacier against the vertiginous blue of an August heat and seemed to supply ice and water to Milan's numerous coffee-houses. At last a narrow square set me at its foot. I craned back my head, and the cathedral cascaded into me with its entire rustling chorus of pilasters and turrets, like a plug of snow slithering through the jointed column of a drain-pipe.

However, I could barely stand on my feet, and the first thing I promised myself on arrival in Venice was to catch up on all the sleep I had lost.

13

When I emerged from the station building with its provincial awning roof in Customs and Excise style, something smooth slid softly beneath my feet – something malignantly dark, like offal, and touched by the sequins of two or three stars. It rose and fell almost imperceptibly and resembled a time-blackened painting in a swaying frame. I did not realise immediately that this depiction of Venice was actually Venice itself, that there I was in it, and this was not a dream.

The station canal went like a blind gut, away round a corner to witness further wonders of that floating gallery of sewerage. I hurried off to the mooring point for the cheap steam-boats which here took the place of tramcars.

The boat sweated and panted and wiped its nose and spluttered. And across the same serene surface where it trailed its water-logged moustaches the palaces of the Canale Grande drifted in a semi-circle and gradually fell away behind us. Palaces they call them, and they could well be noble halls. Yet no words convey any idea of those hangings of hued marble which have been dropped plumb into a night-bound lagoon as if on the arena of some mediaeval tournament.

There is a special Orient – that of the Pre-Raphaelites, which has all the character of Christmas celebration. There is an image of starry night, based on the legend of the Wise Men's Adoration. There is an ancient Christmas scene carved in relief – the surface of a gilded walnut splashed with dark blue candle-wax. And there are words like *khalva* and Chaldea, Magi and magnesium, India and indigo. The nocturnal colouring of Venice and its watery reflections belong in the same company.

And as if to stress its range of walnut qualities to the Russian ear, as the boat drew in now at one bank now at another, shouted announcements were made for the passengers' information: "Fondaco dei Turchi! . . . Fondaco dei Tedeschi!" Of course, the names of the city quarters have nothing in common with *funduki*, the Russian word for hazel-nuts. They contain memories of the caravansaries established here long ago by Turkish and German merchants.[37]

I do not recall which of those innumerable Vendraminis, Grimanis, Corneros, Foscaris and Loredanos we were in front of when I saw my first gondola – or the first one that struck me. But it was certainly on the far side of the Rialto. It emerged into the canal noiselessly from a side-inlet and cutting across, it began to moor at the nearest palace portal. It appeared as though dispatched from an inner court to the main entrance on the rounded belly of a gently rolling wave. Behind it a dark crevice remained, full of dead rats and dancing melon peel, while before it unfurled the lunar desolation of a broad waterway. The gondola had a feminine hugeness – just as everything is huge which is perfect in form and incommensurate with the space it occupies. Its bright crested halberd flew airily across the sky, borne high on the round nape of the wave. The black silhouette of the gondolier ran with the same ease among the stars, while in the saddle between stern and prow the small cowl of the cabin disappeared as though pressed into the water.

From G-v's accounts of Venice, I had already decided it would be best to find lodgings in the region of the Academy. So that was where I alighted. I cannot recall whether I crossed over the bridge on to the left bank, or whether I stayed on the right. I do recall a tiny square surrounded by palaces similar to those on the canal. Only these were greyer and more severe, and they rested firmly on dry ground.

On that moon-bathed square some people stood or strolled, or half-reclined. There were not many of them and they seemed to drape the square with bodies that moved, moved little, or moved not at all. The evening was unusually calm. My gaze was caught by one pair in particular. Enjoying a mutual silence and without turning to one another, they gazed intently at the distant opposite bank. Probably they were servants from the

70

palazzo taking a rest. I was first attracted by the calm bearing of the valet, his close-cropped grizzled hair and the grey hue of his jacket. There was something un-Italian, almost a breath of the north, about them. Then I caught sight of his face. I seemed to have seen it once before, but I could simply not recall where.

Going up to him with my suitcase, I explained to him my concern to find lodgings, speaking in a non-existent dialect which I made up from earlier attempts to read Dante in the original. He listened politely, thought for a moment and put some question to the housemaid standing next to him. She shook her head negatively. He took out his watch and looked at the time, then clicked the lid shut and returned it to his waistcoat pocket. Then, still looking pensive, he motioned me to follow him. We left the moon-bathed façade and turned a corner into pitch darkness.

We went along stone-paved alleys no wider than a household passage. From time to time they took us up on to short bridges of humpback stone. The dirty branches of a lagoon stretched on both sides, the water so confined that it looked like a Persian carpet rolled and crammed into the bottom of a crooked crate.

On the humpbacked bridges we encountered passers-by, and a Venetian woman's approach was heralded a long time before by the rapid clack of her shoes on the flagstones of the quarter.

High above the pitch-black clefts through which we roamed, the night sky glowed and constantly receded. The down of a shedding dandelion seemed scattered along the entire Milky Way. And apparently just in order to let through a column or two of this shifting light the alleys occasionally moved apart to form squares and crossroads. Surprised at my escort's strange familiarity, I chatted away with him in my non-existent dialect and rolled from pitch into down and from down into pitch as I searched with his help for the cheapest possible lodgings.

But on the embankments by the exits on to open water other colours reigned and the stillness gave way to uproar. People crowded on the arriving and departing *vaporetti* and the oily black water erupted in a spray of snow like shattered marble, broken to pieces in the mortars of those engines which hotly pounded or abruptly died. And next to the water's gurgling, burners hissed brightly in the fruiterers' stalls, tongues were at work, and fruits were crushed and bounced in the vacuous columns of some half-cooked compote.

We received helpful directions in one of the restaurant sculleries by the shore. The address we were given sent us all the way back to the start of our wanderings. As we headed there, we retraced our whole journey in reverse. So when my guide finally installed me at one of the hotels near the Campo Morosini, it felt as if I had traversed a distance equal to the Venetian starry sky, travelling round to meet it in the opposite direction. If I had been asked just then what Venice was, I would have answered: Bright nights and tiny squares, and placid people with a strange familiarity.

14

"Well then, my friend!" the landlord roared at me as though I was deaf. He was a vigorous old man of about sixty in a dirty open shirt. "We'll fix you up like one of the family!" The blood rose to his face, he measured me from under his brow, and with his hands threaded in the buckles of his braces he drummed his fingers on his hairy chest. "Like some cold veal?" he bawled with the same hard look, and gathered nothing whatsoever from my reply.

He was probably a genial fellow who with his moustaches à la Radetzki made himself out to be a terror. He could remember the days of Austrian rule and, as I soon discovered, he spoke a little German. But since he thought of it mainly as the language of Dalmatian warrant-officers, my fluent speech prompted him to reflect sadly on the decline of German since his soldiering days. In addition to that he also probably suffered from heartburn.

He rose from behind the counter as though on stirrups, roared a bloodthirsty remark to someone out of sight, and made a springy descent into the little yard where we made one another's acquaintance. There were several small tables there with grubby tablecloths. "I took to you as soon as you came in," he grated with malevolent glee. He waved a hand inviting me to be seated while he settled himself on a chair two or three tables away. I was brought some beer and meat.

The little courtyard served as a dining-room. The hotel patrons – if there were any – had probably had supper long ago and retired to their rooms. Only one squalid little old man still sat in a far corner of gluttons' arena and obsequiously expressed agreement whenever the landlord addressed him.

As I tucked into my veal, I noticed once or twice that the moist pink slices vanished and kept reappearing on my plate. I must have been dozing off and my eyelids were gumming together.

All of a sudden, as in a fairy-tale, a kindly, withered old lady appeared at the table and the landlord briefly informed her of his furious affection for me. I immediately followed her somewhere up a narrow stair and was then left alone. I groped and found the bed and after undressing in the darkness I lay down without another thought.

After ten hours of headlong, uninterrupted sleep I awoke to a bright sunny morning. Gradually the incredible was confirmed. I was in Venice. It was announced to me by patches of bright reflection that swarmed on the ceiling like in the cabin of a river steamer. And they also told me I was to get up immediately and rush to look around.

I examined the room where I lay. Skirts and blouses hung on nails hammered into the painted partition. There was a feather duster on a ring, and a carpet-beater hooked on its nail by a plaited loop. The windowsill was cluttered with various ointments in tins, and an empty sweet carton contained some unrefined chalk.

Behind a curtain stretched right across the attic I could hear the knocking and scrubbing of a shoe-brush. It had been going on for a long while. They were obviously cleaning shoes for the whole hotel. I could also hear the lisp and murmur of a woman and child. I recognised the whispering as that of the little old woman of yesterday evening. She was a distant relative of the landlord and worked as one of his housekeepers. He had let me have her poky little kennel to sleep in, and when I wanted to set matters right, she herself besought me in alarm not to interfere in their family affairs.

Before getting dressed, I stretched myself once more and surveyed everything around me. Suddenly a moment's clarity illuminated the previous day's events. My escort of yesterday reminded me of the head waiter in Marburg – the one who had hoped he might yet be of some use to me. The hint of imputation in his request had probably increased the resemblance further – this was the reason for my instinctive preference of one individual to all the other folk.

I was not surprised to discover this. There was nothing miraculous about it. Our most innocent hello's and goodbye's would be meaningless if time were not sewn through by the unity of life's events – by the crossing inter-effects of a day-to-day common hypnosis.

15

So I too learnt the touch of this happiness. I too had the fortune to learn that day after day one could go out to a rendez-vous with some built-up space as though it were a live personality.

However one approached the Piazza, along every path, a moment lay in store when breathing quickened and one's legs carried one towards it of their own accord and with speeding step. From the direction of the Merceria or the Telegraph Office, at a certain point the road became as it were a threshold, and the square flung wide its own broadly planned world and led forth the Campanile, the Duomo, Doges' Palace and the gallery as though to some reception.

Gradually, as one grows attached to it, one has the sensation that Venice is a city inhabited by buildings – the four I have mentioned and several others of their type. Nor is this a figurative statement. The speech pronounced in stone by architects is so sublime that no rhetoric can reach such height. Moreover, it is overgrown by centuries of travellers' delight as though encrusted with seashells. And this ever increasing rapture has removed from Venice all trace of declamation. In those empty palazzi there are no empty spaces. Everywhere is filled with beauty.

Before they sit in the gondola hired to take them to the station, Englishmen linger for one last time on the Piazzetta in postures that would be natural if they were bidding goodbye to a living person. One envies them that square all the more since it is well known that no European culture has come so close to that of Italy as the English.

16

Beneath these standard-bearing masts with generations intertwined like golden threads there crowded once upon a time three centuries, magnificently woven one into another. And not far from the square the fleet of those centuries slumbered, a motionless thicket of ships which seemed like an extension of the city's plan. Rigging jutted from behind garrets, galleys peered surreptitiously, and whether on board ship or dry land movements were identical. On a moonlit night some three-decker would stare directly at the street and fix it with the thunderous frozen menace of its immobile unfurling thrust. Frigates also rode at anchor in the same funereal grandeur and chose the quietest, deepest halls to admire from their position on the roadstead. For those times it was a mighty fleet. Its size was astonishing. In the fifteenth century already it numbered three and a half thousand merchant ships alone, not counting military ones, and there were seventy thousand sailors and naval workmen.

This fleet was Venice's tangible reality, the prosaic lining of its fairy-tale exterior. To put it paradoxically, one could say that the fleet's maritime shifting tonnage formed the city's terra firma, its territorial holdings and its subterrain of trade and prisons. The air sorrowed and sighed, held captive in ships' rigging. The fleet was something that enervated and oppressed. But, as in a couple of connecting vessels, something redemptive arose from the shore as an equal response to its pressure. And to understand this means understanding how art always deceives the client who commissions it.

A curious thing is the origin of the word "pantaloons". At one time, before its later meaning of "trousers", it denoted a character in Italian comedy. But even earlier, in its original meaning, "pianta leone" expressed the idea of victorious Venice and meant "hoister of the lion" (the one on its banner), in other words, Venice the Conqueror. There is a passage about this even in Byron's *Childe Harold*:

> Her very byword sprung from victory,
> The "Planter of the Lion", which through fire
> And blood she bore o'er subject earth and sea.

Concepts are capable of being transformed in amazing fashion. Once horrors have become part of people's habit, they even form the foundations of good taste. Can we ever appreciate how the guillotine for a time provided the pattern for a ladies' brooch?

The emblem of the lion has figured in Venice in a variety of ways. Thus, on the Censors' staircase right next to paintings by Veronese and Tintoretto, the slit for depositing secret denunciations was sculpted in the shape of a lion's maw. It is well known what terror this "bocca di leone" struck into the hearts of contemporaries, and that gradually it became a sign of ill-breeding to mention any persons mysteriously fallen through that exquisitely carved orifice when the authorities themselves expressed no regrets.

While art erected palaces for enslavers, people trusted it. They thought it shared the commonly held views of the day and would share a common future fate. But that is precisely what failed to happen. The language of the palaces turned out to be a language of oblivion, and not at all the *pianta leone* language that was erroneously ascribed to them. The aims of pantaloonery decayed. The palaces remained.

And Venetian painting has also remained. From childhood I was familiar with the taste of its hot well-springs from reproductions and the exported overflow from museums. But one had to go to the geological source in order to see not separate pictures, but painting itself like a golden marshland, a primordial pool of creativity.

75

17

At the time, I viewed this spectacle more hazily and profoundly than my present formulations of it might convey. I did not attempt to make sense of what I saw in the way in which I shall now interpret it. But over the years my impressions have of their own accord settled in this form, and the concise conclusion I shall now offer will not be far from the truth.

I saw which observation it is which first strikes our pictorial instinct. I saw how the object is grasped all of a sudden, and what it is like for it when it begins to be viewed. Once noticed, nature moves aside like the obedient expanse of some tale, and it is then quietly transferred to the canvas in this condition, as in a state of sleep. One has to see Carpaccio and Bellini in order to realise what depiction means.

Furthermore, I discovered the syncretism accompanying a flowering of artistry, whereby once there is complete identity between the artist and his medium it becomes impossible to say which of the three is more actively manifest on canvas and in whose favour – the executant, the thing executed, or the subject of that execution. Owing to this confusion one envisages misunderstandings in which, as the artist's era poses for him, it might imagine it is elevating him to its own ephemeral greatness. One has to see Veronese and Titian in order to realise the meaning of art.

Finally, while understanding these impressions at the time, I recognised how little a genius requires in order to erupt. All around there is the haunting sight of lions' muzzles, nosing into every privacy, sniffing everything, lions' jaws that devour one life after another in the secrecy of their lair. All around there is the leonine roar of an imaginary immortality, conceivable without laughter only because everything immortal rests in its hands and is held on a stout lion's rein. Everyone senses it and everyone endures it. To feel *only this* requires no genius – it is seen and endured by everyone. But since it is endured in common by all, it means that this menagerie must contain something that is seen and felt by *no one*. And this is precisely the droplet which causes the genius' patience to overflow. Who would believe it? It is the identity between depiction, depicter, and the subject depicted – or, to put it more broadly, an indifference to immediate truth – which arouses genius to fury. It is like a slap in the face of the humanity which he personifies. And into his canvases blows a storm which purifies craftsmanship's chaos by the definitive strokes of passion. One has to see the Venetian Michelangelo – Tintoretto – in order to realise the meaning of genius, that is, the meaning of the word "artist".

18

But in those days I did not go into such details. In Venice at the time, and even more strongly in Florence – or, to be quite exact, in the Moscow winters following my journey – other more specific ideas came to mind.

The main thing that everyone takes away with him from an encounter with Italian art is a sense of the tangible unity of our culture, wherever he may have seen it and however he might describe it.

For instance, what a lot has been said about the paganism of the Humanists. And how variously it has been described both as a legitimate tendency and otherwise. And it is true, the collision of faith in the resurrection with the age of the Renaissance is an unusual phenomenon and a central one for all of European culture. Moreover, who can have failed to observe the anachronism – often an immoral one – in the treatment of canonical themes in all those "Presentations", "Ascensions", "Weddings in Cana" and "Last Suppers" with their licentious high-life luxuriousness?

It was here, precisely in this incongruity, that I became aware of the millennial peculiarity of our culture. Italy crystallised for me what we unconsciously breathe in from our cradle. Its painting automatically completed what I had still to think out for myself on the subject, and as I went day after day from one collection to another it cast at my feet an observation distilled from the paint, ready and complete.

I realised, for instance, that the Bible is not so much a book with a hard and fast text as a notebook of humanity, and that everything long-lasting is like that: it is vital not when it is enforced but when it is amenable to every comparison drawn in the retrospective review of later ages. I realised that the history of culture is a chain of equations in the shape of images which form pairs linking the already known with the next unknown. And the known element, which remains constant for the whole series, is the legend underlying the tradition, whereas the unknown which is new each time is that actual moment in the stream of culture.

This is what interested me then, and this is what I then understood and loved. I loved the vital essence of historical symbols – in other words, the instinct with whose help we have constructed a world, like Salangane swallows building their immense nest, glued together from earth and heaven, life and death, and from two different times – the present and the absent. And I realised that what prevents it from falling apart is a cohesive force contained in the figurative quality which permeates all its parts.

But I was still young then and failed to realise that this does not completely embrace the fate and the nature of genius. I did not realise that the essence of genius rests in the experience of his own life and not in a symbolic system of refracted images. I did not realise that, unlike the Primitives, his roots lie in the rude immediacy of moral intuition. One of his features is remarkable. Although every flash of moral aberration is acted out within a culture, it always appears to the rebel that his revolt is something that rolls along the street outside culture's boundary fence. I did not realise that the iconoclast leaves the most time-tested images undisturbed only in those rare cases when he is not born empty-handed.

Pope Julius II once expressed displeasure at the impoverished colouring of the Sistine Chapel's painted ceiling. But in a reference to its scene of the world's creation and the figures belonging there, Michelangelo justified himself with the remark that "In *those* days men were not decked out in gold. The people represented here were *not* men of wealth." Such is the thunderous yet childlike speech of men such as he.

The frontiers of culture are reached by the man who conceals within himself a tamed Savonarola. But Savonarola untamed is culture's destroyer.

19

On the evening before my departure there was a concert and illuminations in the Piazza of a sort frequently held there. The building façades surrounding the Piazza were adorned from top to bottom with sharp points of electric light, and it was illuminated on three sides by a black and white banner. The faces of those listening under the open sky seemed broiled in the bath-house glare of a wonderfully illuminated enclosed building. Suddenly, from the roof of the imaginary ballroom a light rain began falling. But hardly had the shower started before it abruptly ceased again. The glow of reflected lighting simmered above the square in a coloured haze. The belfry of Saint Mark's sheared like a rocket of red marble into the pink mist that half shrouded its pinnacle. A little further off whirled dark-olive vapours that provided a fairytale concealment for the five-headed frame of the cathedral. The far end of the square appeared like an underwater realm. And surmounting the cathedral porch in a glitter of gold was a team of four horses, which swept at a gallop from ancient Greece and seemed to halt there on the brink of an abyss.

When the concert was over, a steadily shuffling millstone could be heard which had earlier been turning in the encircling galleries but was drowned out by the music. It was the mingled noise of strollers' footsteps as they circulated, and it sounded like the rustle of skates in the bowl of a frozen rink.

Among the strollers, women walked by with angry, rapid step. They seemed to threaten rather than radiate charm, and they kept turning round as they went, as though to repulse and annihilate. Bodies curved provocatively, they disappeared quickly beneath the porticoes, and as they looked back they fixed one with the stare of a deathly mascara face under a black Venetian kerchief. Moving with a rapid *allegro irato*, their gait corresponded strangely with the illuminations' black shivering amid white scratches of diamond light.

I have twice tried to express in verse a sensation which for me is forever bound up with Venice. During the night before I left, I was roused in my hotel by the sound of an arpeggio played on the guitar, which broke off the moment I awoke. I rushed to the window. The water was splashing down below and I began gazing intently into the depths of the night sky, as though to discover some trace of that suddenly extinguished sound. From the way I gazed in my semi-wakeful state, an onlooker might have thought I was investigating whether some new constellation had risen over Venice, and I had a vague preconception of it as the "Constellation of the Guitar".

Part Three

1

The path cut through Moscow by its chain of boulevards was screened in winter by a double curtain of blackened trees. In the houses, lights glowed yellow like stellate circles of lemon cut through the centre. A blizzard-laden sky hung low over the trees, and all around everything white was blue.

Poorly dressed young people hurried along the boulevards, their heads bent forward as if ready to butt. I was acquainted with some of them. The majority I did not know. But all of them together were people of my age, countless faces of my childhood.

They had only just started to be addressed formally, invested with rights and initiated into the secret of such verbs as to "acquire", to "profit" and "appropriate". And they all displayed an urgency that deserves closer analysis.

There exist in this world both death and foreknowledge. We are fond of the unknown, what we know in advance is terrifying, and any passion is a blind leap to one side as the inevitable bears down upon us. Common time – a time in which our universe is gradually destroyed – common time goes bowling down a common road, and if passion had nowhere to spring aside from this common road, living species would have nowhere to exist and reproduce themselves. But there *is* a place for life to live and for passion to leap, because alongside common time there exists an unending infinity of roadside customs and observances, immortal in their self-reproduction, and each new generation is one of them.

Bending forward as they ran, young people hurried through the blizzard, and though each one had his reasons for haste, more than by any personal promptings they were goaded along by something they had in common. And this was their historical integrity, their surrender to the passion with which humanity had just rushed into them, fleeing from the common road and for one more countless time avoiding its own end.

And to shield them from the ambiguity of their flight through the inevitable, and so that they would not go mad and abandon what they had begun and all hang themselves to a man, a force stood watch behind the trees along all the boulevards, a force that was terribly tried and experienced and which followed them all with its intelligent gaze. Behind the trees stood art, which has such wonderful understanding of our make-up that one is always at a loss to know from what unhistorical worlds it has derived its ability to see history in outline. It stood behind the trees and bore an awful resemblance to life and was for that reason tolerated within it – just as portraits of wives and mothers are tolerated in scientists' laboratories devoted to the natural sciences, i.e. to a gradual solution of death's mystery.

So what kind of art was this? It was the youthful art of Scriabin, of Blok, Kommissarzhevskaya[38] and Bely, enthralling, advanced and original. And it was so striking that not only did it evoke no thoughts of its own replacement. On the contrary, to increase its durability one felt like repeating it from the very foundation, only more swiftly, heatedly and wholly. One wanted to retell it all again in a single burst – and that was unthinkable without passion. But passion leapt to one side, and in this way something new was created. Only the new did not come to replace the old, according to the usual idea. Quite the contrary, it arose from a rapturous reproduction of its model.

Such was the art. But what of the generation?

The boys close to me in age were thirteen years old in nineteen five,[39] and they were in their twenty-second year just before the war. Both these critical times coincided with red-letter days in the history of our homeland. Their boyhood's maturing and their coming of age for call-up went straight to form the tie-bars in an age of transition. Our time is sewn through length and breadth with their nerves and has been graciously placed at the disposal of old men and children. But to appreciate their character fully, one must recall the state system whose air they breathed.

Nobody knew that it was the Stuart King Charles I or Louis XVI on the throne. Why is it that it is always the last monarchs who seem to be monarchs *par excellence*? Evidently there is something tragic in the very essence of hereditary rule.

A political autocrat engages in politics only in those rare instances when he is a Peter the Great. Examples like these are exceptional and are remembered for thousands of years. But often Nature limits a sovereign more completely because she is not a parliament and the limitations she imposes are absolute. As a rule sanctified by centuries, "hereditary monarch" is the term for a person ceremonially charged with no more than one of the chapters in the dynastic biography. And here there is a relic of sacrificiality which is even more nakedly emphasised in this role of theirs than in the beehive. What happens to people of this dread calling if they turn out not to be Julius Caesars? If their experience does not boil over as political activity? If they lack the quality of genius, the only thing which liberates them from fate in their own lifetime in favour of a posthumous one?

Then instead of skating they skid, instead of diving they drown, and they do not live but develop a set of touchy responses which reduce life to a state of ornamental vegetation. At first such responses come hourly, then by the minute. First they are genuine, then they are invented. They appear first of all without outside assistance, and later on with the help of table-turning. At the sight of the boiler they are scared of its bubbling. Ministers assure them that this is in the order of things, and that the more perfect the boilers the more dreadful the bubbling. A technique of state reforms is elaborated consisting in the transfer of heat energy into motive force and stating that a state flourishes only when it threatens to explode yet does not actually do so. So then they screw up their eyes in fear, grab for the whistle safety-valve and with the meekness natural to them they lay on a Khodynka,[40] a Kishinyov pogrom[41] or a Bloody Sunday.[42] Then they turn away in confusion and return to their temporarily interrupted diary and their family.

The ministers clasp their heads. It finally emerges that territories sited afar are governed by those that are not far-sighted. Explanations have no effect, and counsel fails to achieve its purpose. These men are slaves of the nearest and most obvious things, and they concluded by analogy that one thing is like another. It is too late to reschool them. Catastrophe approaches. And as supporters leave in obedience to orders of dismissal, these men are abandoned to its mercy.

They see the catastrophe approaching. And from its threats and demands they rush away to the most dread and demanding thing in the household. The voices of Henrietta Maria, Marie-Antoinette and Aleksandra sound ever louder in the fearful chorus. The progressive aristocracy are kept at a distance – as though the public in the square were interested in the life of the palace and required a reduction of its comforts! Appeals are made to Versailles gardeners, to lance-corporals of Tsarskoye Selo and self-taught men of the people. Then one sees the appearance and rapid rise of the Rasputins, totally unrecognised capitulations by the monarchy to a people understood in purely folkloric terms, concessions to trends of the time that are monstrously at variance with anything required of genuine concessions because these are only self-inflicted injuries which bring not the slightest benefits to others. And usually it is precisely this incongruity which reveals the doomed nature of their terrible calling, decides their fate and by the tokens of its own weakness gives the rousing signal to revolt.

When I returned from abroad, it was the centenary of the war with Napoleon. The Brest Railway Line had been renamed the Aleksandrovskaya.[43] Stations had been whitewashed and the watchmen manning the signal-bells were dressed in clean shirts. The station building at Kubinka was festooned with flags and the guards on the doors were reinforced. An imperial review was taking place nearby, and the platform was ablaze for the occasion with a bright scattering of sand which had not yet been stamped down.

For those in the train none of this conjured up any recollection of the events being celebrated. The jubilee decorations were redolent of the chief feature of that reign – indifference to our national history. And if the festivities were reflected in anything, it was not in the train of men's thoughts but the train in which we were riding and which was held up at stations and halted by signals in open country more often and longer than it should have been.

I could not help recalling Serov,[44] who had died the previous winter, and I remembered his stories about the time he painted the imperial family, the caricatures produced by artists attending the Yusupovs' sketching evenings,[45] the curious incidents accompanying the Kutepov edition of *The Tsar's Hunt*,[46] and a host of other apposite trivialities linked with the School of Painting which came under one of the imperial ministries and had been our home for about twenty years. I might also have recalled the year nineteen five, the drama in the family of Kasatkin,[47] and my own twopenny-halfpenny revolutionism, which went no further than a show of bravado in the face of a Cossack's whip and a lash across the back of my quilted overcoat. And finally, with regards to the station guards and the flags, they too of course presaged a drama of high seriousness, and they were not at all the innocent vaudeville that I imagined in my frivolous apoliticism.

I might have said that the generation was an apolitical one, were I not aware that that insignificant section with which I had dealings is insufficient to judge the whole intelligentsia by. I can say, though, that this was the side which it presented to me. And the generation also turned the same side towards the times in its first emergence with pronouncements about its own particular science, philosophy and art.

2

However, culture does not simply fall into the embrace of the first to come seeking it. All that I have enumerated had to be battled for. The concept of love as a duel is also relevant here. Art could be transferred to an adolescent only by experiencing its forceful attraction with the full excitement of a personal event. The literature of budding writers at the time bore all the vivid signs of this. The novices banded together in groups. And the groups divided into those of epigones and innovators.

Unthinkable in isolation, these were the elements of an impulse sensed so urgently that it pervaded everything around with an atmosphere of romance that was not merely anticipated but already happening. The epigones represented impulse without fervour or talent, and the innovators – a militancy animated by nothing but castrated hatred. These were the words and gestures of serious discourse overheard by an ape and distributed haphazardly in verbatim fragments without the faintest idea of what meaning had aroused and inspired the storm.

Meanwhile, already hanging in the air was the fate of some still unidentified chosen one. It was almost possible to say what he would be like, though nobody could say yet who it would be. In outward appearance dozens of young people seemed identically restless, thought identical thoughts, and raised identical claims to originality. As a movement the innovators were marked by an apparent unanimity. But like the movements of every age, this was the unanimity of lottery tickets whirling in a swarm as they were mixed ready for the draw. And the movement was fated forever to remain a movement, a curious instance of mechanically shifting odds, as soon as one of those tickets emerged from the lottery wheel and blazed up with the flame of victory and acquired a face and a name. The movement was called Futurism.

And the victor who justified the draw was Mayakovsky.[48]

3

Our first meeting took place in the inhibited atmosphere of group prejudices. Long before that, in the way that one poet shows off another, Yulian Anisimov had shown me his verses printed in *The Judges' Hatchery*.[49] But that was in the epigone circle called "Lirika". The epigones were not ashamed of their sympathies, and in their circle Mayakovsky was discovered as a phenomenon of promising proximity, like a colossus.

On the other hand, in the innovatory "Tsentrifuga" group of which I soon formed part (this was in the spring of 1914),[50] I learned that Shershenevich,[51] Bolshakov[52] and Mayakovsky were our enemies and that a deadly earnest confrontation was in store. I was not in the least surprised at the prospect of a quarrel with the man who had already astonished me and whom from a distance I found increasingly attractive. That was all there was to the innovators' originality. All winter the birth of "Tsentrifuga" was accompanied by endless rows. All winter I was aware of doing nothing but playing a game of group discipline, and all I had done was sacrifice both taste and conscience to it. Now I prepared once again to betray anything and everything when the time came. But on this occasion I overestimated myself.

It was a hot day in late May, and we were already sitting in a teashop on the Arbat when the three men just mentioned staged a noisy, youthful entrance from the street. They handed their hats to the attendant and without toning down their conversation, which up till now had been outdinned by tramcars and cart-horses, they approached us with relaxed dignity. They had beautiful voices – this marked the beginning of what later became the declamatory manner in poetry. Their dress was elegant, whereas ours was slovenly. Our adversaries' position was in every way superior to our own.

It all hinged on the fact that they had once provoked us, we had answered even more rudely, and now the whole matter had to be cleared up. Whilst Bobrov[53] wrangled with Shershenevich, I watched Mayakovsky without taking my eyes off him. I believe it was the first time I saw him at such close quarters.

His open letter "e" instead of "a" was an actor's trait which rocked his diction like a piece of sheet iron. His deliberate brusqueness could easily be imagined as the hallmark of other professions and situations. He was not alone in this striking manner. His companions sat next to him. One of them played the dandy as he did. The other, like him, was a genuine poet. Yet these similarities did not diminish the exceptional quality of Mayakovsky but only emphasised it. Instead of playing one game, he played all of them at once. And instead of playing roles, Mayakovsky on the contrary played at life itself. This much could be sensed at first glance without any thought of his eventual fate. And it was this that riveted one's attention and also scared one.

Although any person can be seen at full height when he walks or stands, whenever Mayakovsky appeared it seemed miraculous and every head turned in his direction. What was natural in his case appeared to be supernatural. The reason for this was not his stature, but a more general elusive quality. To a greater extent than with other people, his whole being was there in his personal manifestation. He contained within him all the expression and finality which are lacked by the majority, who rarely emerge from the murk of their half-brewed intentions and barren conjectures – and then only do so when particularly jolted. He seemed to exist as on the day after completing some immense spiritual life that had been lived through already in reserve for all future occasions, and

85

everyone now encountered him wreathed in its irreversible consequences. He would sit down on a chair as though mounting a motorbike. He bent forward, cut and quickly swallowed his Wiener Schnitzel. He played cards with sidelong glance and never a turn of the head. He walked majestically along the Kuznetsky and dully intoned through his nose some particularly profound snatches of his own and other people's verse, like extracts from the liturgy. He scowled, he grew, he travelled and he gave public recitations. And just as behind the upright stance of a speeding skater, always in the background one seemed to glimpse some day of Mayakovsky's own, preceding all others, on which he had taken that amazing run-up which set him so unconstrainedly and massively erect. Behind his bearing one had a vision of something akin to a decision which had been put into effect and whose consequences could not be revoked. This decision was the fact of his own genius. And at some point he was so astonished on encountering it that it had prescribed a theme for him for all time, and he surrendered the whole of himself to its embodiment without mercy or hesitation.

But he was still young. The forms which this theme was to take still lay ahead of him. Yet the theme itself was an insatiable one and brooked no delay. So, as an initial gesture of deference to it he was obliged to anticipate his own future, and when realised in the first person such self-preemption is an act of posing. From these poses – natural in the highest realm of self-expression as everyday rules of propriety – he selected one of outward integrity, which is the hardest pose for an artist to maintain and the noblest one vis à vis his friends and those close to him. And he maintained this pose with such perfection that it is now almost impossible to describe what lay behind it.

But the mainspring of his brashness was a farouche timidity, and his pretence of willpower covered up a lack of will, phenomenally suspicious and prone to a quite gratuitous gloom. And just as deceptive was the function of his yellow blouse.[54] He used it not to campaign against jackets worn by the middle classes, but to combat the black velvet of talent within him, whose dark-browed saccharine forms began to outrage him earlier than they would less gifted men. For nobody knew like him the utter vulgarity of a natural fire that is not gradually roused to fury by cold water. No one knew as he did that the passion which suffices to continue the race is insufficient for creativity, since the latter requires the passion needed to continue the race's *image* – i.e. a passion which inwardly resembles any human passions and one whose novelty has the semblance of a new divine promise.

Suddenly the discussions came to an end. The enemies we were meant to annihilate went away undefeated. And in fact the terms of the truce that had been concluded were humiliating for us.

Meanwhile it had grown dark outside and a drizzle had begun falling. After our foes had left, the teashop was drearily empty. One began noticing the flies, half-eaten cakes and glasses blinded with hot milk. But no thunderstorm came. The sun struck sweetly at the pavement snared in a network of fine mauve spots. It was the May of nineteen fourteen. The reverses of history were so very close. Yet who spared them a thought? The crass city was aflame with foil and enamel as in *The Golden Cockerel*.[55] The lacquered greenery of poplars glistened. For the last time colours had that poisonous herbal quality which they were soon to part with for ever. I was crazy about Mayakovsky and already missing him. Need I add that the people I betrayed were not at all the ones I intended?

4

Chance brought us together the following day beneath the awning of the Greek coffee-house. The great yellow boulevard lay flat outspread between the Pushkin monument and Nikitskaya Street. Lean, long-tongued dogs yawned and stretched themselves and settled their muzzles comfortably on their front paws. Nannies in garrulous pairs prattled on, constantly carping and lamenting at this and that. Butterflies folded their wings for a few moments, dissolving in the heat, then suddenly they spread themselves, drawn sideways by irregular ripples in the sultry air. A little girl in white and probably wringing wet hung suspended in the air, whipping herself about the heels with the swishing circles of a skipping-rope.

I caught sight of Mayakovsky from a distance and pointed him out to Loks. He was with Khodasevich[56] playing heads or tails. Then Khodasevich got up, paid off his gambling debt, walked from under the awning and set off towards Strastnoy Boulevard. Mayakovsky was left sitting alone at his table. Loks and I went in and greeted him and fell into conversation. After a short while he offered to recite one or two poems for us.

The poplars glowed green. The lime-trees were a dryish grey. Driven into a fury by fleas, the dozing dogs kept springing up on all four paws, calling on heaven to witness their moral impotence against brute force, then they would roll back on to the sand in an exasperated torpor. On the now renamed Brest Railway Line locomotives sounded raucous whistles, and all around people were cutting hair and shaving, baking and frying, trading and travelling – all of them totally unaware.

It was his tragedy *Vladimir Mayakovsky*, which had then just appeared. I listened with bated breath, my whole heart seized in rapture and completely forgetting myself. I had never heard anything like it before. Everything was there in it – the boulevard, the dogs, the poplars and the butterflies, the barbers, bakers, tailors and locomotives. Why bother to quote from it? We can all remember that sultry, mysterious and summery text, which is now available to everyone in its tenth edition.

Far away in the distance locomotives roared like bulls. In the laryngeal territory of his art there was that same absolute distance as on earth. Here was an unfathomable inspiration without which there is no originality; here, opening up at any point in life in any direction, was that infinity without which poetry is no more than a misunderstanding that merely needs to be clarified.

And how simple it all was! Art was called tragedy – the right name for it. And the tragedy was called *Vladimir Mayakovsky*. The title concealed a simple discovery of genius – that a poet is not the author, but the subject of a lyricism addressing itself to the world in the first person. The title was not the name of the author, but the surname of the contents.

5

As I left the boulevard that day, I carried the whole of him away with me and took him into my life. But he was gigantic. Parted from him there was no way of retaining him. And I kept losing him. Then he would remind me of himself – with poems called "Cloud in Trousers", "The Backbone Flute", "War and the Universe" and "Man". And what was eroded away in the intervals between was so immense that extraordinarily immense reminders were required. And such they were. Each of the stages I have mentioned caught me unprepared. Each time he had grown beyond recognition and was completely born anew, as on the first occasion. It was impossible to get accustomed to him. What was it about him that was so unusual?

He was endowed with some qualities that were relatively permanent. And my enthusiasm too was fairly constant. It was always ready for him. This being the case, it might seem that the process of growing accustomed to him need not have proceeded in such leaps, but that was how it was. While he continued to exist creatively I spent four years trying to get used to him, but I failed. And then I did so in the space of just two and a quarter hours, the time required to read and examine his uncreative "150,000,000".[57] After that I languished in this acclimatised state for more than ten years. Then, all at once, the condition cleared and left me with tears in my eyes as he again reminded me of himself "at the top of his voice"[58] as once he used to do, but this time from beyond the grave.

What one failed to grow accustomed to was not Mayakovsky himself but the world which he held in his hands and which, when the fancy took him, he could either set in motion or bring to a standstill. I shall never understand what he gained by demagnetising his magnet, after which, though still outwardly preserving its appearance, the horseshoe that once used the "feet of his lines"[59] to make any imagination stand on end or attract any weights failed to stir so much as a grain of sand. In all history there can hardly be another example of a man advancing so far in a new experience and then so completely rejecting it, at the very hour he himself predicted and just at a time when this experience could have fulfilled such a vital need, albeit at the price of discomforts. Outwardly so logical yet inwardly hollow and unspontaneous, his place in the Revolution will always remain a mystery to me.

It was impossible to get accustomed to the Vladimir Mayakovsky of his tragedy, to the surname of its contents, to the poet eternally contained within poetry, to a potential realised only by the strongest, and not merely the so-called "interesting personality".

Charged with this unfamiliarity, I left the boulevard and went home. I was renting a room with a window overlooking the Kremlin. At any time Nikolai Aseyev[60] was likely to turn up from over the river. He would come from visiting the S- sisters,[61] a family of profound and varied talents. In the man who entered I would recognise a brilliant, unkempt imagination, an ability to make music out of triviality, and the wily sensitivity of a true artistic nature. I was fond of him. He was a Khlebnikov[62] enthusiast. I shall never understand what he discovered in me. In our art as in life we were in pursuit of different things.

6

The poplars glowed green and reflections of white stone and gold ran lizard-like across the surface of the river as I drove via the Kremlin to the

Pokrovka and headed for the station. From there I travelled with the Baltrušajtis family[63] to the Oka in the Province of Tula. Vyacheslav Ivanov[64] was living close by, and the other folk renting dachas out there were also from the artistic world.

The lilac was still in bloom. It ran far out into the road and without any music, bread or salt[65] laid on a lively welcome at the broad entrance to the estate. Beyond it an empty area worn down by cattle and overgrown with patches of grass sloped down towards the houses.

It promised to be a hot and opulent summer. I was translating Kleist's comedy *The Broken Jug* for the newly created Chamber Theatre. There were lots of snakes in the park. People talked about them every day. They talked about them as they ate their fish soup and bathed. But whenever I was invited to say something about myself I started on about Mayakovsky. It was no mistake on my part. He had become my god. I saw him as a personification of my spiritual horizon. As I recall, it was Vyacheslav Ivanov who first compared him with the hyperbolic style of Hugo.

7

When war was declared the weather spoilt itself. Rains came and the first women's tears were shed. War was still something new and its novelty struck quaking terror. People were at a loss how to react and they entered it like stepping into icy water.

The passenger trains taking local men to the mustering points still departed according to the old timetable. The train would start, and beating its head on the rails in pursuit there surged a wave of ululation quite unlike weeping, unnaturally tender and bitter as rowan. An elderly woman muffled in unsummery clothing was gathered up in someone's arms, and in monosyllables the recruit's kith and kin coaxed her and led her away beneath the vaulted roof of the station.

This keening, which continued only for the first few months, was broader than the grief of young wives and mothers that sustained it. It was introduced along the line as an exceptional emergency measure. As it passed through, station-masters touched their caps and telegraph-poles made way for it. It transformed the district and was visible everywhere in its pewter icon-cover of ill-weather, for it was an unfamiliar thing of burning brightness which had lain untouched since wars gone by. It had been retrieved from a hiding-place the previous night and brought on horseback to the train that morning, and when it had been led out by the hand from under the station vaulting it was transported back home through the bitter sludge of a country road. This was the send-off the men were given as they left with fellow villagers, or singly as volunteers, and departed for the city in green railway carriages.

But the soldiers already formed into marching units and heading directly for the real terrors were met and seen off without lamentation. Kitted out in close-fitting uniform, they seemed quite unlike peasants as they sprang down into the sand from the high trucks with their spurs jingling and greatcoats thrown on askew and flapping in the air. Others stood at the barrier-rails of the trucks and patted the horses as they gouged the dirty, partly rotten wood flooring with haughty hoofbeats. The platform was not giving any apples away and was never lost for an answer, and the young girls blushed crimson and laughed into the corners of their tightly pinned kerchiefs.

It was the end of September. A hazel grove glowed garbage-golden in the hollows like a mud-quenched fire. It was bent and broken by winds and by climbers after nuts – a chaotic image of ruination, sprained all out of joint in its stubborn resistance to disaster.

One August noon, knives and platters on the terrace had turned green, twilight descended on the flowerbed, and the birds had gone quiet. The sky began stripping off the deceptive bright network of night which had been flung over it like an invisible cap. The deathly park cast a sinister skyward squint at the humiliating puzzle which made something superfluous of an earth whose resounding praise it had been drinking so proudly with every root. Out on to the path rolled a hedgehog. A dead viper lay there like a piece of cord, knotted in the shape of an Egyptian hieroglyph. The hedgehog stirred it then suddenly left off and froze. Again it broke and scattered a bundle of dry needles, poked out its pig's snout then withdrew it again. Throughout the eclipse, that ball of prickly suspicion bunched itself now like a bootee and now like a fir-cone, till finally a sign of returning certainty drove it back into its hole.

8

In the winter, Z. M. M-va,[66] one of the S- sisters, removed and came to live on Tverskoy Boulevard. People used to visit her. One of her callers was the remarkable musician Isay Dobrovein,[67] with whom I was friends.

Mayakovsky too used to visit her home. By that time I was already accustomed to regard him as the foremost poet of our generation. Time has shown I was not mistaken.

It is true, there was Khlebnikov with his fine authenticity. But to this day some of his merits are beyond me, because poetry in my understanding is an event in history and interacts with real life. There was also Severyanin,[68] a lyricist whose outpourings came in ready-made stanzas like Lermontov's[69] and who, for all his slipshod vulgarity, impressed me with the rare structure of his open, uninhibited talent.

But it was Mayakovsky who marked a pinnacle of poetic destiny, and this has subsequently been confirmed. Each time when the generation later expressed itself dramatically, lending its voice to a poet – be it Esenin,[70] Selvinsky[71] or Tsvetayeva[72] – an echo could be heard of Mayakovsky's intimately vital note in their links with it, that is, in their way of addressing the world from the platform of their own time. I make no mention of such masters as Aseyev and Tikhonov,[73] because from now on I shall limit myself to this dramatic line of writing which is closer to me, whereas they have chosen a different one.

Mayakovsky rarely turned up on his own. Usually his following was made up of Futurists, men of the movement. It was in M-va's household at about that time that I first set eyes on a primus stove. As yet the invention did not give off any stench – who could have guessed it would become so widespread and so befoul our lives? The clean, roaring container emitted a high-pressure flame and over it chops were fried one by one. The elbows of our hostess and her lady-helpers were covered in chocolate Caucasian sunburn, and when we came through from the dining-room to visit them, the little cold kitchen turned into a settlement in the Tierra del Fuego and like technically innocent savages from Patagonia we bent over that copper disc which for us embodied something bright and Archimedean. Then off we would rush to fetch beer and vodka. In the drawing-room a tall Christmas tree in secret connivance with the trees on the boulevard stretched out its paws towards the grand piano. The tree was still wrapped in solemn gloom, but the whole settee was covered in piles of glittering tinsel like sweetmeats, still partly packed in cardboard boxes. The guests had been specially invited for the decoration of the tree – "in the morning if possible", which meant about three in the afternoon.

Mayakovsky recited, made the whole company laugh, and hurriedly downed his supper, scarcely able to wait for the card play to begin. He was caustically polite and showed great skill in concealing his agitation.

Something was happening to him. He was undergoing some crisis. He had realised his purpose in life. He was openly striking a pose, but he did so with such hidden anxiety and feverishness that beads of cold sweat stood out on his adopted mask.

9

But Mayakovsky did not always appear in the company of innovators. He was often accompanied by a poet who emerged with honour from the test usually posed by his proximity. Of the many people I saw him with, the only one whom I would place alongside him without any sense of strain was Bolshakov. Both of them could be listened to in any order without jarring one's hearing. Like the subsequently even stronger bond with his lifelong friend Lili Brik,[74] this friendship was a natural one. It was easy to understand. One's heart never ached for Mayakovsky in the company of Bolshakov. He was not divided within himself and he was not lowering himself.

But more usually his sympathies aroused only bewilderment. As a poet of strikingly ample self-awareness, he had gone further than any in his lyrical revelation and shown mediaeval valour in linking it to a theme in whose huge inventory poetry spoke out almost in a language of sectarian identifications. Moreover, he had shown the same amplitude and strength in taking up another, more local tradition. He saw beneath him a city which had gradually risen up to him from the depths of *The Bronze Horseman*, *Crime and Punishment* and *Petersburg*[75] – a city wreathed in a mist which was described with unnecessary vagueness as the problem of the Russian intelligentsia, although in fact it was a city surrounded by a perpetual haze of conjecture about the future, a precariously vulnerable Russian city of the nineteenth and twentieth centuries.

He embraced views such as these, yet along with reflections of such immensity he kept faith, almost like a duty, with the pigmy-like projects of a fortuitous clique that was hastily recruited and always quite indecently mediocre. Despite an almost animal instinct for the truth, he surrounded himself with petty eccentrics, men with fictitious reputations and false and unwarranted pretensions. To state the main point: Till the very end he continued discovering something in the veterans of a movement which he himself had long ago and permanently outgrown. Probably these were the consequences of his fatal isolation. And once having established it, he then intensified it deliberately and with a pedantry with which humans will sometimes pursue a path they recognise to be unavoidable.

10

However, all this was only to register later. At that time the signs of strange things to come were only faint. Mayakovsky recited Akhmatova,[76] Severyanin and his own and Bolshakov's verse about war and the city. And the city where we emerged late at night after visiting friends was a city situated deep in the rear.

We were already failing in those things that an immense and animate Russia has always found difficult – transport and supplies. The first maggots of profiteering were starting to hatch from new words such as "warrants", "medications", "licences" and "refrigeration". And while speculators thought in terms of waggonloads, the same waggons were involved day and night in bringing large, song-singing consignments of fresh population in exchange for the damaged loads returning in the hospital trains. And the best of our girls and womenfolk signed on as nurses.

The site of genuine positions was the front, and even had it not cultivated deliberate falsehood, the situation of the rear would in any case have been a false one. The city hid behind phrases like a thief at bay, even though no one had yet tried to arrest it. Like all hypocrites, Moscow lived an intensified external life and was bright with the unnatural brightness of a florist's in winter. At night it seemed the living image of Mayakovsky's own voice. What went on there and what that voice erected or destroyed were as alike as two drops of water. Yet this was no resemblance dreamt of by naturalism. It was the link connecting cathode and anode, the artist and life, the poet and his age.

Opposite where M-va lived was the house of the Moscow police chief. It was there on several days in the autumn that Mayakovsky and I – and Bolshakov too, I believe – were brought together by one of the formalities for enlisting volunteers. We had all been concealing the procedure from one another, and despite my father's approval I never actually completed it. If I remember rightly it also failed to lead anywhere for my friends. It was the son of Shestov,[77] a handsome ensign, who entreated me to give up the idea. He told me with sober seriousness what the front was like and he warned me I would discover the exact opposite of what I expected to find there. Soon after that he perished, in his first engagement after returning from leave. Bolshakov entered the Tver Cavalry School, and eventually Mayakovsky was also called up as his turn came. But after my own discharge in the summer just before the war I was turned down again each time my case was re-examined.

A year later I went away to the Urals. Just before doing so I spent a few days in St Petersburg. There one was less conscious of the war than in Moscow. Mayakovsky had been settled there for some time already and had by now received his call-up notice.

As always, the lively movement of the capital was moderated by its generous, dreaming spaces, which life's necessities could not exhaust. The avenues themselves were the colour of winter and twilight, and in order to send them sweeping and twinkling into the distance their silvery urgency required little in the way of extra snow or lamplight.

Mayakovsky and I walked along Liteiny Prospect. He trod miles of streets with sweeping stride, and as always I was astounded at his ability to appear as the border or frame for any landscape. In this respect he matched up with Petrograd's grey sparkle even more than with Moscow. . . . This was the period of "The Backbone Flute" and the first sketches for "War and the Universe", and "Cloud in Trousers" had come out as a booklet in an orange cover. . . . He told me about the new friends he was taking me to see, about his acquaintance with Gorky,[78] and about how social themes were invading his ideas more and more and enabling him to work in a new fashion, at set times and in measured amounts. It was then that I also paid my first visit to the Briks.

But even more naturally than in the two capitals, my thoughts of Mayakovsky settled into place in the winterly, half-Asiatic, "Captain's Daughter"[79] landscape of the Urals and in Pugachov's region of the Kama.

Soon after the February Revolution I returned to Moscow. Mayakovsky came from Petersburg and stayed in Stoleshnikov Lane. One morning I called to see him at his hotel. He was just getting up, and as he got dressed he recited his new "War and the Universe" to me. I made no attempt to enlarge on my impressions – he could read it all in my eyes. And in any case he was already aware of the effect he had upon me. I started talking about Futurism and said how wonderful it would be if he now publicly sent the whole thing to hell. He laughed and almost agreed with me.

95

11

In what I have written so far I have described my own perception of Mayakovsky. But there is no love without scars and sacrifice. I have already described what Mayakovsky was like as he entered my life. It remains for me to recount how my life changed in consequence, and I shall now fill in this gap.

I returned home from the boulevard that day utterly shaken and unable to think what to do next. I felt that I was totally bereft of talent. But that was only half the trouble. I also felt a sort of guilt before him and could not make sense of it. Had I been younger, I would have given up literature. But my age prevented that. After so many transformations I had not the resolve to change course a fourth time.

Something else happened instead. The age and influences we shared established a kinship between Mayakovsky and myself. We had certain similar features in common. I noticed this and I realised that if I did not do something they would become more frequent in future. I had to protect him from their vulgarity. Unable to put a name to it, I resolved to renounce the thing which gave rise to them. I renounced the romantic manner. And hence came the non-romantic poetics of *Over the Barriers*.[80]

But the romantic manner which I henceforth forbade myself concealed a whole way of viewing life. It was a conception of life as the life of a poet. It came down to us from the Symbolists, and the Symbolists adopted it from the Romantics, chiefly the Germans.

This conception of life had a hold on Blok, although only for a certain time. In the form that came naturally to him it failed to satisfy him. He was obliged either to intensify it or else to abandon it. And in fact he parted company with the idea. It was Mayakovsky and Esenin who intensified it.

The poet who posits himself as life's measure and pays for this with his life has a romantic conception of life which is overwhelmingly brilliant and irrefutable in its symbolism – i.e. in everything about its imagery which has any bearing on Orphism and Christianity. In this sense something permanent is embodied in the life of Mayakovsky and in the fate of Esenin – a fate which defies all adjectives and self-destructively pleads to be registered and disappears in the realm of myth.

But outside the legend this romantic scheme is a false one. The poet on whom it is founded is inconceivable without non-poets to set him off.

Because this poet is not a living person absorbed by moral perception, he is a visual biographical emblem which requires a background to make his contours visible. Unlike Passion plays, which need a heaven in order to be heard, this drama needs the evil of mediocrity in order to be seen, just as the romantic always needs the philistine and with the disappearance of bourgeois mentality loses half its content.

The concept of biography as spectacle was characteristic of my age, and I shared it together with everyone else. I parted company with it at a stage when it was still a mild option with the Symbolists and before it yet presupposed any heroics or smelt of blood. I escaped from it first of all unconsciously, by renouncing the romantic devices which were based upon it. But, secondly, I also consciously avoided it as a piece of glamour that ill-suited me, because by confining myself to craftsmanship I was afraid of any poeticising which might put me in a false or inappropriate position.

And when *My Sister Life*[81] appeared, in which some totally uncontemporary aspects of poetry found expression which were revealed to me in the summer of the Revolution, the name of the force that produced the book became a matter of complete indifference to me, because it was a force immensely greater than myself or the poetic conceptions surrounding me.

12

The winter twilight, the terror, and the roofs and trees of the Arbat gazed from Sivtsev Vrazhek Street into a dining-room which lay uncleared for months on end. The owner of the apartment, a bearded journalist of extraordinary absent-mindedness and geniality, gave the impression of being a bachelor although he had a family somewhere in Orenburg Province. At moments of leisure he used to rake up from the tabletop the previous month's worth of newspapers, covering every shade of opinion, and carried them in armfuls from the dining-room to the kitchen together with the fossilised breakfast remnants which accumulated in regular deposits of bacon-rind and breadcrusts between the pages of his morning reading. Till I lost all conscience about it, on the thirtieth of each month a brightly roaring, fragrant flame flared up under the hotplate, just as in Dickens' Christmas tales of roast geese and counting-house clerks. When darkness fell, the sentries on duty began enthusiastically firing off their revolvers. Sometimes they fired salvoes, sometimes just an isolated, rare enquiry into the night, loaded with pathetic, irrevocable deadliness. And since they could never pick up any rhythm and there were many deaths from stray bullets, in order to ensure safety in the lanes one felt that metronomes should be stationed out there instead of the militia.

Sometimes their crackling turned into a savage wail. And in those days it was so often impossible to tell immediately whether the sound came from the street or inside the house. But in a few moments of lucidity amid general delirium there was a call for attention from the sole inhabitant of the study, a portable one complete with a jack-plug. From here came a telephone invitation to attend a gathering of all the poetic forces in Moscow at the time at a private house in Trubnikovsky Lane. On that same telephone I had also had an argument with Mayakovsky, though this was much earlier, before the Kornilov revolt.[82]

Mayakovsky informed me that he had put me on a poster announcing my appearance together with Bolshakov and Lipskerov[83] and also with the most faithful of the faithful, including, I believe, the man who used to break inch-thick planks across his forehead![84] I was almost glad of the chance to speak to my favourite for the first time as if to a stranger, and I became more and more exasperated as I parried each of the arguments he produced in his defence. I was surprised not so much by his lack of ceremony as by his poor imagination, because, as I told him, the incident was not over his using my name without permission but his irritating conviction that a two-year absence had in no way altered my fate or the objects that concerned me. He should therefore have inquired first of all whether I was still alive and whether perhaps I had not abandoned literature for something else. To this he replied reasonably enough that since returning from the Urals I had already seen him that spring. But surprisingly this argument failed to impress me. I showed quite unwarranted insistence and demanded a newspaper correction of the error on the poster, which was quite impossible because of the closeness of the date. And since no one knew me at that time, it was in any case a piece of senseless affectation on my part.

But although I was then still hiding *My Sister Life* and concealing what was happening to me, I could not endure it when everyone around me assumed that things remained with me as before. Apart from that, I probably still had a dim memory of our springtime conversation to which Mayakovsky had vainly alluded, and after everything that was said then I was annoyed by the inconsistency of this recent invitation.

13

He reminded me of our angry exchange over the 'phone a few months later at the house of the amateur poet A-.[85] Those present were Balmont,[86] Khodasevich, Baltrušajtis, Ehrenburg,[87] Vera Inber,[88] Antokolsky,[89] Kamensky,[90] Burlyuk,[91] Mayakovsky, Andrei Bely and Marina Tsvetayeva. Naturally, I could not have known at the time what an incomparable poet Tsvetayeva would develop into. But even without knowing her remarkable *Mileposts*,[92] written at about that time, I instinctively singled her out from among the other folk present because of her striking simplicity. I detected in her a kindred quality we shared, a readiness at any moment to abandon all habit and privilege should anything lofty suddenly inflame her and arouse her admiration. We addressed a few frank and friendly words to one another on that occasion, and at that evening gathering she was to me a living palladium against the Symbolists and Futurists, people of two movements that crowded the room.

The recital began. Poets performed in order of seniority and without much apparent success. When it came to Mayakovsky's turn he got up, curved one arm round the edge of the empty shelf at the back of the divan and began reciting "Man". Like a bas-relief against the background of his age, such as I had always seen him, he towered above the people that were seated or standing there. And now with one arm propping his handsome head, now bracing his knee against the bolster, he recited a work of uncommon profundity and exalted inspiration.

Opposite him, next to Margarita Sabashnikova, sat Andrei Bely. He had spent the war in Switzerland, and the Revolution had brought him back home. Possibly this was the first time he saw and heard Mayakovsky. He listened like a man entranced, betraying no sign of his rapture. His face was thus all the more eloquent. Filled with astonishment and gratitude, it seemed to rush out to meet the poet as he declaimed. Some of the audience, including Ehrenburg and Tsvetayeva, were out of my sight. But I could observe the rest of them. The majority stayed safe inside the bounds of their enviable self-esteem. They all felt that they were names to be reckoned with, and all regarded themselves as poets. Only Bely listened with total abandon, completely carried away by a joy that was utterly ungrudging, because at the heights where such joy feels at home there exist only sacrifices and a perpetual readiness to make them.

Before my gaze, chance was thus bringing together two men of genius

99

who justified two literary movements that had successively exhausted themselves. In Bely's proximity, itself a proud and gladdening experience, I sensed the presence of Mayakovsky with doubled force. His essence was revealed to me with all the freshness of our first encounter. That evening I experienced it for the last time.

Many years went by after that. One year passed, and when I recited to him the poems of *My Sister Life* before anyone else, I heard from him ten times more than I expected ever to hear from anyone. Another year passed. He read his "150,000,000" to a small circle of friends, and for the first time I had nothing to say to him. Many more years passed, in the course of which we met at home and abroad, tried to be friends and attempted to work together, and all the time I understood him less and less. About this period other people can tell, because in these years I came up against the limits of my understanding – limits which, seemingly, I shall not overcome. My recollections of this period would emerge as pale and add nothing to what has already been said. I shall therefore go straight on with the rest of what I have to recount.

14

I am going to tell of a curiosity which repeats itself from age to age and which can be termed the "last year of the poet".

Projects that have not reached completion are suddenly ended. Often nothing is added to their incomplete state except for a new and only now admissible certainty that they *are* finished. And this certainty is passed on to posterity.

The poet changes his habits, busies himself with new plans and has never done boasting about some new sense of uplift. Then all of a sudden comes the end – sometimes violent, more often natural – and even then, because he showed no desire to resist, it still looks very much like suicide. Then suddenly people realise and begin making comparisons. The dead man was busy with new plans. He was publishing *Sovremennik*[93] and preparing to found a peasant journal. He was mounting an exhibition of twenty years' work and trying to secure a passport for travel abroad. Yet it turns out that during those selfsame days he was observed by other people and seen to be complaining, depressed and weeping. After entire decades of self-imposed solitude he had suddenly acquired a fear of it, like a child scared of the dark, and had clutched at the hands of chance visitors, seizing on their presence simply in order to avoid being left alone. Those who observed him in this state refused to believe their ears. A man who had received more affirmative answers from life than she bestows on most began arguing as if he had never even begun to live and had derived no experience or support from his past.

But who will ever understand or believe that the Pushkin of 1836 might suddenly recognise himself as the Pushkin of any year? As the Pushkin, say, of 1936? Who can understand that a time comes when one expanded and regenerate heart suddenly blends the responses that have long been coming from other hearts in answer to the main one which is still alive and pounding, still thinking and wanting to live? Who will believe that the constantly multiplying interference of these heartbeats finally comes so thick and fast that they suddenly settle and coincide with the main heart's tremors and begin to live one life with it and share the same rhythm? Who will understand or believe that this is not a parable? That this is really experienced? That this is an age in life which is real and felt impulsively in the blood although still not yet named? That this is a youthfulness not of human kind but one which sunders life's earlier continuity with such piercing joy that, because this age is nameless and comparisons are unavoidable, its piercing quality makes it resemble death more than anything else? Who will appreciate or believe that it does resemble death – *resembles* death, but *is not* death, not death at all? And if only, if only people did not require such a total resemblance. . . .

And together with the heart, a displacement occurs in memories and works, in works and hopes, in the world of the created and that which still remains to be created. "What was the man's personal life like?" people sometimes want to know. You shall now be enlightened: A vast area of ultimate contradictions is drawn together, concentrated and made level, and suddenly, with a simultaneous shudder in every part, it takes on a physical existence. It opens its eyes, heaves a deep sigh and casts off the last traces of the pose which it earlier acquired as a temporary aid.

And if one recollects that all this sleeps at night and keeps watch by day, and that it walks around on two legs and is called a human being, it is natural to look for corresponding phenomena in its behaviour.

The large city is there, real and actually existing. It is winter there. It grows dark early and the working day continues by the light of evening.

Once, long, long ago the city used to terrify. It had to be conquered, its refusal of recognition had to be broken. But much water has flowed by since then. Its acknowledgement has been extorted, and its submissiveness has become a habit. It now requires a great effort of memory to imagine how at one time it could inspire such alarm. The city lights twinkle, people cough into a pocket handkerchief and click their abacus, and the city is covered in snow. Yet its alarming immensity might well sweep by unnoticed but for this new and wild impressionability. What is adolescent coyness beside the vulnerability of this new birth? And once again, just as in our childhood, everything gets noticed – lamps and typists, swing-doors and galoshes, storm-clouds, moon and snow. A terrible world![94]

It bristles on the backs of sleighs and fur-coats. It rolls on its rim along the rails, like a ten-kopeck piece across the floor, and bowling away into the distance it collapses gently in the mist where a signal-woman in a sheepskin bends down to pick it up. It gets shifted around, becomes smaller, and teems with chance events. It is easy to stumble in this world over a slight lapse of attention. These troubles are deliberately imagined. They are consciously blown up out of nothing. But even when blown up, they are utterly insignificant compared with the wrongs over which people strode triumphantly not so long ago. Yet the whole point is that there can be no comparing, because it all happened in that earlier life which people took such joy in tearing apart. But if only this joy was steadier and more true to life!

Yet it is an unbelievable, incomparable joy. Nothing in life has ever hurled us from one extreme to the other in such a way as this joy has done.

But what despondency people suffer here! How the whole of Hans Andersen and his wretched duckling repeat themselves! How many great mountains are made out of molehills here!

But perhaps some inner voice is lying? Perhaps the terrible world is right?

"You are requested not to smoke." "You are requested to state your business briefly." Are these not incontrovertible truths?

"Him? Hang himself? Don't you worry!" – "Love? Him? . . . love? Ha-ha-ha! He's only in love with himself!"

The large city is there, real and actually existing. It is winter there and it is freezing. A squeaking wickerwork of air gripped by twenty degrees of frost stands across the road as though on stilts driven into the ground. Everything in the city mists over, sinks and disappears. But can things be so sad when there is such joy? Is this not a second birth? Is this really death?

15

In public registry offices there is no equipment for measuring truthfulness and no X-ray test for sincerity. In order for a record to be valid, nothing is needed but the firm hand which makes the entry. And then no doubts or disputes can arise.

Before he dies, the poet writes a last message in his own hand, leaving a legacy of treasure to the world as patent evidence. He measures his own sincerity and X-rays it with a speed that permits no alteration . . . and then people all around start discussing, doubting and making comparisons!

They compare that last message with earlier examples, whereas it is comparable only with him alone and with the whole of his previous existence. People make conjectures about his feelings and are unaware that it is possible to love not just in a space of days (albeit for eternity) but (albeit not forever) with the entire accumulated force of the past.

There are two expressions which have long been marked by an equal banality: "man of genius" and "woman of beauty". How much they have in common!

From childhood she is constricted in her movements. She is lovely and realises it early on in life. What we commonly call God's good earth is the only entity with which she can be completely herself, because with others she cannot take one step without causing hurt or else being hurt herself. When still a young girl she goes out of the house. What does she have in mind? She already receives letters via a mail-box. Only two or three friends are let into her secrets. All this is already here. So let us suppose she is going out to keep some tryst. . . .

She goes out of the gate. She would like the evening to notice her. She would like the heart of the air to be wrung for her and the stars to pick up something of her story. She would like the same renown enjoyed by trees and fences and all things on earth when they exist not in the mind but in the open air. Yet if one ascribed such wishes to her she would simply laugh and deny any such thought. But she has a distant cousin in this world, a person of immensely ordinary habit, who is there in order to know her better than she can know herself and ultimately to answer for her. She has a healthy love of healthy nature and is unaware that she constantly expects the universe to reciprocate this feeling.

It is springtime, a spring evening, old women sit out on the benches, and there are low fences and shaggy white willows. The sky is wine-green, weakly infused and pale. Here is her homeland, here are dust and dry, splintering voices. The sounds fall dry as woodchip, and their splinters fill the smooth hot silence. A man comes along the road to meet her – the very man it would be natural for her to meet. In her joy she keeps on telling him that she has come out just in order to meet him. Partly she is right. Who after all is not to some degree dust and homeland and a quiet spring evening? She forgets why she came out, but her feet remember. He and she walk together and the further they go the more people they encounter. And since she loves her companion with all her heart, her feet cause her more than a little distress. But they still carry her onwards, and the two of them can hardly keep pace with one another. But the road leads them unexpectedly to a wider space where it seems less crowded and where they might pause for breath and look around. Yet often at this very moment her distant cousin makes his own way there and they meet. And whatever happens now, it is all the.same. All the same, some blissfully perfect "I am thou" binds them with every tie this world can conceive. And proudly, youthfully and wearily it stamps one profile on another like on a medal.

16

The beginning of April surprised Moscow in a white stupor of returning winter. On the seventh it began to thaw again, and on the fourteenth when Mayakovsky shot himself not everyone was yet used to the novelty of spring.

When I heard of the tragedy I summoned Olga Sillova[95] to the scene. Something suggested to me that this shock might provide an outlet for her own grief. Between eleven and twelve the circle of waves caused by the shot was still spreading outwards. The news shook telephones, shrouded faces in pallor and sent people rushing to Lubyansky Passage, through the courtyard and into the house. There folk from the town and other tenants were already perched all the way up the staircase, huddled and weeping, hurled and splattered against the walls by the flattening force of the event. Yakov Chernyak[96] and Romadin,[97] who were first to tell me of the tragedy, came up to me. Zhenya[98] was with them. As I caught sight of her my cheeks started twitching convulsively. She was weeping as she told me to hurry upstairs. But at that moment they carried the body down past us on a stretcher, completely covered.

Everyone rushed downstairs and blocked the exit, so that by the time we made our way out, the ambulance was already driving out through the gateway. We followed after it and went to Gendrikov Lane.

Life outside the gates pursued its course and was indifferent as some folk wrongly claim. There still remained the concern of the asphalt courtyard, forever a participant in such dramas. The weak-legged air of spring wandered through the rubbery mud as though still learning to walk. Cockerels and children proclaimed their presence for all to hear. Their voices carried strangely in the early spring, despite the busy rattling of the town.

Slowly the tramcar made its way up Shvivaya Hill. There is a place there where first the right-hand and then the left-hand pavement approach so close below the window that you seize the strap as you move involuntarily and bow down over Moscow. It is as though one were stooping to assist an old woman who has slipped, since the town suddenly drops on all fours, dolefully sheds watchmakers and cobblers, and raises and rearranges a few rooftops and belfries before suddenly standing up, shaking out its skirt-hem and launching the tramcar down a level and quite ordinary street.

This time its movements were such an obvious excerpt from the man who had shot himself, they so strongly recalled a vital part of his essence, that I quivered all over and the famous phone call from the "Cloud"[99] thundered inside me as though someone was speaking it loudly right next to me. I stood in the gangway next to Sillova and bent over to remind her of those eight lines, but. . . .

"And I sense that my 'I' is too small for me. . . ."

My lips shaped the phrase like gloved fingers, but in my agitation I could not pronounce a single word.

Two empty cars stood by the gateway at the end of Gendrikov Lane. They were surrounded by a small inquisitive gathering. In the hall and dining-room people stood and sat. Some wore hats while others were bareheaded. He was lying further away, in the study. The door leading from the hall to Lili's room was open and on the threshold Aseyev stood weeping with his head pressed against the door-frame. In there, over by the window, Kirsanov[100] quivered finely as he sobbed in silence, his head drawn into his shoulders.

Even here the damp mist of mourning was interrupted by low murmurs of anxious conversation – just as after a requiem service thick as jam the first whispered words are so dry that they seem to come from beneath the floorboards and reek of mice. During one such interruption the concierge came cautiously into the room with a chisel slotted in his boot-top. Taking out the winter window-frame, he slowly and noiselessly opened the casement. Anyone outside without a coat must have shuddered with cold, and the sparrows and children kept rallying one another with inconsequent cries.

Someone tiptoed out from the room where the dead man lay and quietly asked whether a telegram had been sent to Lili. L.A.G.[101] answered that it had. Zhenya took me to one side and commented how courageously L.A. was bearing the awful burden of the tragedy. She burst into tears. I squeezed her hand firmly.

The apparent unconcern of a boundless world came pouring in at the window. Across the sky, as though between earth and sea, grey trees stood and guarded the boundary. As I looked at the boughs covered in a fluster of buds I tried to picture far away beyond them that improbable city of London where the telegram had gone.[102] Soon someone over there would be bound to give a cry, stretch out their arms towards us and fall down in a faint. My throat tightened. I decided to go back into his room in order this time to weep my fill.

He lay on his side with his face to the wall, sullen, tall, covered by a sheet up to his chin, and with his mouth half-open like someone asleep. Proudly turned away from everyone, even as he lay there, even in this sleep he stubbornly strained to get away and escape. His face reminded one of the time when he once described himself as a "handsome twenty-two-year-old", for death had ossified a facial attitude that scarcely ever falls into its clutches. It was an expression with which people begin their life, not one with which they end it. His face was pouting and indignant.

Then there was a movement in the hall. The dead man's younger sister, Olga Vladimirovna, had turned up at the apartment independently of his mother and elder sister, who were already there, silently grieving among the crowd. Her entry was noisy and demanding. Her voice floated into the room ahead of her. As she came up the stairs alone, she was talking loudly to someone, obviously addressing her brother. Then she actually appeared, walking past everyone as if they were so much rubbish, and as she reached her brother's door she threw up her hands and stopped.

"Volodya!" she screamed, and her voice rang through the entire house. A moment passed. "He won't speak!" she shouted even louder. "He won't say anything! He won't answer! Volodya! Volodya! How horrible!"

She began to collapse. They caught her and quickly tried to bring her round. But she had hardly come to herself when she greedily moved towards the body and hastily renewed her unquenched dialogue, sitting at his feet. I finally burst into the fit of weeping for which I had been longing.

It had been impossible to weep like this at the scene of the event, where a herd-like sense of drama was quickly ousted by the fresh-fired fact. The asphalt yard there had stunk of deified inevitability, like saltpetre, which means that it reeked of a false urban fatalism that was founded on apelike mimicry and viewed life as a series of amenably recordable sensations. They had been sobbing out there too, but only because the stricken throat and its animal sixth sense had reproduced the convulsions of apartment blocks, fire-escapes, a revolver case, and all the other things that made one sick with despair and vomit murder.

His sister was the first person to weep for him of her own will and choice, as people weep for something great, and to the sound of her words, like a roaring organ accompaniment, one could weep insatiably and expansively.

She continued unrelenting. "They wanted a Bath-house!" Maya-kovsky's[103] own indignant voice could be heard strangely transposed to his sister's contralto. "They wanted it as funny as possible! And they had a good laugh! 'Called him out on stage! . . . And look what was happening to him! . . . Why didn't you come to *us*, Volodya?" she wailed on, sobbing. Then she took a grip on herself and made an impulsive move to sit closer to him. "Do you remember? Can you remember, Volodya dear?" she suddenly reminded him, almost as though he were alive. And she began to recite:

> And I sense that my 'I' is too small for me.
> Someone stubbornly tries to break out of me,
> Hallo!
> Who is speaking? Mother?
> Mother! Your son is splendidly ill.
> Mother! His heart is on fire.
> Tell his sisters Lyuda and Olya.
> Now he's nowhere to go.

17

When I went there in the evening he was already lying in his coffin. The faces that had filled the room during the day were now replaced by others. It was fairly quiet. Hardly anyone was weeping now.

Suddenly down below the window I imagined I could see his life, belonging now entirely to the past. It stretched away obliquely from the window in the form of a quiet road planted with trees like Povarskaya Street. And the first thing on that road, right by the wall, was our Soviet State – this impossible, unprecedented State of ours, bursting in upon the centuries and taken up by them for ever after. It stood right there below. One could have called and reached out one's hand to it. In its tangibility and extraordinariness it somehow resembled the dead man. So striking was the link between them both, they could have seemed like twins.

And then it also occurred to me quite spontaneously that in fact this man had been the only citizen of our State. Others had struggled, sacrificed their lives and created things, or else they had endured and been perplexed, but still they had all been natives of a past epoch and despite their differences they were relatives and kinsmen of that age. Only this man had had the climatic newness of the times flowing in his veins. And the whole of him was strange with the strange features of our epoch, half of which had still to be realised. I began recalling the traits of his character and his independence, utterly unique in many ways. And all of these were explained by his adjustment to conditions which, though implicit in our age, had not yet assumed a forceful relevance to the present. Since childhood he was the spoilt favourite of a future that yielded to him quite early on and seemingly with no great effort.

THE APELLES MARK

It is said that on finding his rival Zeuxis out one day, the Greek artist Apelles drew a mark on the wall by which Zeuxis could guess who had called in his absence. But Zeuxis did not remain in debt for long. He selected a time when he knew Apelles was away from home and he too left behind a mark, which has since become a byword for artistry.

1

It was one of those September evenings – why, I remember the date exactly, it was the evening of the 23rd of August. It was one of those evenings when the Leaning Tower of Pisa leads an entire army of leaning sunsets and shadows to launch an assault on the town, an evening when the scent of bayleaf bruised in the fingers was borne from all Tuscany by a teasing vesperal breeze. And on that evening Emilio Relinquimini failed to find Heine at his hotel. From an obsequiously grovelling footman he required paper and a light, and when the man returned with pen and ink and a stick of sealing-wax and seal in addition to what was requested, Relinquimini fastidiously waved his services aside. Removing the pin from his tie, he heated it in the candle flame. Then he pricked his own finger, and seizing one of a pile of cards bearing the hotelier's letter-head, he used that finger to bend over one edge of the card. Then he nonchalantly handed it to the ever-attentive footman. "Give this to Mr Heine," he said. "I shall call on him again about the same time tomorrow."

The Leaning Tower breached the cordon of mediaeval fortifications. The number of people in the street who witnessed it from the bridge increased every minute. Sunset crept across the squares like a troop of partisans. Some streets were barred by inverted shadows, while others fought hand to hand in narrow passages. And the Leaning Tower made no distinction and mowed every object down with slashing swing, until the point when a single gigantic stray shadow passed over the sun . . . and day was brought to a sudden end.

But before the sun set completely, the footman still had a few moments to give Heine a brief, disjointed account of his recent visitor and to hand the impatient guest a card bearing a stain that had now dried and turned brown.

"Here's an eccentric for you!" mused Heine, but he immediately guessed the true name of his visitor. It was the author of a well-known poem called "Il sangue".

It struck the wandering Westphalian poet Heine as no strange coincidence for Relinquimini to turn up from Ferrara precisely when an even more haphazard whim on his own part had brought him to Pisa. He remembered an anonymous writer who had recently sent him a carelessly written and provocative letter. The stranger's claims had gone quite beyond the bounds of the permissible. While going on in casual and vague terms about the bloodstock and generic roots of poetry, he had demanded from Heine a proof of his identity in the style of Apelles.

"Love," wrote the anonymous correspondent, "that bloodstained cloud which often completely befogs our cloudless blood – you must tell of it in such a way that your account is as succinct as Apelles' mark. Remember, the only thing that Zeuxis is curious about is your membership of the aristocracy of blood and spirit (inseparable concepts).

"P.S. I have taken advantage of your stay in Pisa, of which I was duly informed by my publisher Conti, in order once and for all to allay the doubts that have been tormenting me. In three days' time I shall pay you a personal call to view your Apelles signature. . . ."

The servant who answered Heine's summons was authorised to act as follows. "I am leaving on the ten o'clock train to Ferrara. Tomorrow evening the person you know already who presented this card will come and ask for me. You will hand this package over to him personally. And now, please, let me have my bill and call the *facchino*."

The insubstantial weight of the apparently empty parcel was in fact due to a thin slip of paper which had evidently been cut from some manuscript. The scrap of paper bore only part of a phrase without a beginning or ending: ". . . but discarding their former names, Rondolfina and Enrico managed to exchange them for hitherto imaginary ones. 'Rondolfina!' he shouted wildly. 'Enrico!' came her responding cry."

2

The citizens of Pisa burnt up the fragrant night of Tuscany on pavement flagstones, asphalt squares, on balconies and on the embankments of the Arno. Its dark combustion made breathing even harder in the already stifling passages beneath dusty plane trees. Its sweltering oily gleam was added to by scattering sheaves of stars and bundles of spiky nebulosity. And these sparks strained the Italians' patience beyond endurance. Pronouncing oaths with fanatic fervour as though they were prayers at the first glimpse of Cassiopeia, they wiped the dirty sweat from their brows. Pocket handkerchiefs fluttered in the gloom like thermometers being shaken. Evidence of these cambric indicators moved along the streets like a depressive bane. They spread sultriness like a rumour overheard, an epidemic or some panic terror. And just as the stagnating town disintegrated unprotesting into blocks and courtyards and houses, so the night air too was reduced to individual immobile encounters, exclamations, altercations, bloody clashes, whispers, laughs and murmurs. The sounds stood in a dusty, fine interlacement above the pavements. They stood in ranks and took root in the footpaths like roadside trees gasping for breath and colourless in the light of the gaslamps. It was with such power and caprice that night in Pisa imposed firm limits on human endurance.

And at that point began the chaos, an arm's length from the frontier. Chaos reigned at the railway station. Here handkerchiefs and curses disappeared from the scene. Here people who a moment ago found natural movement almost a torture gripped suitcases and cardboard boxes, milled around the ticket office, stormed the charred carriages like madmen, besieged the carriage steps; and besmutted like sweeps, they burst into compartments divided by hot brown plywood that seemed to buckle with the heat, the swearing and the heavy buffeting of bodies. The coaches blazed, the rails blazed, oil tankers and locomotives on the sidings blazed, and the signals too blazed, like the steam-squashed wails of locomotives far and near. With scuttering flares and like an irritant insect the open fire-box's heavy breath dozed on the cheek of the driver and the leather jerkin of the stoker. Both men were ablaze. And also blazing were the clock-face, the watchmen, and the cast-iron shoals of intersecting tracks and points. All this was beyond the limits of human endurance. Yet it could all be endured.

.

He had a seat right by the window. The totally empty platform was made entirely out of stone, entirely of sonority and the guard's shout of "Pronti!" At the last moment the guard himself ran past in pursuit of his own shout. Smoothly the pillars of the station slipped aside. Points of light scurried criss-cross like knitting needles. Caught up by the air-stream, the rays of reflectors sprang in at the carriage windows, passed through the compartment and out of the windows opposite, and then they stretched shuddering along the tracks, tripping over rails, rising again and disappearing behind the store-sheds. Dwarf-like lanes and ugly mongrel alleyways were swallowed sonorously by yawning viaducts. There was a blustering of gardens coming right up to the blinds, the restful expanse of a carpet of curling vineyards, and then the open fields.

Heine was travelling on an off-chance. He had no thought to occupy him. He tried to doze and closed his eyes.

"Something might come of this. There's no sense in guessing in advance – no possibility of that. All I have ahead of me is total, intoxicating uncertainty."

Probably the wild oranges were in bloom. The fragrant spread of orchards overflowed. A breeze from out there rushed in to suck a droplet of moisture on the passenger's gummed eyelashes.

"It's bound to work. Something must come of it. Or else why should . . . ? Aaah!" Heine yawned. "Why should every one of Relinquimini's love poems be marked invariably 'Ferrara'?"

Cliffs and chasms, sleep-shattered neighbours, stench of carriages, and a tongue of gas-flame burning in the lamp. It licked the rustlings and shadows from the ceiling, then licked its own lips and gasped as cliffs and chasms were followed by a tunnel. Thundering, the mountain crawled along the carriage roof and spread the engine smoke flat, driving it in at the windows and clinging to coathooks and luggage nets. There were tunnels and valleys. The single-gauge track wept mournfully over a mountain stream that smashed on the rocks after plummeting from some incredible heights that glimmered faintly in the darkness. And waterfalls out there fumed and smoked, and all night long their dull roaring circled round the train.

"An Apelles mark . . . Rondolfina. . . . Probably I shall not achieve anything in twenty-four hours. But there's no more time. I have to vanish without trace. And tomorrow he'll rush straight to the station as soon as the hotel footman tells him which route I took!"

Ferrara! Dawn of blue-black steel. Sweet-scented mist soaked in chill. How sonorous the Latin dawn!

3

"Impossible. The next issue of *Il Voce* is already in page-proof."

"Yes, but I won't hand over what I've found to anybody else at any price, and I cannot stay in Ferrara for more than a day."

"And you say it's his notebook which you've found under a seat in the train?"

"Yes, it's Emilio Relinquimini's notebook. Moreover, it's a notebook which among a mass of day-to-day records contains an even greater quantity of unpublished poems, several drafts and jottings and aphorisms. The entries cover the whole of this year, and most of them – to judge by the notes on them – were made in Ferrara."

"Where is it? Do you have it with you?"

"No, I've left my things at the station. The notebook is in my travelling bag."

"What a pity! We could have delivered the book to his home. Our editors know Relinquimini's address in Ferrara. But he's been away now for almost a month."

"What? Relinquimini isn't in Ferrara?"

"That's the whole point. Personally, I don't see what you're hoping to achieve by placing an announcement of your find."

"I merely hope through your paper to establish reliable contact between myself and the notebook's owner. And Relinquimini can use the kind offices of *Il Voce* at any time concerning the matter."

"What are we to do with you?! Have a seat then, please, and kindly compose your notice."

"I'm sorry to trouble you, but I see you have a 'phone on your desk. Can I make a call?"

"Certainly. Go right ahead."

"Is that the Hotel Torquato Tasso? . . . What rooms do you have available? . . . Which floor? . . . Splendid. Please reserve number eight in my name."

"*Ritrovamento*. Found: the edited manuscript of a new book by Emilio Relinquimini. Occupant of room 8 at Hotel Tasso will await owner of manuscript or his representative all day until 11 p.m. As of tomorrow, *Il Voce* editors and hotel management will be regularly and promptly informed of further changes in address of finder."

Tired out by the journey, Heine fell into a lifeless, leaden slumber. Heated by the breath of morning, the venetian blinds in his room blazed like the brass reeds of a harmonica. By the window a network of rays fell on the floor like a piece of dishevelled straw matting. The blades of straw crowded, pressed and huddled close to one another. Out on the street there was the sound of indistinct talking. One man rambled, another stammered, and a whole hour went by. The lengths of straw already lay close packed and the matting melted across the floor in a pool of sunlight. Out on the street people were carried away by chatter and nodded off to sleep and tongues tripped over themselves. Heine slept. The sunny pool expanded as though soaked up by the parquet flooring. And once more it became a thinning mat of scorched and plaited lengths of straw. Heine slept on. There was talking on the street. The hours passed and lazily grew along with the growth of black breaks in the straw matting. There was talk out on the street. The matting faded, gathered dust and dimmed. Already it was a little twisted tangle made of string, and its stitches, threads and loops all merged into one. There was still talk out on the street. And still Heine slept.

At any moment, though, he would wake up. Any moment now he was going to jump to his feet – just mark my words. Any moment. Just let him see the end of that last fragment of dream. . . .

A wheel that had dried in the heat suddenly split open right to the hub and the spokes poked out like a cluster of chewed-off pegs. The cart fell on its side with a rumble and bang and out spilled piles of newspapers. There was a crowd of folk, parasols, shop-windows and sun-blinds. The newspaper boy was carried off on a stretcher. There was a chemist's shop close by.

You see! What did I tell you? Heine leapt up.

"Just a minute!" he called.

Somebody was knocking with furious impatience at the door. Half awake, with his hair in a tousle and still drunk with sleep, Heine reached for his dressing-gown.

"Sorry, just a moment!" With an almost metallic clank his right foot landed on the floor. "Right away!"

Heine went to the door.

"Who's there?"

It was the voice of the footman.

"Yes, yes, I do have the notebook. Please present my apologies to the signora. Is she in the drawing-room?"

The footman spoke again.

"Ask the signorina to wait ten minutes. In ten minutes' time I'll be at her service. Do you hear?"

The footman spoke again.

"Wait a moment, *cameriere*!"

The footman again.

"And don't forget to tell mademoiselle that the signore expresses his sincere regret that he cannot come out and join her immediately.

114

He feels most guilty, but he will attempt. . . . Can you hear me, *cameriere*?"

The footman again.

". . . But he will attempt in ten minutes' time to make full amends for his unpardonable solecism. And be as polite as you can, *cameriere*. I'm not one of your folk from Ferrara."

"Very well, very well," the footman said.

"*Cameriere*, is the lady in the drawing-room?"

"Yes, signore."

"Is she alone there?"

"She is, signore. This way, please. To the left, signore. To the left!"

"Good afternoon. How can I be of service to signora?"

"Pardon me, but are you from room number eight?"

"Yes, that's my room."

"I've come for Relinquimini's notebook."

"Allow me to introduce myself: Heinrich Heine."

"Excuse my asking, but are you related to . . . ?"

"Not at all. A mere coincidence. And a regrettable one even. I also have the fortune to. . . ."

"You write poetry?"

"I have never written anything else."

"I know German and I spend all my leisure hours on poetry, but even so. . . ."

"Do you know *Verses Unpublished in the Poet's Lifetime*?"

"Of course. So you wrote that?!"

"Excuse me, but I'm still longing to hear your name."

"Camilla Ardenze."

"Delightful to meet you. So, signora Ardenze, you saw my notice in *Il Voce* today?"

"Yes, I did. About the notebook you found. Where is it? Let me see it."

"Signora! Signora Camilla, it may be that with your whole heart, celebrated by the incomparable Relinquimini. . . ."

"Enough of that. We're not on the stage. . . ."

"You are mistaken, signora. All our life we are on the stage. And by no means everyone achieves that naturalness of performance which is allotted to each man as his role at the moment he is born. Signora

115

Camilla, you love your native town. You love Ferrara. But for me . . . this is the first town that actually repels me. You are lovely, signora Camilla, and my heart shudders at the thought that you and this repulsive town are conspiring against me."

"I don't understand you."

"Don't interrupt, signora. I tell you, you are in league with a town that has put me to sleep like a poisoner who drugs his drinking companion when the latter's lady-love arrives. He drugs him in order to rouse a spark of scorn for the unfortunate man in the eyes of his beloved just as she enters the tavern. And she goes and betrays the man who has been drugged. The poisoner addresses the lady as she comes in. 'Milady, pray take a look at this lazy-bones. He is your beloved. As he waited he whiled away the time with stories about you, and they have pricked my imagination like spurs. Were you not mounted on my fantasy as you came galloping in here? Why did you lash it so cruelly with that fine whip of yours? It's all in a lather and overheated. Oh, the stories he told! But just take a look at him. He's drugged by his own stories about you, milady. You can see that separation from you works on him like a lullaby. However, we can wake him.' – 'There's no need to do that,' the drugged man's beloved answers the poisoner. 'Don't bother. Don't disturb him. He's sleeping so sweetly. Maybe he's dreaming about me. You'd do better to get me a glass of punch. It's so cold outside. I'm frozen stiff. Please rub my hands for me. . . .'"

"You're a very strange person, Mr Heine. But please do carry on. I find your elevated speech most amusing."

"I am sorry. We mustn't forget Relinquimini's notebook. I'll just go up to my room. . . ."

"Don't worry. I won't forget it. Please, carry on. You're an amusing fellow. Do continue. 'Please rub my hands for me,' I think she said?"

"Yes, signora Camilla. You've been listening attentively. I am grateful."

"Well?"

"The town has treated me in the same way as the poisoner treated his companion. And you, my lovely Camilla, you are on its side. The town has eavesdropped on my thoughts of dawns as old and as remote and as ruined as brigands' castles. And it has drugged me in order to make use of me on the sly. It has allowed me to talk to my heart's content about gardens sweeping into the open night, unfurling their scarlet sails of evening air. And look, now it has hoisted its sails and left me lying in

116

some port-town tavern. And as you know, if that rascal suggests waking me, you won't let him."

"Listen, my good fellow. Where do I come into all this? I hope that the footman did wake you properly?"

" 'No,' you will say. 'Night is coming. We must hurry to avoid the storm. It's time to go. Don't wake him.' "

"Oh, signor Heine, how very mistaken you are! I shall say 'Oh yes! Yes, Ferrara, come and give him a shake and rouse him if he's still asleep. I've no time to wait. Wake him quickly, assemble all your crowds. Rumble and roar with all your streets until you wake him. Time won't wait.' "

"Yes, you're right. The notebook!"

"Later, later."

"Oh, dear signora Camilla, Ferrara has miscalculated. Ferrara has been made a fool of. The poisoner is in flight. I'm waking up. I'm awake and on my knees before you, my love!"

Camilla leapt to her feet.

"That's enough! Quite enough! . . . It's true that all this suits you very well. Even these banalities . . . especially these banalities! But really you cannot behave like this! You are just a strolling entertainer! We hardly know one another. It's only half an hour since. . . . Heavens, I find it funny even to discuss it! Yet here I am discussing it all the same. I have never in my life felt so stupid. The whole of this scene is like one of those Japanese flowers that open out immediately you put them in water. That's exactly what it's like. But those flowers are only made of paper, you know. And they don't cost much either!"

"I am listening, signora."

"But I would far rather listen to *you*, signore. You are very intelligent, and you're also apparently rather sarcastic. And yet you still indulge in banalities. And it's strange, but there's no contradiction in that. Your dramatic pathos. . . ."

"I beg your pardon, signora, but pathos is the Greek work for passion, and the Italian for blowing a kiss. Sometimes there are kisses which can only be blown. . . ."

"There you go again! Spare us the play-acting. It's intolerable. There is something you are concealing. Just explain yourself. And listen, please, dear Mr Heine, don't be angry with me. Behind all this you really are just – you won't condemn my familiarity? – you are just a sort of unusual child. No, that's not the word. You are a *poet*. That's right, why didn't I think of the word at once? One glance at you is enough. You're a sort of divinely elected idler, a spoiled darling of fate."

"Eviva!" Heine jumped up on the sill and leaned his whole body out of the window.

"Be careful, signor Heine!" Camilla shouted. "Be careful! I'm afraid!"

"Don't worry, dear signora. Hey, *furfanto*! Catch this!" He dropped some lire down on to the square below. "You'll get the same again and perhaps ten times the amount if you can plunder a few of Ferrara's gardens. One soldo for every hole in your breeches! On your way now! And watch you don't breathe on the flowers as you carry them. The Contessa here has a mimosa sensitivity. Off you go at the double, you rogue! Did you hear that, enchantress? The boy will come back dressed as Cupid. But to return to the subject: How perceptive you are! You have summed up the whole of my being, the whole essence of the situation in a single stroke, a single Apelles mark!"

"I don't understand you. Or is this another of your sallies on the stage? What is it you want exactly?"

"Yes, we're on the stage again. But why can't I be allowed to enjoy a bit of the limelight. It's not my fault after all that the most dangerous places in life are lit up the brightest – bridges and crossings. And what harsh lighting it is! All the rest is plunged in gloom. But on such a bridge – or let's suppose it's a stage instead – a man flares up when he's illuminated by those alarming lights. It's as though he has been put on exhibition to everyone and surrounded with railings, precipices, town-scapes, and signal lamps on shore. . . . signora Camilla, if we had not run into each other in such a dangerous place you wouldn't have heeded half what I had to say. And one must assume that it's dangerous, although personally I wouldn't know. But one has to assume that, because people have expended such a vast amount on illumination, and it isn't my fault that we have been lit up so cruelly and clumsily."

"Very well. Have you finished? What you say is all true. But it's an incredible piece of nonsense! I'd like to confide in you. And it's not just a whim of mine. It's almost a basic need. Your eyes don't lie. So what was it I wanted to say to you? . . . I've forgotten. Wait. . . . Yes, just listen, my good fellow, only an hour ago after all. . . ."

"Stop! Those are just words. But there are such things as hours and eternities. There are many of them and not one has any beginning. They break out at the first opportunity, and it's a matter of pure coincidence. But then it's away with all words! Are you aware, signora, when words are overthrown? And who it is that overthrows them? Away with words! Are you familiar with such rebellions, signora? All the fibres of my being are rebelling against me, signora, and I shall be forced to give way to them, as one yields to a mob. And one final point: Do you remember what you called me just now?"

"Of course. And I'm prepared to repeat it."

"You needn't. But there is such vitality in the way you view things. You have already mastered a line that is unique as life itself. So don't lose it or let it break off with me. Extend and draw it out for as long as possible. Continue tracing this mark and what do you get, signora? How do you turn out? Profile? Half-facing? Or in some other attitude?"

"I understand you." Camilla held out her hand to Heine. "And yet. . . . Heavens, no! I'm not a schoolgirl after all. I must pull myself together. This is like some form of hypnosis."

"Signora!" Heine exclaimed theatrically, kneeling at her feet. "Signora!" His voice rang dully as he hid his face in his hands. "Have you made that mark already? . . . What torture this is!" he sighed in a half-whisper, tearing his hands away from his suddenly blanching visage. And looking into the eyes of an increasingly disconcerted signora Ardenze, he noticed to his utter astonishment that. . . .

4

. . . He noticed that this woman was truly beautiful – almost unrecognisably lovely, that the beating of his own heart was gurgling like water in the wake of a boat. Its level rose, flooding her closely approaching knees, its successive waves lapped lazily about her figure. It rippled her silks, it covered her shoulders beneath its smooth surface, it raised her chin – oh miracle! – it raised it slightly, raised it higher, and the signora now stood up to her neck within his heart. One more wave like that and she would drown! And Heine seized her as she sank. Their kiss – and what a kiss! – bore them away. But it sighed a deep sigh under the pressure of their excited hearts, it jerked and tore aloft and onward, devil knows where. And she offered no resistance, none at all. "No!" sang her body, bridled, drawn and extended by that kiss. "If you wish, I'll be the boat to convey such kisses. Only carry it, carry me, carry me away . . . !"

"Someone's knocking!" The words escaped her in a hoarse cry. "Someone's knocking!" And she broke free from his embrace.

She was right.

"Hell and damnation! Who's there?"

119

"Signore should not have locked the door of the drawing-room. It is not our custom here."

"Silence! I shall do as I please."

"I think you must be ill, signore."

A stream of Italian abuse followed, fanatical and passionate as prayer. Heine unlocked the door. Out in the corridor the footman was completing his curses and a little way behind him stood the young ragamuffin engulfed in a forest of lianas, oleanders, orange blossom, lilies. . . .

"This young rascal. . . ."

. . . Roses, magnolias, carnations. . . .

"This young rascal has been demanding that he must at all costs be let into the room whose windows face on to the square – and that can only mean the drawing-room."

"Yes, yes, the drawing-room," the boy growled gruffly.

"Of course he's to be let in," Heine agreed. "I told him to come myself."

"Because," the footman continued hastily, "he can't possibly have any business in the office, or the bathrooms, or especially in the reading-room. But because of his totally unsuitable dress. . . ."

"Oh yes," Heine exclaimed, as though only now awakening. "Rondolfina, just look at his pantaloons! Who sewed you these fishnet breeches, transparent creature?"

"Signore, each year the thorns of Ferrara's bramble hedges are sharpened up with special gardeners'. . . ."

"Ha-ha-ha!"

"In view of his completely indecent dress," the footman continued hastily, specially emphasising the words as he saw the signora approaching with a shadow of sudden puzzlement on her face which conflicted with a ray of irrepressible merriment. "In view of his totally indecent dress we told the boy to hand the signore's commission over to us and wait for an answer outside in the street. But then the young varmint started. . . ."

"Yes, yes, he's right," Heine cut the orator short. "I told him to present himself to the signora personally. . . ."

By now the irascible Calabrian had lost control of himself. "The young scoundrel started uttering threats," he gabbled.

"Oh yes? What sort of threats?" Heine inquired. "What a colourful scene this is, signora! Don't you agree?"

"The little varmint referred to you. 'The signore,' he threatened, 'The signore merchant will start patronising other hotels next time he passes through Ferrara if you go against his wishes and don't let me in to see him.' "

"Ha-ha! He's a real comic! Don't you agree, signora? You can take this tropical plantation. . . . No, wait a moment." Heine turned, awaiting Camilla's instructions. "Take it to number eight for the time being," he went on without waiting for her reply.

"Yes, to your room for the moment," Camilla repeated, blushing slightly.

"Certainly, signore. And as for this boy here. . . ."

"And now, you monkey, how much do you think your trousers are worth?"

"Giulio is all covered in scars. Giulio is blue with cold. Giulio hasn't anything else to wear, and he hasn't a papa or a mama," the rascally ten-year-old snivelled tearfully and broke out in a sweat.

"So how much then? Come on, tell me!"

"A hundred soldi, signore," the youngster said in an uncertain, dreamy voice as though suffering hallucinations.

"Ha-ha-ha!" everyone laughed. Heine laughed, and Camilla laughed, and even the footman burst out laughing – the footman especially when Heine produced his wallet, took out a ten lira note and still laughing handed it to the young ragamuffin.

The boy shot out a grasping paw to seize the outheld note.

"Wait," Heine said. "I imagine that this is your first venture in the field of commerce. So good luck to you. . . . Listen, *cameriere*, I can assure you that your laughter on this occasion is very misguided. You're really hurting the feelings of this young trader. But I'm right, aren't I, young man? In your next few dealings in Ferrara you'll not be showing your face at the inhospitable door of the Hotel Tasso, will you?"

"Oh no, signore, on the contrary. . . . How many more days is signore staying in Ferrara?"

"I'm packing up and leaving in two hours' time."

"Signor Enrico. . . ."

"Yes, signora?"

"Let's go outside. We really don't want to go back into that stupid drawing-room."

"Very well. . . . *Cameriere*, take these flowers up to room eight. Wait, this rose has still to open out. Ferrara's gardens entrust it to you for this evening, signora."

"Merci, Enrico. . . . But this black carnation is totally uninhibited.

121

Ferrara's gardens entrust you, signore, with the care of this licentious bloom."

"Your hand, signora. . . . So, *cameriere*, this goes to number eight. And I need my hat – it's in my room."

The footman went away.

"You mustn't, Enrico."

"I don't understand, Camilla."

"You will stay. . . . Oh, don't bother to answer! . . . You will stay just another day at least in Ferrara? . . . Enrico, Enrico, you've smudged your eyebrow with pollen. Let me dust it off."

"Signora Camilla, there's a fuzzy caterpillar on your shoe. Let me knock it off. . . . I'll send a telegram home to Frankfurt. . . . And your dress is all covered in petals, signora. . . . And I shall keep on sending letters express every day until you tell me to stop."

"Enrico, I see no wedding ring on your finger. Have you ever worn such an ornament?"

"I noticed one on yours, Camilla, a good long while ago. . . . Ah, my hat. Many thanks."

5

All Ferrara's alleyways brimmed with an evening fragrance which lapped through the labyrinth of streets like a sonorous liquid globe – just like a droplet of sea-water which stops up an ear and floods one's skull with muzziness.

It was noisy in the coffee-house. But there was a quiet fragility in the lane that led up to it. That was the main reason why the stunned, astonished town held its breath and surrounded it on every side. The evening had retreated into one of its lanes, precisely the one where the coffee-house stood on one corner.

Camilla became lost in thought as she waited for Heine. He had gone to the telegraph office next door to the coffee-house.

"Why did he absolutely refuse to compose his telegram in the coffee-house and send it next door by messenger?" she wondered. "Couldn't he be content to send an ordinary express letter? Is this another liaison founded totally on feelings? But on the other hand he would have forgotten all about the telegram if I hadn't reminded him. And this Rondolfina . . . I must ask him about her. But can I do that? It's his private affair. Good Lord, I'm just like a schoolgirl! I must ask him, I have to! Today I have the right to do anything, and at the same time I'm losing that right. These artists have certainly messed you about, my dear! And what about this man? And what about Relinquimini? . . . How distant he seems! Ever since the spring. No, even earlier, maybe at that New Year's party?! . . . No, he never has been close to me. . . . But what about this man?"

"A penny for your thoughts, Camilla!"

"Why are you looking so sorrowful, Enrico? Don't be sad. I'll let you go if you wish. There are some telegrams that can be dictated and taken down by a servant. Send an express letter home that you've overstayed by just three hours. There's a train going to Venice from Ferrara tonight, and another to Milan. You won't be delayed by more than. . . ."

"What is all this about, Camilla?"

"Why are you so sad, Enrico? Tell me something about Rondolfina."

Heine started and jumped up from his chair.

"How do you know? Is he here? Has he been here while I was away? Where is he? Where is he, Camilla?"

"You've gone quite pale, Enrico. Who are you talking about? I was asking you about a woman, wasn't I? Or am I pronouncing the name wrongly? Is it Rondolfino? It's all a question of that last vowel. Sit down. People are looking at us."

"Who told you about her? Have you had some news from him? But how could it have got here? It's quite by chance that we're sitting here after all. What I mean is that nobody can know that we're here."

"Nobody's been here, Enrico, and nothing has happened while you were away. I can give you my word of honour. But this all gets more and more curious every minute. So there are *two* of them?"

"This must be some miracle! It's quite beyond me. . . . I must be losing my wits. Who mentioned that name to you, Camilla? Where did you hear it?"

"I heard it last night in a dream. Heavens, it's a common enough name! But you still haven't answered me. Who is Rondolfina? Plenty of miracles happen in this world, but let's leave them out of it. Who is she, Enrico?"

"Oh, Camilla, Rondolfina is *you!*"

"You dissembling play-actor! . . . No, no! Let me go! . . . Don't touch me!"

Both of them jumped to their feet, Camilla as part of a single sweeping manoeuvre. Only the table stood between them. Camilla grasped the

THE VOICE OF PROSE

back of a chair. But something had come between her and her resolve, something had come over her. Then all of a sudden the coffee-house lurched round in a wave, up and away like a merry-go-round. . . . She was lost! . . . She had to tear it off, that necklace. . . . The row of faces also started moving and flowing down the same carousel-twirling path . . . faces . . . imperial beards . . . monocles . . . lorgnettes . . . more and more of them directed at her every second. At all the other tables conversations tripped over this wretched one. She could still see it, still prop herself up. Maybe it would pass off. . . . But no. . . . the orchestra went off pitch and lost the beat. . . .

"*Cameriere*, water! Over here!"

6

She was slightly feverish.

"What a tiny room you have! . . . Yes, that's right, like that, thank you. I'll lie here a little longer. It's malaria. . . . Later one. . . . You see, I've got a complete apartment. But you mustn't leave me. It might come over me again any minute. Enrico!"

"Yes, my love?"

"Why don't you say something? . . . No, no, don't, it's better like this. . . . Ah, Enrico, I can't even remember whether there was a morning today. Are they still there?"

"What, Camilla?"

"The flowers. They must be taken out for the night. What a heavy perfume! How many tons does it weigh?"

"I'll have them removed. . . . What is it, Camilla?"

"I'm getting up. . . . I can manage, thank you. There, it's gone completely. I just needed to stand up. . . . Yes, they must be taken out. But where? Wait, I have a whole apartment on the Piazza Ariosto. You can probably see it from here. . . . "

"It's nighttime. It seems to be a little cooler."

"Why are there so few people on the streets?"

"Hush! They can hear every word."

"What are they talking about?"

"I don't know, Camilla. They seem to be students. It's some sort of showing off. Perhaps they're talking about our. . . . "

124

"Do let me go. They've stopped on the corner. Good Lord, he's chucked the little fellow head over heels! . . . But now it's quiet again. How oddly the light catches in the branches! Yet you can't see the lamp. Are we on the top?"

"How do you mean, Camilla?"

"Is there another floor above us?"

"Yes, I think so."

Camilla leaned out of the small window and looked up from beneath the overhang.

"No. . . ." But Heine didn't let her finish. "No, there's nobody there." She wrenched herself free and repeated what she had said.

"What is the matter?"

"I just thought that there was a man standing there with a lamp at the window, and he was throwing crumpled leaves and shadows through the window into the street. I wanted to lean out and catch them on my cheek. But there's nobody there."

"That is true poetry, Camilla!"

"Really? I don't know. . . . There it is over there, by the theatre. In the lilac glow!"

"Who's there, Camilla?"

"You are a strange one! It's my house, of course! But I keep having these bouts. If only we could somehow arrange. . . ."

"A room has already been reserved for you."

"Really? How thoughtful of you! At long last! What is the time? Shall we go and look what my room is like? I'm curious to see."

They went out of room number eight smiling and excited as schoolchildren playing at the siege of Troy in the backyard.

7

Long before it came, the Catholic church bells began their garrulous announcements of approaching dawn, jerking and bowing frigidly from their somersaulting beams. Only one single lamp glowed in the hotel. It flared on suddenly as the telephone bell gave its acid trill, and afterwards it was left burning. The lamp was witness as a sleepy night-porter ran to the 'phone and then placed the receiver on the desk after some altercation with the caller, disappearing into the depths of the corridor and re-emerging shortly afterwards from the same half-darkness.

"Yes, the signore is leaving this morning. If it's so very urgent, he'll ring you in about half an hour. Give me your number and tell me who to ask for.''

The lamp was still burning when the ''man from number eight'', as he was described on the 'phone, emerged into the main corridor from a side-passage and made his way on stockinged tiptoe, still fastening his buttons.

The lamp stood exactly opposite his room. But to reach the telephone the man from number eight had to go on a promenade down the corridor. The start of his walk was somewhere around the rooms numbered in the eighties. During a brief discussion with the porter his expression changed from anxious excitement to one of carefree curiosity. Then he boldly picked up the receiver and after going through the usual formalities he found himself speaking to the editor of *Il Voce*.

''Look here, this is outrageous! Who told you that I suffer from insomnia?''

. . .

''You shouldn't be on the telephone – your place is shouting from the rooftop! Why are you sounding off like this? What's the matter?''

. . .

''Yes, I've been delayed by one day.''

. . .

''The footman was right. I didn't give them my home address and I've no intention of doing so.''

. . .

''Give it to *you*? I shall not do that either. I wasn't intending to publicise it at all – and certainly not today, as you seem to imagine.''

. . .

''You'll never need to use it.''

. . .

''Don't get hot under the collar, dear editor. Just try and stay calm. It will never occur to Relinquimini to use you as a go-between.''

. . .

''Because he has no need of that.''

. . .

''May I remind you again that I'd greatly appreciate it if you kept calm. Relinquimini never lost any notebook.''

. . .

''Pardon me, but that's the first unambiguous thing you've said. And the answer is: No, most definitely not.''

. . .

126

"Are you still on about that?! Very well, I admit it. But it's only blackmail in the context of yesterday's *Il Voce*, certainly not otherwise."

. . .

"Since yesterday. Since six p.m."

. . .

"If you'd caught the slightest whiff of what has come frothing up on the yeast of my inventiveness, you'd choose a slightly more piquant name for it. And it would be still further from the truth than the one you've just come up with."

. . .

"Willingly. With pleasure. I see no objection to that today. The name is Heinrich Heine."

. . .

"Precisely."

. . .

"Most flattering to hear it."

. . .

"Goodness me!"

. . .

"With pleasure. But how can we manage it? I regret that I must leave today. Come to the station. We could spend an hour or so together."

. . .

"At nine thirty-five. Although time is a never ending train of surprises. It would be better if you didn't come."

. . .

"Come to the hotel in the afternoon. That will be more reliable. Or come up to my apartment in the evening. In tails, please, and bring flowers."

. . .

"Yes, yes, dear editor. You truly have the gift of prophecy."

. . .

"Or tomorrow at the duelling ground, outside town."

. . .

"I don't know. Maybe it's not a joke."

. . .

"Or else, if you are completely booked up for the next couple of days, then come to the Campo Santo the day after tomorrow."

. . .

"Do you think so?"

. . .

"Really?"

. . .

"What a weird conversation at this ungodly hour! Well, you must excuse me. I'm tired. I want to get back to my room."

. . .

"I can't hear. . . . Number eight? Ah yes. Yes, yes, number eight. It's a wonderful room, dear editor, with a climate entirely of its own. It has been perpetual spring in there for four hours now. Goodbye, dear editor."

Heine mechanically turned off the light.

"Leave it on, Enrico," a voice sounded from the dark depths of the corridor.

"Camilla?!!"

SUBOCTAVE STORY

Part One

1

The service was over. A swelling wave of prim hooped skirts and tumid flounces surged towards the door of the church, and as the last lady parishioners' dresses made their blustering exit, only a cold and senseless void remained beneath the vaulted arches. The congregation which had been the soul of that whitewashed vaulting disappeared. Now the church's lifeless interior resembled the glass bell of a gigantic air-pump. Sucked in by the building's immense vacuity, chill streams of sterilised white midday poured through the long windows' narrow ventils and fell on the backs of pews and carved ornamental scrolls. Like toppled columns, they pressed the weight of their light on the broad benches' wooden trims so as to slide across the smooth stone floor and avoid crashing on the dusty planks of the choirstalls. God was abandoned in His church, and either He was unable to warm the frozen limbs of that Lutheran colonnade barehanded, or else He never saw fit to concern himself.

Meanwhile the organist stoked the fires of his art. After the grumbling whine of a delayed and protracted cadenza, as the peasants and townswomen rose from their seats and crowded towards the doors with a hollow, shuffling echo, he unleashed and gave free play to his instrument.

In the doorway a jostling began as the hot breath of a fine dry Maytime stirred and came to meet the folk as they emerged. The throng issued on to the church steps, and in the open air there was the usual sudden, loud and crowded chorus of chattering, drenched by sunlight and scalded with chirruping birdsong. But above all the chatter out on the square, Knauer the organist could still be heard through the open doors as he bade the congregation a joyous farewell. The inner parts of his jubilant improvisations could easily have been crushed and trampled underfoot as they leaped about and sprang up at the dispersing crowd like frisking setters. And they were besides themselves with joy that so many of them belonged to just one master, for it was at the end of the service that Knauer usually loosed the entire pack of his countless registers.

The church gradually emptied.

The organist played on.

Any force spontaneously growing and increasing is bound eventually to reach a stage where it looks around and sees nothing other than itself. The melodic line of Knauer's invention improved with each moment. It grew more and more lovely and swelled with ripeness and strength. And then, as it was stricken with solitude and its whole body racked by a sickening force with no adequate fulcrum, Knauer shuddered at a sensation familiar only to the artist. He shuddered at the affinity between himself and the line of his cantilena, and he was vaguely aware that it knew him as well as he knew it. They were drawn together by the attraction of equals. He took pride in his melody, little realising that their feelings were mutual.

The organist played on and was lost to the world as one improvisation followed on another. There was one in which the whole acoustic aristocracy of the treble was imperceptibly transferred piece by piece down to the bass. And there in a barony of noble octaves, one more noble and powerful than all the rest asserted itself and ruled over the theme unchallenged. And as the theme noisily worked up an unprecedented, menacing speed, it moved towards a pedal point. Successfully negotiating the final link of a sequence, it was only a few steps from the dominant when all at once, in the twinkling of an eye, an irreparable catastrophe occurred. The entire improvisation was suddenly dispossessed and orphaned. It was as though the notes had had their hats knocked off, or suddenly bared their heads. At the most perilous point of a statement in the bass, two keys on the instrument failed to respond and from behind the majestic rampart of pipes and ventils arose an inhuman shriek – inhuman precisely because it seemed to have a human source.

But the unaccountable wail was soon obscured and drowned by other sounds, and although one sprained key now yielded nothing but the knock of wood against wood, the organist bore bravely with his loss. Half an hour earlier his wife had been unable to tear him away from the console, and now the disobedience of just one key could still not halt his outpourings. Half an hour ago she had come in by the side-door and called up to him in the gallery. She shouted across the empty church to tell him that his sister Augusta was there already and that he had better come down and see her – she was down there in the churchyard waiting and was in a hurry to see little Gottlieb, but Knauer had for some reason taken the boy with him and the child was probably starving by now, and if Knauer was staying on to play he should at least let her take the boy and they would go home with Augusta, and why should the child suffer because his father . . .

Knauer cut her short without turning round. "Gottlieb isn't here," he called. "He was around here earlier but I don't know where he is now. He's probably at the Pockennarbs. I saw him playing with Therese and Fritz. . . ."

"The verger's children again! How many times have I said . . ."

"Can't hear you! Go back home, Dortchen! I can't hear a thing you're saying!"

Knauer paid no more attention to the crippled key than he did to his wife. From the bass he transferred his concern to the middle register, and there a series of concluding chords finally restored his composure and calm. He rose from the organ-stool, locked the console, and dismissed Seebald who had been working the bellows. Then he climbed behind the casing into the organ chamber to examine the G sharp and A sharp valves and ascertain the damage.

2

It was Whitsunday evening. Contours of gable peaks, angular cornices and overhangs and other wonders of twilit and time-smutted mediaeval architecture were cramped and compressed to a state of blackness in the poorly lighted parts of the town, where they detached themselves from the glowing sky like words spoken in an even voice against a background of utter silence. And their black edges turned feverish on contact with a celestial lake whose depths were fed with dark chill from two floating lumps of broken ice – two large melting stars filled to overflowing a sky that already brimmed with undulating luminosity. The proximity of such spring-sources sent the black edges of ridge-tiles and eaves into a fine shiver which was all the keener because every single curvature and hollow in the roofing could be reached and probed by the rippling flood of that pale, unsettled night.

In those parts of town it was still, and the stillness had a weirdly arousing effect on the sky, which tensed and trembled as it listened in to something far away.

But it only needed a tavern lantern to glow among the horse-chestnuts in the garden for the dull beams to light up an entire anthill of rustlings. The anthill clumped together and turned suddenly into a pile of dreamy monotonous verbiage as the thrifty citizens of Ansbach[1] with their families and households made their way to the Wirtsgarten, pushed back the chairs and sat down at the tables, still chewing away at conversations brought in from the street. The sky parted the gnarled branches of the horse-chestnuts and bent low over the people as they talked. The citizenry might well have raised many a squabble over spare seats (of which there were none, nor were there likely to be any), if squabbling had been the custom with these peaceable folk, and if passers-by in the street had not been merely wound-up clockwork people. But here no change of established custom was tolerated. And one such custom was that the family of Tuch senior sat at the table commanding the best view of the river, and that his family and household exchanged remarks with the Sturzwages at the next table, while Arthur Rosarius and family sat like his ancient namesake at the table encircling the thick trunk of an old horse-chestnut tree.

The sky was swarthy and scorched olive by the garden lanterns glowing here and there. Like a supple gymnast, it clung to the tips of twigs and hung right down to the tablecloths. Pyramids of chestnut blossom, accidentally caught by the sky, dropped an occasional bloom from their erect steeplets. The petals fell into the tankards, twirled and finally settled on the beer's surface in lacy circlets of froth that dissolved in a network of loops like the lost eye of a bull. Night chucked palmfuls of beetles, gnats and moths on to the linen tablecloths. And swarms of brittle-winged bugs smashed against the sides of the lanterns with a dry crackle like handfuls of greasy beans against the glowing walls of a coffee-roaster. And like rich, heavy granules in the roasting chest, the conversations in the garden scattered and fragmented as someone mixed and stirred them with an iron ladle which made a clinking sound that was dull and soporific.

Down there at the tables all the talk was of the Knauer family tragedy. As soon as it was mentioned, people lost all desire to enjoy themselves. The news had swept the town in a trice. Everyone admitted that it spoilt their holiday and hypocritical concern had obliged everyone to give up their holiday habits. So the artisans and shopkeepers and their wives and children did their energetic utmost to spoil the last remnants of festivity for one another. They wearied each other with repetitive discussions as to whether or not there was good reason why the Lord had visited such a punishment on the arrogant town organist. And if there was, then surely they themselves – simple souls who had only that evening confessed their simplicity with such satisfaction – surely they themselves must be more pleasing in the sight of their Creator? With the instinctive flair of domestic animals they felt that Whitsuntide was the feast of their own station; the chestnuts' weighty, knotted arches provided them with their fitting shade; and the beer dissolving in clasping loops and foaming rings and resembling a tawny bull's eye they felt to be the drink befitting folk of their station. And since providence had punished the standoffish organist precisely on that day and on the common ground of their native town, they all believed Knauer had been punished in their presence not by mere accident, but by some deliberate design. And hence, by a natural train of thought, they naively concluded that they were collectively called upon to judge Knauer and condemn him. And condemn him they did. They condemned and sentenced him to what had already happened without their intervention a few hours earlier on that warm Whitsunday – a peaceful, unpretentious day which thus consorted so well with their own station. The entire town talked of nothing but the organist. And late that night when Julius Rosarius on his way back from Lollar rode in through the old Grafstor, he followed his old custom and without alighting asked the watchman whether there was anything new in town. And the answer he heard was roughly as follows: Knauer the organist had crushed his own child to death; they said it happened during one of his furious extemporisings; the child had got inside the organ chamber and had been strangled by some lever. God alone knows how it happened. It was hard to credit, but it was true.

3

All night long in the Knauers' apartment the armchairs and cupboards, clocks and books, and the sayings worked in wool on canvas which hung framed on the wall felt as if they had been shrouded with dust-covers. The master and mistress seemed to be away and the doors were locked. Yet in fact the outside door had never closed all day, and the master and mistress were both at home and had never been to bed. There was an element of truth only in the dust-sheets. Down to the floor from all the furnishings and fitments hung shrouds that were fashioned from soft footfalls, rapid whimperings and stifled sobs. And in the dining-room which directly adjoined the room where all those shrouds

were meticulously woven, the swaying canopy of muted weeping transformed every object into a catafalque.

Up in the hills whose distant sighs came in at the wide-open windows,
it took a long time to waken the dawn. But finally it was roused and it
stretched and stirred its chilled bones. It arose in a greyish-white strip
and with a broad ogre's gape set off on its usual treck. It arrived from
beyond Rabenklippe and was terribly weary after walking on an empty
stomach for seven miles along the dark and desolate post-road. It arrived
exhausted, still short of sleep, and with its boot-soles caked in damp
sand from the road. Usually it stopped by the window and through the
pane its large, hungry eyes devoured everything in the dining-room. It
was specially fond of the cheese, still uncleared from yesterday's supper,
and it cunningly made eyes at the young mice which it found resembling
wisps of warm grey cottonwool. But it had never set eyes on the owners
of the house. So it was most surprised as it hitched up to the window
and discovered it wide open. And instead of mice glimpsed through a
window-pane, it discovered a candle burning freely in the open air. For
the dining-room itself was open to the air and smelled of the street, and
following the dawn there came filing through the window remote,
perfume-drenched kitchen plots and flower gardens, distant peat-bogs
and even more distant hills. Swum about by so much, such rapturous
space, the flame made salute and excitedly rushed from its candle with
the wick in tow. It fled, surrendering its post. . . . And then it resumed
again, pale, pinched, and straight as a rod. Having burned all night, the
candle was dying of fatigue. It no longer shone and its little tongue of
paralysed, enfeebled flame floated in the current, belly upwards like a
little fish – a cold, dead bleak washed by the cool stream of dawn.

Before the morning light had taken even a couple of steps inside the
room, it collided with Aunt Augusta in the doorway. Candle in hand,
she was heading straight for the light without noticing it. She closed the
door right in its face and blew out both candles, then with a loud sigh
she went through to see her brother. So the long-sought door retained
its secret.

But in the bedroom beyond that mysterious door, in the room where
the most sumptuous and heavy tassels and trimmings on the canopy of
mourning hung to the very floor – in that room the following took place
behind closed curtains: There lay the corpse of the child, and above it
dimly swayed and fluttered the ruin of his mother. Once she had fed
him from her breast. But now it was her own breast, convulsed in starving
spasms, which she nourished with the rich offerings of generous grief.

Her anguish was insatiable as a half-crazed bitch and its fangs gnawed bare everything that suffering could feed upon. Not a single feature of her memories or of her child's little point-nosed face had escaped them. Everything was etched and gnawed by them. Yet the furious hunger of her torment showed no sign of abating. Sifting her memory for the still intact details of former motherhood, she noticed a toy standing in the corner. And she fastened on it with a new, still more urgent craving. It was a little wooden horse which Aunt Augusta had intended for the boy. But he hadn't been able to enjoy the gift. He hadn't even seen it, poor mite. . . . O Lord, what on earth had happened?! . . . Oh! . . .

The sight was indeed one to draw tears – and it claimed them by extortion.

Throughout the night the boy's face had been lit by the pallid glow of death. It was as if death had shone deliberately for the mother's benefit, so that a bundle of rays from its horrid lampion fell just on her child's tiny face. His face was the only object in the whole room, and it immediately caught one's gaze and was terrifying in its whiteness. Expiring alcoholics in their dying delirium have often down the ages had the same vision of a severed head tied in a barber's snow-white napkin. And the weight of that lifeless child's head could now have been told at a glance, moulded as it was from a mass of white tallow like a candle-stem cast from a pound of white wax. And as it parted from life – that rich assemblage of every sort of grimace, smile, wry look and laughter – the child's face had chosen for its road to the world beyond an expression only of childish terror. And on that journey, since no others were available, the expression never left the little waxen visage. And no other expression would ever come to replace it. None.

There were many toys lying in the nursery, and in the mother's memory so many looks and expressions were stored that she felt an urge to run and give him something for the journey, something he might need or have use for. She wanted to give it to him before it was too late, while he was still there. Because soon it would be too late – irrevocably, forever. . . .

And how she thrashed in her anguish! What? Leave him now, when he was all on his own with no one to watch over him? Could he be allowed such awful freedom? . . . Once upon a time she could console him. Then there was just a partition between them and she had only to run across the corridor to reach him. But now, when they were parted and the whole of him, his eyes and mouth, his hands and little ringing voice would be buried in the earth . . . now she had to abandon him and leave him all unconsoled, frightened and confused. . . .

The mute, hysterical cries of a mother's soul crushed and disfigured her breast like folds of a Heraclean shirt. And had they been thoughts and had her brain been able to control them, the idea of suicide would have appeared as a divinely sent viaticum. But she thought of nothing. Or else she was unaware that hysterical ideas were irrepressibly writhing and raging inside her like a mass of blind white maggots. Infested and weary with sobbing, her face and body both collapsed. Her hands dangled as though not part of her. And with a blank gaze she surrendered awkwardly and clumsily to silent tears which she herself was no longer aware of and which flowed without her knowledge or consent. The tears rolled lazily of their own accord and spread across the whole of her already moist countenance. Her features were affected by these new tears like some view shrouded with a mournful reticle of rain and ill-weather. Her face was already bereft of sense and doomed to a long narcosis. And tears, chased from one remote source to another remote distance, misted and distended it into a mask of incomprehension. The dead child resembled his mother – so much was clear from one glance at the pair of them.

At that moment the door half-opened and Knauer appeared on the threshold and addressed his wife from there without looking at her or entering. He spoke quietly and with evident self-restraint.

"Go out and let me spend a while with him alone," he said.

"Amadeus! You! And now, Amadeus . . ." his wife shouted incoherently and rose jerkily from her seat. But she never finished her sentence. All the strength left her and she reeled and fell into the arms of Augusta who rushed to assist and support her as she left the room. Knauer closed the door behind them. He approached the body of his son slowly and sat down in the armchair just vacated by his wife. He propped his head on his right hand and with his left began deftly carressing the little body which lay there festively decked out. He closed his eyes and was unaware that soon it would be thirteen hours since he lost his reason and that the place where it happened was in the inner workings of the organ.

Knauer's position was that of a man who had learned for the first time – learned for himself and not merely heard from others – that he had a soul. And he could sense and feel where it was within him, because it ached. Something was happening to it akin to a sclerotic degeneration. His soul was turning hard within him and slowly gathering like muscle fibre. It was tightly knotted, clung to every internal cavity of his body and suffered the delirium of any morbific organ. And without any actual change in size, it seemed in its delirium to assume utterly shameless, improbable dimensions – just like a cavitied tooth which never leaves the jaw or alters its proportions yet swells to an infinity of nightmarish pain and extrapolates a crazy fable of Goliath's jawbone. . . . But Knauer did not lose his composure. His soul stirred in him like a tapeworm. Yet it was an all-invading tapeworm whose contractions failed to nauseate him only because every particle of his body was sick with its own particular sickness, and their different varieties cancelled one another. Consequently, although racked by nausea, he suffered no vertigo – simply because being subject to the law of specific gravity he was drowning in the maelstrom of his soul, a maelstrom that was tangible and therefore nauseating. . . .

As he sat by the corpse of his son, Knauer was filled with the sound of an incessant, steady humming – the same indistinct, imaginary noise that fills the body of a bell when the ringer is away and people down below imagine the bells are silent. . . . But how he started when, suddenly, through the dense darkness of oblivion he noticed what his left hand was doing to the body of his child! He snatched his hand hastily away as though it were a viper, or as if he had burnt his fingers plucking a blazing log from the carpet and had to blow on them. That incorrigible hand of his had been carressing his son in octaves! It had been playing on his corpse in octaves!

Knauer straightened up. Then he bent and kissed the boy's forehead and went to the door. On the threshold he stopped and looked back, recollecting or trying to summon some thought. Then he turned and went back to the body. He bent and kissed him again. This time his kiss lasted longer than the first by a whole eternity, and it outrageously prolonged the execution of an evidently solemn, startling decision known only to himself. And during the whole of that illicitly protracted instant he endeavoured to transfer something from his lips to the boy's waxen forehead. But instead a film of cold deposit passed from the child's brow to his own lips, like a blurred transfer slipping from its wet mount on to dry paper. Then Knauer raised a handkerchief to his eyes, bit his lip hard and rushed out of the room. He walked quickly through into the entrance-hall, grabbed his cane and hat and ran out of the house without closing the door.

The damp morning vapoured up into his eyes and evaporated, leaving them dry. The aroma of grass and lilac and the rancid breath of poplars and dusted raindrops rushed to his head. And there were birds too. They chirruped and twittered endlessly. He could hear them all the time – all the time just them.

From that day onward he was never seen in town again. So he never heard how they buried little Gottlieb.

Part Two

1

"Well? . . . Still nothing? . . . Not back yet?"

The impatient travellers plied postmaster Schlippe with these and similar questions every time he tried to shrink and tiptoe back to his quarters at the rear of the posting-station's huge twilit vestibule. And each time he would stop and raise both hands as though to fend off an impending attack.

"The express courier isn't back yet," he answered in a loud whisper. "Lemke hasn't any horses. We've inquired already. And as you already know, we haven't a single one here at the station. They've all been taken by His Excellency's suite – you must have passed them on the way. But it's a long ride to the next station, gentlemen. You'll have to spend the night here."

"It isn't a question of staying overnight, Herr Postmeister," the gentleman in wig and riding-boots repeated for the tenth time. "Many of us, you know," he went on, turning to the young honeymoon couple – "Many of us," he smiled as if he had caught the postmaster out – "Many of us make a point of staying at a hotel overnight when we travel. But we could have been spending the night at Treysa. Instead of which, Herr Postmeister, we have wasted ten hours here all for nothing. . . ."

But by this time the postmaster was stealing back to his quarters. He gestured helplessly from the doorway and in a loud whisper addressed the entire hall, as though it were some important official. "There's nothing I can do, gentlemen. His Excellency . . ." – and with that he disappeared and locked the door from the other side as a defence

138

against the impatient travellers. The latter remained huddling in the corners, looking diminutive and unsightly. But the vestibule with its four windows facing the street and two round hatches looking on to the courtyard was huge and empty, an inveterate twilight stood from floor to ceiling in airy grey pillars, and the travellers had no lamp to place between themselves and the crepuscular colonnade which never moved yet always seemed to close in on them.

Meanwhile outside the rainstorm roared. With its flanks of chestnuts raging, the post-road trailed its sumptuous, rushing garment across a field, through the roaring summer downpour. Then, speeding at full tilt, it turned off sharply into the Posthof where its five-mile train swung and shattered against the panes of the hollow vestibule. In flashes of lightning all the veins and fissures of the grey marbled walls shuddered like the legs of a galvanised frog, and in the gateway a pallid façade of clean faces sprang into sight, each resembling a flattened moon. A glance at the window at that instant would have shown sinewy skies agush with rivulets of dull blackness. Quicklime blazed and lashed the heavens with pails of soapy water and swilled them with waves of suds that scudded in pursuit of one another. And at each new celestial flash six white faces leaped above six collars – the gentleman in the wig and riding-boots, the young couple, and . . .

And the rain poured down with redoubled force. It ranted and choked itself in the throat of the foliage, and the leaves were throttled and gave vent to pealing plaints. Out in the courtyard the mass of lush and rustling luxury was like a chorus of worship. But when a rumble of stone rolled up to the gateway of the courtyard, the six travellers could still distinguish the sonorous exertions of twelve heavily hammering hooves from the fanfare of thunderclaps that blended with them.

2

/This section of Pasternak's manuscript is missing. Maybe the author himself excised it when revising the text. It appears likely that it contained an account of the incident in which lightning struck dead one of the horses as it drew a coach into the yard of the posting-station. By some miracle the vehicle's occupants, including a young aristocrat and his elderly tutor, were unscathed. The episode probably ended with all the travellers' decision to stay overnight in the town, whereupon a servant escorted them away to the hotel./

3

Their escort's swaying lantern broke the darkness into abrupt lumps, yet still failed to disperse it. The rest of them discussed the promise of a dry bed for the night in tones of anticipated bliss, inhibited only by weariness and caution as they crossed the wet flagstones in fear of stumbling or treading on something live. The rest of them also discussed the amazing [good fortune]* that had deflected the thunderbolt away from both travellers. The young man following the servant and walking in arm with the elderly gentleman turned and looked back at the lowborn folk in the rearguard of the procession. Even by daylight the travellers had hardly been distinguishable and now they had blurred into a single sodden smudge. The young man dropped back slightly, causing the others to stub their toes on his heels. Addressing no one in particular, he mouthed a few courteous remarks. In the presence of such a [friendly nobleman] they felt free to choose their own subject of conversation, and they talked also of the little town's beauty and its splendour. . . .

"Tell me," the old man asked the servant. "Is it still the same man who owns the hotel here?"

"His name's Würzenau," the servant mumbled. "Why? Do you know him?"

"No, no. But I . . . I was told . . . I thought his name was Markus."

"Markus? He used to be the owner," the servant continued. "But he died back in . . . er . . . eighteen ten. No, wait. . . . That's right, ten years ago, when the French came. It was a right bad day, that was. In summer it was. I can remember it like yesterday. Dusty and windy it was. The wind regular scorched you. And when it dropped, the dust settled and the trees stood stock-still. And you could hear it going bang-bang-bang – the crackle of gunfire from Kronwerk yonder. Well, of course, you wouldn't know anything about that. But it was a dozy sort of firing, sort of anyhow . . . like someone having a little set-to after dinner. It wasn't at all frightening. It was just like in the kitchen next door – just one step away — as though they were chopping meat or clattering saucepans. Noonday it was. There wasn't a soul in the street. But the wind was terrible – awful hot it was. And when it dropped, the gunpowder smoke

---

*Gap in original manuscript; text supplied here and elsewhere by conjecture – Translator.

caught up your nostrils. And there was this bitter smell, and you could quite clearly hear them going bang-bang-bang. . . . It all carried on the wind. . . . It was blowing in that direction. . . . I only realise all this now, of course. I didn't then. I was still a young lad – about nine I'd be. The town was deserted. . . . Anyway, what was I talking about? . . . Oh yes, Markus. They buried him one day in the morning, and that same evening the French entered town and they took the hotel over for about a month. After that there's only been Würzenau. . . ."

"He tells a good tale, doesn't he, Georg?"

"You call that a good tale? It's quite amazing, I'll grant you. But completely incoherent!"

"What's that, milord?"

"Never you mind. Carry on."

"It was Würzenau who did the place up again. What's the matter, sir? Why do you keep on staring so hard at the houses? I suppose you've been here before, haven't you? Was that why you mentioned Markus, eh?"

The old man made no answer. He was fighting down an inner turmoil which refused to stay within the lantern beam that lit their way, and it strained ahead, anticipating the appearance of something to the right of them on the far side of the street. Suddenly, without warning, the swath of bright light was invaded by the gigantic, looming plinth of a Gothic church which traversed it without shifting a stone, and while its breast and pinnacle stayed wrapped in darkness it forded the beam like a yellow stream and swam across the yellow flagstones. And when the church had completed its transit of the band of yellow, I can tell you that the old man started behaving strangely. A loud, dry noise issued from his larynx. And had its brevity not recalled the click of a tongue or an unstifled hiccup, the vocalic escaping his lips would have resembled laughter. Apparently electing at this point to blow his nose, he stopped and produced a handkerchief from inside his old-fashioned frock-coat. But halfway between coat-lap and nose his outstretched hand stopped in midair and his handkerchief fell to the ground.

"Pick . . . it . . . up." In the silence the syllables sounded osseous and detached. The groomsman set his lantern on the ground and picked up the handkerchief. As he handed it back he looked at the old man in surprise.

"What's the matter?"

But the old man had managed to raise the sole of one boot from the magnetised pavement. He took one step, and then another, and another. . . . And the procession moved on its way again.

141

4

"Heavens above, what is the matter with you? Has that accident with the horse scared you so much?" the young man asked him. "You really shouldn't let it. Come, calm down. Put it behind you. Think of something else. Let's talk about something more cheerful. By the way, you never answered when he asked how you got to know that Herr Markus – the one who was buried on a hot summer's day with that awful wind and the sound of rattling crockery. No, seriously, don't laugh."

But the old man never heard what his young pupil said. He moved along as if every step was a conscious effort, made with deliberate intent. The young man shook him by the arm.

"Come on, wake up! . . . There! . . . You've travelled through these parts before, I dare say, haven't you?"

"I . . . been here? . . . Yes."

"Ah, so you *have* been here before. I didn't know that. But in that case how is that before the storm, when we were in the coach, you were so opposed to the idea of stopping here?"

But the old man's agitation was straining ahead again. And it only faded when all of a sudden their escort turned off to the left, causing the strip of lantern light to swing round and lick the crossroads in a broad circle. At this point the old man felt slightly easier, and his agitation either forgot or failed to notice that to reach the hotel from Elisabethstrasse meant turning off at the corner of Marktstrasse.

"Oh dear, oh dear! The hotel's full," said the servant in annoyance. At the end of the street which sloped steeply down to the river, a dark, lopsided building had appeared with lights burning in every window. "See for yourselves – lights everywhere! We've got the fair starting soon, and hordes of folk have come rolling in. Anyway, perhaps you can find your own way from here. I'm going back home. Good night, gentlemen." And with a low bow to the young nobleman their escort turned and set off back home.

"We'll manage somehow."

A side-alley quickly engulfed the retreating band of light and the travellers found themselves in darkness.

Now clear of the storm, the sky rolled back, breathing deeply and stirring the treetops. Majestically and with increasing speed it flattened out along the mainstream of the river. Like remnants of a fleet which had suffered some distant defeat, the shreds of former clouds were torn, tugged low and tormented as they swept across the sky. And at the point where their husks of former splendour were washed away by an eddy of water – perhaps some deep spring of cold black clarity welling smoothly from beyond the clouds – there in the mouth of that cold stream a star shone sharp and brittle, talonned and gleaming like a shell revealing its pearl, incisive and hard as a glass-cutter's diamond. And the gelid points that shivered around that glistening prong were those of profoundest depth and blackness.

"Why have we stopped? My dear Amadeus, is it because of you again? . . . Oh yes, is there a lady among us?" The nobleman spoke in a loud, resonant voice as he addressed the tail-end of the party. "If there is any room in the hotel, gentlemen, then I surrender my share of our communal rights to a bed for the night to Madame. . . ."

"Madame Scherer. But she is my wife, milord."

"To Madame Scherer and to her husband of course – obviously, because of their . . . begging your pardon . . . their family relationship."

"Mille graces, monsieur, but my husband and I certainly wouldn't presume. . . ."

"Please, not a word more. It's already decided, Madame . . . Madame Scherer. But you, what about you, Herr Amadeus? What do you say? You must have your night's rest as well. Have no fear. Why worry? With the Lord's help we'll arrange it. That's right, isn't it, gentlemen? You shall have a bed to lie on as well."

"They're all so worked up. Of course, we'll all be glad if that's possible. Oh, le pauvre, Dieu le bénisse – but . . ."

"Well, gentlemen, this is our journey's end. Hark how loudly the water's roaring. Where is . . . Herr Amadeus, where is the door-knocker?"

"Allow me, sir."

"Wait, I'll find it myself. Herr Scherer, this is my tutor Herr Amadeus. Have you a light? . . . Ah, here's a plank of wood. . . . One! Two! Three! . . . 'Can't knock any louder than that. I think someone's coming. Hark! . . . Herr Amadeus, you know, I hardly seem to recognise you today. . . ."

At that late hour the rustlings and other sounds in the hotel were all slumbering – as usual in houses where many are asleep and goodness knows how many others try to fight off sleep, and a brigade of dreams blindly spreads torpor over everything, even over those who stay awake.

And as for rustlings in the hotel, there were not many of them. It was impossible to tell where the skittle-alley was – Was it far away or close by, just beyond that empty room? Nor could the billiards-room be located. From the weird nooks and groping crannies of halls and vestibules one inevitably emerged in a large assembly room, and there on the wall a clock was ticking. Its pendulum swung behind a glass panel. And as it moved it sowed the whole chamber with ticking, frequent and fine like millet. But the arc of its swing was deathly dull and weary, like the tired, aching arm of the sower at the end of his day's work.

Next door – or maybe several rooms away – scruples of tightly corked rumbling were monotonously weighed on a chemical balance. Play was in progress. The men were playing there and maybe also loudly discussing their game. They were bowling heavy spheres, and the spheres kept clouting varnished wood and dumpy skittles made a racket as they tumbled to the ground. Then there was a pronounced shuffling. After that a numbed and paralytic silence resumed again. Next door, or maybe several rooms away, the play yawned loudly and infectiously. Perhaps they were discussing the spheres that kept clicking and colliding. But the voices were tightly corked, sealed in with blue tobacco smoke and guttering lamp-wicks, and packed in sawdust by the ticking clock and the dreams of those sleeping on the floor above. And the voices which audibly followed the bowling spheres were also sealed in finally by the lateness of the hour – like premises sealed after the occurrence of some incident. And that night the hotel was surely indeed the scene of an incident – one which took the form of three loud raps on the outer door, followed by a long pause and then by deafening and even more insistent hammering, the tramp of shoes along a corridor, the clink of a lock, and a scuffle of voices on the doorstep, in which one sleep-enfeebled, swollen, hoarse and felt-lagged voice had to contend with a whole chorus from the street that was icy-fresh and chillingly refreshing.

"We've no room. Why do you ask?"

"Oh no, my good fellow, I'm not used to dealing with some flunkey. Where is this what's-his-name? Where's Herr Markus?"

"Herr Würzenau. Georg Würzenau."

"Yes, that's right, Würzenau. Call your master down."

"Oh, I don't know that I can do that. . . ."

"You don't need to know anything. Just you go to Herr Würzenau and send him down here. . . ."

". . . And now, gentlemen, you shall witness how eagerly Herr Würzenau will give up his own room and his bed to Frau Scherer . . . who is – ha-ha! – my sister!"

"What an honour this is!"

"And you, my brother-in-law, permit me to inquire: Do you fall asleep very quickly, if that isn't . . . si ce n'est pas une indiscrétion exagérée?"

"Oh yes, and especially tonight. I'll be asleep inside five minutes."

"In that case, brother-in-law, you'll only enjoy being my relative for five minutes! And the rest of us, gentlemen . . . we'll make ourselves comfortable here somehow or other. Although actually I sense that there might well be a special display of kindness and consideration from Herr Würzenau to me personally as Madame Scherer's brother – Prince Georg Kunz von Wölflingen in case you've not already guessed."

"Oh! . . . Ah! . . . So that's it! . . . I thought as much ! . . . Deeply honoured, I'm sure."

"Please, think nothing of it. Sit down, gentlemen. Here are some chairs. Allow me to offer you an armchair, Madame. I'm used to . . ."

"Georg!"

"Yes, Herr Amadeus?"

"Listen, Georg. I shall have to leave you for a while. I must, you understand. I've gone and lost my purse in the street. What a thing to happen! But I know where to look. You remember, by the Elisabethkirche, by the church, I took out my handkerchief. . . ."

"Is it your own purse you have lost?"

"Yes, indeed."

"I never realised before that you. . . . Anyway, do you really want to go off and search for it right now, without a lantern?"

"It's only a stone's throw from here, Georg."

"Herr Amadeus, you're not quite your usual self today. I've never known you like this. I never imagined the effects of that accident would last so long. Listen, Herr Amadeus. Believe me, what you intend doing is – begging your pardon – sheer madness. What you have lost is . . ."

"Georg . . ."

"What you have lost is a mere trifle if . . ."

"Georg . . ."

"Just think what my father told you . . ."

"Let me finish, Georg . . ."

"You and I share the same purse, Herr Amadeus. You can take the amount you have lost out of my funds. I'll be hurt if you refuse, Herr

Amadeus. It's not worth going out without a light to look for such a trifling sum. Tell me, why is it you are so worked up over nothing?"

"Never you mind, Georg. It's a bit stuffy in here. I don't feel quite myself. Something has upset me. I'm just going out for a little walk. I'll be back shortly. . . ."

5

The seventeenth of July may not have been a memorable date for every inhabitant of that small town, but for many at least it was no ordinary day. It was a day that was quite unusually protracted. Many were agreed about its length. On that day a meeting of the town council had been fixed to discuss various matters concerned with the forthcoming fair. The meeting took place in the large hall of the Rathaus, whose windows faced the sunset, and matters were already drawing to a close when a sudden announcement by one member of council confronted the assembly with a quite new and unexpected item of business. In fact, Kurt Seebald's announcement so puzzled and perturbed some council members that after first deluging him with impatient questions and exclamations, they forgot the formalities of public debate for a moment and broke into animated private conversation. Their disjointed exchanges bore all the signs of their loud and utter astonishment. Moreover, the councillors displayed a vivacity in this unscheduled debate of theirs which quite belied their years – in fact every one of them was approaching or had already passed his three score years and ten.

The sun was halted in its path by the general confusion of that strange and sickly day and it hung in the air outside one of the dusty window-panes, bathed in fire. The bright crimson band of its evening glow lay like a ready-cut swath of orange fabric draped across the green cloth covering the council table. Through the five other windows came thick rafters of dense light and pressed in bands against the opposite wall. From inside the council chamber transfixed by these beams the eventide roadway seemed a far more pleasant place and appeared to be propping up the debating chamber. And if that relentlessly illuminated street were suddenly to disappear or be cut short, it seemed as if the council hall itself might wilt and collapse in ruins.

There were seven councillors who initiated that intrusive conversation with Seebald, and their animated discussion was quickly interrupted by their seventeen junior colleagues demanding an explanation of what it was they were talking about. They had failed to understand the older men's agitation just as they failed to grasp their actual words. The elders hastened to satisfy their junior colleagues' curiosity and six of them interrupted one another as they showered them with fragments of a confused tale from the ancient history of the town. Their story emerged as an account of the very affair tabled for discussion by Kurt Seebald. Gradually, however, the older councillors' excitement subsided and the tone fitting their assembly was discovered again and reinstated. And in this tone they wound up the business of the town fair and then turned to discuss the case of the man on whose behalf Seebald had spoken and made the extraordinary proposal that caused so much excitement.

Outside the dusty pane of the end window the sun continued hanging in an atmosphere grey with twilight and refuse. It hung there bathed in waves of fire beneath the lowest spar of the window-frame, halted in its descent by the final confusion of that strange and sickly day.

It was a day of unusual duration. How it began is difficult to reconstruct. From early morning the town was swept by tales of yesterday's thunderstorm. There was talk of a miraculous occurrence in the neighbouring village of Rabenklippe. Lightning had struck a house where a wedding celebration was in progress, and although the bridal couple plus the hosts and guests had escaped with no more than a fright, they had been only an inch from death. There were also tales of another incident. Lightning had killed a horse as it stood harnessed at the entrance to the post-station courtyard right outside the post-master's house – the coach had been damaged, but the travellers had evidently survived unscathed. . . . For many folk the retail and embroidering of these rumours had formed the start to the now declining day.

But for Herr Seebald the day had started much earlier. The appraisals of yesterday's flash-flood found him already on his feet. He was roused from his bed just after five when Anne-Marie, his second wife, went to the door in response to prolonged knocking by some worthy gentleman who had refused to tell her his name. Following a long, yawning parley with her and much annoyed shrugging, Seebald finally emerged and went down into their squalid lobby. His astonishment on seeing the visitor waiting there in the darkness was all the more sudden and immense because from his wife's conjecture he had expected to see one of his late wife Susanne's relatives.

"The old devil looked at me so distrustfully," Anne-Marie said. "I told

147

him I was Frau Seebald. But he probably doesn't realise you've remarried. He goggled at me as if he'd never heard of such a thing. As though there were anything strange about it!"

For a long time Seebald stood speechless. He shook his visitor's hand and embraced him. Both men had tears in their eyes. Then Seebald quickly drew his strange guest inside the house. Once indoors, they both no doubt recovered themselves. Their voices rose in rapid leaps and they soon settled into a lengthy, animated conversation. Of the two voices it was Seebald's that leaped the higher, and after turning in again without the slightest wish to eavesdrop Anne-Marie managed to pick out several disconnected exclamations from her husband: "By chance?! . . . So that . . . but for the weather! . . . Well? . . . And you weren't?! . . ." Seebald exclaimed in amazement. But his remaining words, like those of the visitor, were a dull mutter that remained buried deep within the wall. Their talk was abrupt and undissolving. A brief silence followed. Then the visitor spoke again. Anne-Marie dozed off.

"You?! . . . You yourself?! . . ." Seebald's indignant voice suddenly thundered through the wall. Anne-Marie opened her eyes. Outside the window spread the dry, heated chirruping of birds. The words of their guest crept sluggishly along the wall in layers. Anne-Marie fixed her gaze on the ruddy pattern etched on the claret wallpaper by the gathering dawn. She propped a flushed cheek on her plump bare elbow. The town rang with the crowing exchange of cockerels.

"What? Today?! . . . You've been there already? . . . To play? . . . You were able to? . . . You want me to? . . . On that same organ! . . ."

The visitor probably offered some reassurance, because after Seebald's shouting their elderly voices sounded so steady that it was hard to tell which of them was talking. Their speech kept crumbling, interrupted by the visitor's frequent cough, and embedded itself in the wall and remained there.

Anne-Marie succumbed and dozed off again. For a long while she lay sunk in the remotest wilds of slumberland. She was twenty-five years younger than her husband, and she was a good sleeper and enjoyed it. She heard nothing more.

"Do you think so? . . . No. . . . Agree?! What?! Them – agree?! . . . Never! . . . How can you? . . ."

Then one of the two quite distinctly pronounced the name of Tuch. And after a short interval Sturzwage was also mentioned. But that was only conjecture – the second name was pronounced much more softly and hesitantly.

And that was the early and unusual start of the day for Seebald, the day of the council meeting. Yet in fact that excessively long day had begun even earlier. It was first roused some time after three or thereabouts, by a noise on the forecourt of the Hotel Schützenpfuhl. It was caused by the ring of a scythe amid the deathly immovable hush that heralded a hot day – a scythe that swung steadily and dreamily through the damply steaming grass nearby, behind the hotel. Or maybe the day was suddenly scared by the voices of two men who left the hotel at that hour and themselves heard the ring of the scythe nearby. Or else the day was raised from the meadows like quails from the stubble by the chatter of a blade on the whetstone and by the quiet converse of two voices in the street – the only speech that could be heard at this hour amid the silence. The two men talked quietly, but to the silence their speech was audible on every side, because it was speech of remarkable rarity, precise and sonorous as the voice of Adam in the first days of Creation.

And that unusually protracted July day hanging outside the end window of the Rathaus, blazing with avid sunset passion and lighting up all the adjacent streets with pillars of pungent crimson smoke . . . that day had started with the loud wranglings of two voices in dispute on the street. The two men walked away. And as they hurried off somewhere into the distance, the sound of their speech also receded in abrupt leaps and bounds. There was not a soul about on the ghostly, still sightless streets. The only things that thronged the town were the tiled roofs silently washing themselves like disembodied phantoms in the cold murk of an ill-defined dawn. There was not a soul in the streets where the dew had settled, moistening the bumps on the roadway's brow with cold sweat, and both roadway and buildings emerged through a micaceous layer of haze like the trace of a round open mouth on a misted pane. Not a soul was there, I assure you, when among all the other incorporeal objects a new one was born – a building which had only appeared in the world that very instant and was more disembodied than all the rest, a building which heaved a groan and was shrouded in its own insuperable remoteness. And then its groaning ceased. Not because it had disappeared below ground again in the same way as it had just emerged and reared up from the earth. But it could only be caught in the very act of its appearance, like the inhuman effort of one buried alive to shift a stone slab of stillness. And only for one instant could this spectre of careful symmetry be discerned among the other wraith-like presences of rooftops, air and dew. When that instant had passed, it could no longer be distinguished from the dew. It was nowhere to be found.

Not a soul was there on the Elisabethplatz when the entire stone core of the church's two skyward soaring crags was struck through to the foundation by a wheezing sound, nasal, tremulous, and drawn out imperturbably. Not a soul was there. But had anyone walked past, he might have stopped and realised that someone in there had begun to play the organ. First of all he would have heard pealing avalanches of chromatic scales, rapidly played up and down the full length of the manuals, from lowest bass to highest treble and back down again to bottom C. And he would have recognised it as the method by which a professional player tries out a new instrument to check that everything is in working order.

But not a soul was there on the street.

The first to appear were two men who left the church via a little side-door leading into the churchyard. Before going their ways, they exchanged a few parting words which were hard to make out:

"Splendid! . . . And the main thing is that I'd never have expected that you . . ." drawled one of them.

"Do you have your watch on you?"

"Five past five."

"Good. Now I can go and fetch Seebald. You go and have some sleep."

"But it's not at all tiring pumping. I enjoy it. It's just like in the smithy. And I owe you an apology. I honestly thought you were out of your mind. That was why I ran. Did you notice that door open yesterday?"

"Indeed I did. I told you. I saw it as we walked past. Probably the painters left it open. They are doing some repairs. Off you go now."

"But you . . ."

"I'll look after myself. You go back to bed now."

"Very well. We'll meet again soon. But truly it is remarkable that. . . . The main thing is. . . ."

In fact, though, the day had begun with the fine ring of grinding steel and the chatter of a blade on the whetstone beyond the currant-bushes at the back of the stables in the hotel courtyard. The yard of the hotel directly abutted on the fence of a small orchard that was mounted by a fringe of tall weeds and nettles and besmirched with splodges of chalk. There was still no trace of dawn when the keen, airy ring of a scythe started up beyond the currant-bushes, swing after dreaming swing. The intoxicated grass was raw and damp and had still not recovered its breath. Like heavy earlobes, the lifeless drops of yesterday's rain dragged down the blades of grass. There were countless multitudes of them in the sodden darkness, deadened, immobile, silent, swollen. And their immobility foretokened a day that would be hot and an afternoon swelter that would never shift. . . .

Meanwhile, only the scythe rang beyond the currant-bushes. With only rare hesitation, it flayed the air time and time again with a scalding lash, and. . . .

And it was the scything which roused the day from the dense grass beyond the currant-bushes. It was not those two voices which had started a loud dispute in the street in front of the hotel gateway at such an early hour. It was the scything. Because when the two travellers were let out of the hotel door and stood outside in the middle of the roadway, they could hear someone scything over on the courtyard side. And they guessed someone was mowing the patch of grass beyond the stables which they had glimpsed from their window and which had taken such immense pains to overwhelm the pre-dawn gloom and detach itself as a ghostly grey lozenge. The two men were not arguing at all loudly. But in the completely desolate stillness quartered at every crossroads and in every courtyard and alleyway, their words were such a loudly conspicuous land-mark that one could only wonder at their brazen, intrepid jauntiness, the only two voices in town.

The two men moved away, and their speech receded in leaps like they themselves as they hurried off in the direction of Elisabethstrasse.

"You can work the bellows."

"And who's going to take the responsibility?"

"I will."

"How are you going to get in?"

"The side-door isn't locked."

"How do you know?"

"I noticed it yesterday. You see, we came past that way, and I noticed. . . . Probably the painters have left it open. They are doing some repairs."

"This is madness!"

"Watch your step!"

"I can jump it."

"There! Now do you believe me?"

"Give me your handkerchief."

"It will dry. Then you can brush it off. There are lakes of water everywhere. I can't remember a storm like it."

"We have to go uphill. It will get drier as we go."

The meeting in the Rathaus had finished long ago, and the guildsmen and tradespeople had split into several noisy groups. And still in groups and without interrupting their leisurely conversations, they began leaving the council chamber and only paused in the doorway in order to let the most prominent, respected members leave first. But several remained behind in the chamber together with Burgomaster Tuch. Some wandered around in the free space up at the front of the room, but most crowded around the table where Gruner the town notary was quickly finishing a copy of the latest resolution.

The meeting in the Rathaus had finished long ago and many had gone back already to their homes. In the right-hand corner of the chamber the setting sun still struggled like a huge and ponderous bumble-bee. A gathering of folk on the square attracted the attention of the gentlemen still sauntering in the council chamber. They were joined by those who had been standing by the table urging Gruner on, and gradually they all collected by the window and Gruner was finally left sitting alone at his table. Every now and again he tossed back a smooth lock of tow-coloured hair which kept falling over his forehead, and the thick paper buckled awkwardly and tried to curl into a tube as his goose-quill danced across it in bold strokes.

As it turned off round the corner, the street procession had attracted a resplendent following of gapers and idlers. . . .

The members of council returned to their table.

"What's going on out there?" asked Gruner.

"The gypsies are there. Are you going to be long, Herr Gruner?"

"Ready right away."

"Well, we won't disturb you."

"Do you remember that she-bear at the last town fair, Herr Sturzwage? I don't think I saw it just now."

"I didn't notice it either."

"The bear wasn't there. Pity. It was a magnificent animal."

"But otherwise the procession was the same as in previous years – just the camel and the apes. . . ."

152

"Oh yes. The rest was like it was the last few times – the camel and the monkeys."

"Well, Gruner?"

The crowd stood on the freshly mown grass facing the setting sun. With their backs to the stream of newcomers they cut off the view of gypsies and animals and obscured the bloody sun which crushed the twisted and snapped-off bushes as it rolled straight into the black-currant thicket like a gigantic, smoking, eviscerated carcase. Only the camel's thin muzzle rose and floated above the throng. It paraded around the crowd and its narrow head planted on a swinging neck resembled a hawker's display or a tray carried over the waiter's shoulder on the crooked-back flat of one hand. More and more gaping onlookers came in from the street, drawn in through the gateway by the sound of the barrel-organ. And up they went on to the green to join the crowd already assembled. The entire hotel company was there already. The servants kept their distance from the gentry and stood bunched together on a mound. Visitors arriving singly or in pairs had a less good view. Only a few of the menials were detained by their jobs at the oven or in the cloakroom, and then they dashed quickly across the paved courtyard laughing and shouting to one another, and once they reached the grassy area they never looked back.

The crowd stood with their backs to the newcomers and faced towards the animals and the sun. Its smoky crimson beams flooded the green with a passionate, relentless light. The gypsy's boots sank in the syrupy grass of liquid scarlet. On one of the carts stood a case with iron bars fitted down one side. Naked monkeys frisked and grimaced, rummaging in one another's fur. Their roan-coloured faces had a scorched cast of dark blue – the inevitable dark of an ancient imprint of wisdom permanently crazed. They blinked and simpered gloomily and listened to the barrel-organ as though its droning music had hatched from their own hirsute simian wombs. The crowd stood facing the animals and the sun. The elderly tutor stood on the mound which other serving folk had picked for themselves. The smoky crimson rays of the sun caught on the bramble thorns. Baked in sunset embers, the bark of the wild pear-tree buckled like striated bronze and the nap on the gooseberries was stifling in pink vapour. A Bengal smoulder crept and spread across the grass. Reaching the little barrel-organ, it surrendered up its soul and planted shimmering kisses on the dusty bare feet of the gypsy woman who

153

stood grinding the handle in time to the camel's swaying. And the old tutor also stood there among the crowd. People exchanged expressive remarks about the monkeys and without shifting their position the animals directed a cloud of simian glances back at the crowd. Their eyes screwed up, glinting with a black sheen as they hopped like fleas over people's faces. Content with this, their pupils then took a single leap and jumped back into place in their deep orbits.

The sunset condensed and became rarified as raw nuggets. Separate ingots gradually disappeared in the loose earth of the currant-bush plots. Special curiosity was aroused by the cage on top of which the monkeys had distributed themselves. It was empty. There was nothing in it but a heap of straw and the indeterminable acrid gloom usually found nestling in the deepest recesses of half-dark animal houses in a zoo in winter. The empty cage aroused everyone's special curiosity until eyes became acclimatised and people discovered something lying there in the right-hand corner by the back wall – something like a rich woman's muff, large and black or else dark grey, which had half-burrowed into the straw. After that people's curiosity. . . .

"Knauer!"

The shout came from the hotel.

The elderly tutor turned as though the summons were addressed to him.

"Knauer!"

They were calling from the wooden balcony which overlooked the courtyard and ran the whole length of the building at first-floor level. He left the crowd and made towards the group of men standing at the balustrade. He peered up and recognised them. Tuch, Sturzwage, Rosarius . . . he recognised them all apart from two or three unfamiliar faces. And he grew fearfully excited. Had he worn a hat, he would certainly have removed it and waved from the green as a signal to convey his choking sense of joy to the men up on the balcony who stood there, picked out in the sunset glow. But when he went out to look at the animals he had forgotten to put on his hat. . . .

It is not known exactly what was said up there. The discussion was a brief one. Tuch soon reappeared on the gallery, half-turning to speak to his colleagues who were following him. Then they crossed the courtyard on to the street and went their various ways. The aim of their visit had been to serve Knauer with what they termed an "official notification".

They had come to inform him that his application for reinstatement as town organist had not merely been rejected. Indeed, they regarded it as a uniquely brazen example of his arrogance and dementia. First of all, the post of organist was not vacant, contrary to what he evidently imagined in his irrepressible conceit. But also – and especially – because his continued presence in the town was impermissible, and for various reasons best known to himself it could on no account be tolerated. Moreover, these reasons had today been compounded and aggravated tenfold when without consulting anyone, not even his own conscience (a point which they specially emphasised), he had wantonly presumed to act as though he owned the church and had taken liberties with something (a point which they also laboured) which should for him have been an object of dread and inviolable sanctity.

The aim of their visit had been to notify Knauer of all this, and although it is not known exactly what was said, there is reason to assume that they successfully achieved their purpose.

As they left, their faces showed no sign of their earlier consternation. But as they passed out through the hotel courtyard all their movements were still ruled by the portentous style of the edict which Tuch had just read out to Knauer. Its manner of expression enclosed their elderly figures about like an orthopaedic corset stuffed under their knee-britches, and its air of grave reverence had clamped a muzzle on all of them.

They were still trying to recover from their apoplexy when Gruner suddenly dispelled it all in an instant. "Oh yes," he said, "I forgot: I have asked Ignatz about it. That she-bear has apparently snuffed it."

"Snuffed it?!"

And they walked out of the gate.

Seebald was not among them. Next day, when he called at the hotel to visit him before dinner, he discovered Knauer had already booked out. Both guests had left town that morning.

So ends this story of a suboctave coupler on the organ. It also marks the beginning of the tale of Knauer's ill-fame. But that is not really a tale, it is no more than trivial tittle-tattle.

Martens too was an organist. He had also been in Knauer's hotel room when the councillors' edict was read out. He was a man of keen observation and gentle nature, and for a long time afterwards he kept reminding his colleagues how strangely Knauer had behaved when they called to serve notice on him. He had said nothing at all, but fixed his eyes on Tuch and evidently listened to everything they had to say to him.

"A regular crank he was!" said Martens. "You tell him about the wrath of the Lord, and he never turns a hair. Well, maybe he was an unbeliever. But all the same, I must say that Tuch went a bit far in singing my praises. And I don't say that out of any false modesty. But it is true: a poor woman like that, left in penury and abandoned by her husband. . . . One couldn't refuse to help her, could one? Any of us would have done the same. And then Dorothea, to be fair to her – God rest her soul – was a woman of angelic meekness. But he was just a crank! Then, do you remember? – Tuch pointed at me and called me 'this worthy husband'. I can't remember his exact words. . . . Yes, I can: 'But for this kindly and most worthy man (really far too flattering!) who was her second husband in a manner of speaking, bearing in mind his selfless concern for the fate of your wife, et cetera, et cetera. . . .' And what did Knauer do? It all went in at one ear and out of the other! He's nothing but a crank! Well, even if you allowed for the fact that he's an old man now, slow to react. . . . What does that amount to? Someone happened to mention that I'd taken over his duties or something of the sort, and he flashed me a look and turned out not to be dumb after all! 'Are you an organist?' he asked me. He must have been a crank! And those were the only words he spoke the whole time we were there. Crank – there's no other word! I'm sorry, gentlemen, but you all surprise me. If I'd appeared in Ansbach a little earlier. . . ."

"Well, what of it?"

"If I'd been here in those days like the rest of you, I'd have seen through him at a glance. I could have forecast everything that happened. So there!"

ZHENYA LUVERS' CHILDHOOD

The Long Days

1

Zhenya Luvers was born and brought up in Perm. Just as her little boats and dolls had once done, so later on her memories too sank deep into the shaggy bearskins of which there were many in the house. Her father was business manager of the Lunyev mines and had a large clientele among the Chusovaya factory owners.

The bearskins had been gifts. They were deep brown and sumptuous. The white she-bear in her nursery was like an enormous chrysanthemum shedding petals. This was the one acquired specially for "young Zhenya's room," admired and bargained for at the shop and delivered by special messenger.

In summer they lived at their dacha on the far bank of the Kama. In those days Zhenya was put to bed early. She could not see the lights of Motovilikha. But once something scared the angora cat, and it stirred suddenly in its sleep and woke her up. Then she had seen grown-ups on the balcony. The alder overhanging the railings was dense and iridescent as ink. The tea in the glasses was red, the cuffs and cards were yellow, and the cloth was green. It was like a delirium – except that this one had its name, which even Zhenya knew: they were playing cards.

However, there was no way of determining what was happening far, far away on the other bank. This had no name, and no precise colour or definite outline. And as it stirred it was familiar and dear, it was not delirious like the thing that muttered and swirled in clouds of tobacco smoke, throwing fresh and flighty shadows on the russet beams of the gallery. Zhenya burst into tears. Father came in and explained things to her. The English governess turned her face to the wall. Father's explanation was brief: "That is Motovilikha. For shame! A big girl like you! . . . Go to sleep!"

The little girl understood nothing and contentedly swallowed a rolling tear. In fact that was all she needed to know: what the mysterious thing

157

was called – Motovilikha. That night it still explained everything, because that night a name still had a complete and childlike reassuring significance.

But next morning she started asking questions – what Motovilikha was and what they did there at night – and she learned that Motovilikha was a factory, a government factory, and that cast iron was made there, and from cast iron. . . . But that no longer concerned her. She was more interested in knowing whether the things called "factories" were special countries, and who lived there. . . . But she did not ask these questions and for some reason deliberately concealed them.

That morning she emerged from the state of infancy she had still been in at night. For the first time in her life she suspected there was something that things kept to themselves – or if they revealed it, then only to people who knew how to shout and punish, smoke and bolt doors. For the first time, just like this new Motovilikha, she did not say everything she thought. What was most stirring, essential and vital she kept to herself.

Years passed. Ever since their birth, the children had got so used to their father's absences that in their eyes it was a special feature of fatherdom to lunch only seldom and never to have dinner. More and more often they played, squabbled, wrote and had their meals in completely empty, solemnly deserted rooms. And the cold instructions of the English governess could never replace the presence of their mother, who filled the house with the sweet oppression of her ready anger and obstinacy, like some native electricity. The quiet northern daylight streamed through the curtains. It was unsmiling. The oaken sideboard seemed grey. The silver lay piled there, heavy and severe. The lavender-washed hands of the English governess moved above the tablecloth. She always served everyone his fair portion and had an inexhaustible supply of patience; her sense of justice was every bit as germane to her as her room and her books were always clean and tidy. The maid who brought the food stood waiting in the dining-room and only went away to the kitchen to fetch the next course. It was all pleasant and comfortable, but dreadfully sad.

But for the little girl these were years of suspicion, solitude, a sense of sin, and what in French might be called *christianisme* (because none of this could be called Christianity). And it therefore sometimes seemed to her that matters could not improve – nor, indeed, ought they to in view of her perversity and impenitence, and it all served her right. Yet, in fact – although the children were never aware of it – in fact, it was quite the reverse: their whole beings were shuddering and fermenting, utterly

158

bewildered by their parents' attitude to them whenever they were there – whenever they returned "to the house", rather than returning "home".

Father's rare jokes invariably failed and sometimes they were quite misplaced. He was aware of this and sensed that the children realised it too, and a suspicion of sad embarrassment never left his face. But when he was irritated he became a stranger – a stranger totally and at the very instant when he lost his self-control. And the stranger awoke no feeling in them. The children never answered him back.

But for some time now the criticism emanating from the nursery and silently present in the children's eyes had found him utterly insensitive. He failed to notice it. And *this* father, totally vulnerable and somehow unrecognisable and pathetic, was genuinely terrifying, unlike the merely irritated stranger. He produced a greater impression on the girl. His son was less affected.

But Mother bewildered them both. She showered them with caresses and loaded them with gifts and spent hours with them when they least desired her to. And all this merely stifled their children's conscience because it was so undeserved, and they failed to recognise themselves in the affectionate pet names lavished on them by her thoughtless instinct.

Often, when their souls were visited by a rare, clear calm and they ceased to have the feeling inside them that they were criminals, when their consciences were relieved of all mystery that evaded discovery like fever before a rash, they saw their mother as aloof, remote, and irascible without cause. The postman would come. The letter would be brought to its addressee – Mama. She would take it without a word of thanks. "Off to your room!" The door banged. They hung their heads quietly and miserably surrendered themselves to a long and mournful bewilderment.

At first they sometimes cried. Later, after an especially sharp outburst, they began to take fright. Then, over the years, it turned into a concealed and increasingly deep-rooted antagonism. And everything that passed from parents to children was mistimed and came from outside, elicited not by them but by some external cause. And as always, it had a touch of remoteness and mystery, like whimpering outside the city gates at night when everyone is going to bed.

Such were the circumstances that nurtured and educated the children. They were unaware of it, because there are few adults even who know and sense what it is that creates, fashions, and binds their own fabric.

159

Life initiates very few into the secret of what it is doing with them. It loves its purpose too well, and as it works it speaks only to those who wish it success and love life's workbench. No one has power to assist it, though anyone can hinder. And how can one hinder? If for instance a tree is entrusted with the care of its own growth, it might sprout uncontrollably, become totally absorbed in its own roots, or squander itself on a single leaf, because it has forgotten the surrounding universe that should serve as a model, and in producing one thing in a thousand it will start to produce thousands of that one thing.

So in order to guard against dead branches in the soul – to prevent its growth from being retarded and man from involving his own stupidity in the formation of his immortal essence – several things have been introduced to divert his vulgar curiosity away from life, which dislikes working in his presence and tries every means to avoid him. For this purpose all decent true religions were introduced, all general concepts and human prejudices, and the most resplendent of these and the most entertaining – *psychology.*

The children had already emerged from primordial infancy. The concepts of punishment, retribution, reward, and justice had already penetrated their souls in a childish way, distracting their awareness and allowing life to do with them whatever it thought most necessary, impressive, and lovely.

2

Miss Hawthorn would not have done that. But in one of her bouts of gratuitous tenderness toward the children Madame Luvers had spoken harshly to the English governess on some utterly trifling pretext, and the latter had disappeared from the house. Shortly after, somehow imperceptively, her place was taken by a weakly French girl. Afterwards, Zhenya could recall only that she had looked like a fly, and that nobody liked her. Her name was lost completely, and Zhenya could not even guess which syllables and sounds to search among in order to rediscover it. She remembered only that the French girl had first shouted at her and then taken scissors and shorn away the patch of bloodstained bearskin.

It seemed to her that now people would always shout at her. It seemed her headache would last for ever and never clear, and she would never again understand that page in her favourite book which swam together before her gaze in a dull blurr like her lesson book after lunch.

That day was terribly drawn out. Mama was away. Zhenya was not sorry. She even believed she was glad at her mother's absence. But soon that long day was consigned to oblivion among the forms of the *passé* and the *futur antérieur*, watering the hyacinths, and walks along Sibirskaya and Okhanskaya Street. Indeed, so forgotten was that day that she only noticed and sensed the duration of the other – the second in her life – toward evening, as she read by lamplight and the lazily progressing narrative suggested hundreds of idle thoughts to her. Whenever she later recalled the house on Osinskaya Street where they lived then, she always imagined it just as it seemed on the evening of that second long day. It had certainly been long. It was spring outside. Sickly and ripening laboriously at first, spring in the Urals later broke broad and vigorous in the course of a single night. And after that it continued so. The lamps only highlighted the emptiness of the evening air. They gave no light but swelled up inside like sickly fruits, with a clear lacklustre dropsy that distended their dilated shades. They went missing and then turned up in their places, where they should have been, on tables and coming down from stucco ceilings in the rooms where she was used to seeing them. And yet the lamps had far less to do with the rooms than with the spring sky against which they seemed to have been thrust like drinking water placed by the bed of an invalid. At heart they were out there in the street, where the servants' babbling teemed in the wet earth, and where the sparse droplets of melting snow froze and congealed for the night. That was where the lamps disappeared to in the evenings. Their parents were away. But Mama was apparently expected that day. On that long day, or in the next few days. . . . Yes, probably. Or maybe she had arrived suddenly, unawares. . . . Maybe that was it.

Zhenya started getting into bed and saw that the day had been a long one for the same reason as before. At first she was about to take scissors and shear those pieces out of her nightdress and the sheet. But then she decided to take some of the French girl's powder and rub them white, and she had already seized the powder box when in came Mademoiselle and gave her a slap. Her entire sin became centred on the powder.

"Powdering herself! That really is the limit!"

Now at last Mademoiselle realised. She had noticed it for some time already.

Zhenya burst into tears from the slapping and shouting and a sense of injury, and because while she felt innocent of what the French girl suspected, she knew she had done something – this was what she *felt* – she had done something far viler than she suspected. And she sensed it with stupefying urgency, sensed it in her calves and temples: without knowing why or wherefore, she had to conceal it at any price and no matter how. Her joints ached and fused in a single hypnotic suggestion. Tormenting and enervating it was the work of her organism which concealed the meaning of everything from her. Behaving like a criminal, it made her imagine this bleeding was some foul and revolting form of evil. *Menteuse!* She could only deny it and stubbornly disavow the thing that was most vile of all and that lay somewhere between the shame of illiteracy and the disgrace of a scene in the street. She could not throw herself in the Kama because it was still cold and the last ice floes were still floating down the river. She could only shudder, grit her teeth and press herself against the wall.

Neither she nor the French girl heard the bell in time. The commotion they raised disappeared in the density of the deep brown bearskins, and when Mother come in it was already too late. She found her daughter in tears and the French girl blushing. She demanded an explanation. The French girl announced straightaway that – not Zhenya but *"votre enfant"*, she said – that *her daughter* was powdering herself, and that she had noticed and suspected it for some time already. Mother did not allow her to finish. Her horror was genuine. The girl was not yet thirteen.

"Zhenya! – You?! . . . Good Lord, what have things come to?" (At that moment her mother imagined these words actually meant something, as though she had already known that her daughter was going to the bad, but she had failed to take measures in time and now found her sunk to this low depth.) "Zhenya, tell me the whole truth . . . It'll be the worse! . . . What were you doing . . . ?" "With the powder box?" Madame Luvers probably meant to say, but in fact what she said was "with this thing?" And she seized the "thing" and waved it in the air.

"Mama, don't believe Mademoiselle. I never. . . ." And she burst into sobs.

But her mother detected in her weeping a hint of malice that was not really there. She sensed that she herself was to blame and was inwardly terrified of herself. She would have to put the whole matter right, she believed. Even against her maternal instincts she must show herself capable of taking "prudent educative measures". She decided against yielding to sympathy and proposed to wait till the tormenting flood of tears had subsided.

She sat down on the bed and directed her serene and vacant gaze at the edge of the bookshelf. She smelled of expensive perfume. When her daughter had recovered herself, her mother began again to ply her with questions. Zhenya cast a tearful glance toward the window and gave a sob. Outside, the ice was moving downstream and probably crackling. A star shimmered. The deserted night showed rough and black and was malleable and chill, but unchanging. Zhenya looked away from the window. A menacing note of impatience sounded in Mother's voice. The French girl stood against the wall, the image of solemnity and concentrated pedagogy. She held her hand in adjutant pose, resting on her watch ribbon. Zhenya glanced once again at the stars and at the Kama. Her mind was made up. And despite the cold and the ice floes – in she plunged. Getting tangled in her words, she gave her mother an implausible and terror-stricken account of "it". Mother allowed her to finish only because she was struck by the amount of feeling the child put into her story. She actually guessed everything from Zhenya's very first word. No, even before that – from the deep gulp with which she began her tale. Mother listened, rejoicing, loving and consumed with tenderness for that slender little body. She felt like throwing her arms about her daughter's neck and weeping. But – educational principle! She rose and pulled back the bedspread. She called her daughter to her and very slowly and gently began stroking her head.

"Good girl. . . ." She trotted the words out quickly then swept noisily over to the window and turned away from the two of them.

Zhenya could not see the French girl. Only tears, only her mother – filling the whole room.

"Who makes the bed?"

It was a pointless question. The girl gave a shudder. She was sorry for Grusha. Then in the French tongue that she knew something was said by a tongue she failed to recognise. They were harsh words. Then again to her in quite a different voice: "Zhenya dear, go down to the dining-room, darling, and I'll come myself right away. And I'll tell you what a lovely dacha Papa and I have rented for you . . . for us, for the summer."

The lamps were again themselves. As usual, in winter at the Luvers' home – warm, zealous, faithful. Mama's sable frisked across the blue wool tablecloth. "WON – REMAINING BLAGODAT – AWAIT END HOLY WEEK. . . ." She could not read the rest – the telegram was folded over at the corner. Zhenya sat down on the end of the settee, tired and happy. She sat down modestly and correctly – just as she sat six months later on the end of a cold brown bench in the corridor of the Ekaterinburg *lycée*, when she gained top marks for her answer in the Russian orals and was told she was "permitted to go".

Next morning Mother told her what she must do on such future occasions – it was nothing serious, Zhenya need not be afraid, it would keep on happening. She mentioned nothing by name and gave no explanation, but added that from now on she herself would be coaching her daughter since she was not going away any more.

After only a few months in the family the French girl was dismissed for negligence. When the cab was hired for her and she started down the stairs, she met the doctor coming up on the landing. His response to her nod was very unfriendly and he never said a word of goodbye. She guessed he must know everything. She frowned and gave a shrug.

In the doorway stood the maid who had been waiting to let in the doctor, so that in the hall where Zhenya stood the ring of footsteps and the echoed answer of the stone sounded on for longer than expected. That was how the story of her maidhood's first maturity imprinted itself on her memory: the resonant echo of the chirruping morning street lingering on the stair and freshly penetrating the house, the French girl, the maid, and the doctor – two criminals and one initiate, bathed and disinfected by daylight, chill, and by the sonority of shuffling steps.

It was a warm and sunny April. "Your feet! – Wipe your feet!" The bright, bare corridor echoed the words from end to end. Bearskins were packed away for the summer and the rooms rose clean and transformed and sighed sweetly with relief. Throughout the day, throughout the wearisome, unsetting, clinging day in all the corners, in all the rooms, in panes left leaning by the wall, and in mirrors, glasses of water and the blue air of the garden, the blinking, preening cherry blossoms laughed and raged and the honeysuckle choked and bubbled insatiably, unquench-ably. The boring chatter of the courtyards continued around the clock. It announced the overthrow of night, and all day long the fine patter kept swelling forth and acted like a sleeping potion, reiterating that there would be no more evening and no one would be allowed to sleep. "Feet, feet!" But they arrived hotfoot. They came in intoxicated from the open air with ringing in their ears. So they failed to gather properly what was said and rushed in to gulp and chew as fast as possible before shifting their chairs with an agonising crash and running back once more into the soaring daylight that forced its way through supper-time, where drying wood gave out its brittle tapping, the sky was a piercing chirruping blue and the earth gleamed greasily like baked milk. The boundary between house and courtyard was erased. The floorcloth

164

failed to wipe off all the footprints, and floors were streaked with dry, light-coloured daubs and crunched underfoot.

Father brought them sweets and other marvels. A wonderfully good mood filled the house. Moistly rustling, the stones gave warning of their appearance through the gradually colouring tissue, which grew more and more transparent as the soft, white, gauzy packets were unwrapped layer by layer. Some stones were like drops of almond milk, others like splashes of blue watercolour, while others resembled a solidified tear of cheese. Some were blind, somnolent, or dreamy, while others had a gay sparkle like the frozen juice of blood oranges. You did not like to touch them. They were lovely, displayed on the frothing paper which exuded them like the dark juice of a plum.

Father was unusually affectionate to the children and often accompanied Mother into town. They would return together and seemed full of gladness. Most of all, both of them were serene, even-tempered and friendly, and when Mother on odd occasions cast a playfully reproachful glance at Father, she seemed to draw tranquillity from his small and ugly eyes in order to pour it forth from her own big and beautiful ones upon the children and those around her.

Once their parents rose very late. Then for some unknown reason they decided to go and have lunch on a steamer anchored by the harbour, and they took the children with them. Seryozha was allowed to try some cold beer. All this pleased them so, that they went for lunch on the steamer again. The children failed to recognise their parents. What had happened to them? Zhenya lived in a state of uncomprehending bliss and imagined that now life would always be like this. They were not downcast when told that they would not be taken to the dacha that summer after all. Soon afterwards their father left and there appeared in the house three huge yellow trunks with stout metal bands around them.

3

The train departed late at night. Mr Luvers had moved one month before and had written that their apartment was ready. Several cabs went jogging down to the station. One could tell when they were nearing it by the colour of the road. It turned black and the streetlamps struck against brown iron. At that moment a view of the Kama opened up from the viaduct, and a pit, black as soot, all heavy mass and panic, crashed open beneath them and escaped. It darted off and there in the distance at its farthest reach it took fright, rolled away and trembled in the winking beads of distant signals.

It was windy. The outlines fled from cottages and fences like the frame torn from the grating of a sieve, and they rippled and fluttered in the churning air. There was a smell of potato. The cabman edged out from the line of baskets and carriage backs that jogged ahead and began to overtake. From a distance they recognised the dray with their own luggage. They drew level. Ulyasha shouted loudly to her mistress from the cart but was drowned out by the jolting wheels. She shook and leaped up and down, and her voice leaped too.

With the novelty of all this nocturnal noise, blackness and freshness the young girl was unaware of sorrow. Far, far away something loomed dark and mysterious. Beyond the huts of the harbour, lights were bobbing – the town was rinsing them in water from the boats and shore. Then there were a lot more of them, and they swarmed greasy, dense and blind as worms. At Lyubimov Wharf the funnels, warehouse roofs and decks were a sober blue. Barges lay gazing at the stars. "This is a rat hole," thought Zhenya. They were surrounded by workmen in white. Seryozha was first to jump down. He looked around and was astonished to see that the drayman with their baggage was there already. The horse threw back its muzzle, its collar rose and reared up like a rooster, and the animal leaned to the rear and began to backstep. And all during the journey Seryozha had been wondering how far behind the others would be. . . .

The young boy stood there in his clean white school shirt and revelled in the imminence of their journey. Travelling was a novelty for both of them, but he already knew and loved the words "depot", "locomotive", "sidings" and "through carriage", and the sound of the word "class" seemed to have a bittersweet taste. His sister enjoyed everything too, but in her own way and without the boyish methodicalness that marked her brother's enthusiasms.

Suddenly Mother appeared at their side, as though sprung from a hole in the groung. She gave instructions to take the children along to the buffet. Then she strutted off proudly through the crowd and went straight to a man who was first referred to in the open by the loud and menacing title of "stationmaster". After that he was often mentioned variously in various places and by a variety of folk in the throng.

They were overcome by yawning. They were seated at one of those windows, so dusty, standoffish and huge that they seemed like an institution made of bottle glass where you had to remove your hat. Zhenya looked through the window. She saw not a street but another room, only more serious and gloomy than the one here in this decanter. Into that other room engines slowly came and stopped, spreading darkness. But when they left and cleared the room, it turned out not to be a room because there behind the pillars was the sky, and on the far side – a hill and wooden houses with people going away toward them. Perhaps the cockerels were crowing there right now, and the water-carrier had recently been and left a trail of sludge. . . .

It was a provincial station without the commotion and the glow of those in the capital. Departing passengers turned up in good time from the benighted town. There were long waits and silences and migrants sleeping on the floor, surrounded by their hunting dogs, trunks, engines packed in bast and bicycles without packing.

The children settled down on the top bunks. The boy fell asleep immediately. The train was still standing. It was getting light, and gradually Zhenya realised that the coach was dark blue, clean and chilly. And gradually she realised. . . . But by now she too was asleep.

He was a very portly man. He read his newspaper and swayed about. One glance at him was sufficient to reveal the swaying which soaked and flooded the whole compartment like sunshine. Zhenya surveyed him from above with the lazy attentiveness of a newcomer who is fully awake and thinks or watches something but continues lying there only because he is waiting for the decision to get up to come of its own accord, clear and unforced like the rest of his thoughts. She looked at the man and wondered where he had come from to sit in their compartment, and when he had managed to get washed and dressed. She had no idea of the real time of day. She had only just woken, so it must be morning. She observed him but he could not see her – the upper berth sloped in towards the wall. He could not see her, because occasionally he too glanced up from the news, or aslant, or sideways, and when he looked up at her bunk their eyes never met. Either he could see only the mattress or else . . . but she quickly tucked them up beneath her and pulled up her slackened stockings. "Mama is in this corner. She's already tidied up and is reading a book," Zhenya decided by studying the fat man's gaze. "But Seryozha isn't down there either. So where is he?" She yawned sweetly and stretched. "It's terribly hot." She realised it only now and glanced down from the head of the bunk at the half-lowered window. "But where is the earth?" The question gaped inside her.

What she saw was beyond description. The sighing hazel grove into which their train was sliding snakelike had become an ocean, a whole world – anything and everything. It ran downward, bright and murmuring, broad and sloping. Then fragmenting, condensing and glooming, it fell away sharply, already completely black. And the thing that rose there on the far side of the chasm resembled some enormous green-yellow thundercloud, all curling and whirling, lost in thought and stupefied. Zhenya held her breath and immediately felt the swiftness of the boundless, oblivious air. She immediately realised that the storm-cloud was some country or locality, and that it had a loud and mountainous name that had rolled all around and been cast with stones and sand down into the valley. She realised that the hazel grove was aware only of whispering and whispering that name – here and there, and awa-a-a-ay over there – only that name.

"Is this the Urals?" she asked, leaning over and addressing the whole compartment.

She spent the entire remainder of the journey by the window in the corridor and never left it. She clung to it and constantly kept leaning out. She was greedy. She discovered that looking backward was much more pleasant than looking forward. Majestic acquaintances misted over and receded into the distance. And after a brief separation, during which cold air blew down the nape of your neck as grinding chains served up some new marvel right before you with a precipitous roar, you began to search for them again. The mountain panorama expanded outward, constantly growing and enlarging. Some of them blackened, others brightened. Some of them spread dark, while others darkened. They met and parted, fell and rose again. And all this was accomplished in a slow-moving circle, like the rotation of the stars, with the careful restraint of Titans one hair's breadth from catastrophe and with a concern for the world's entirety. And these complex movements were ruled over by a steady, mighty roar that eluded the human ear and was all-seeing. It surveyed them with eagle eye. Mute and obscure, it held them in review. Thus the Urals were built, rebuilt, and built up yet again.

She went back to the compartment for a moment, her eyes screwed up from the harsh lighting. Mama was chatting with the strange gentleman and laughing. Seryozha was holding on by a wall strap and shifting restlessly about the crimson plush. Mama spat the last seed out into her clenched fist, brushed off the ones that had dropped on her dress, then bent forward swiftly and lithely and flung all the rubbish under the seat. Contrary to what she expected, the fat man had a husky, cracked little voice. He apparently suffered from shortness of breath. Mother introduced Zhenya to him and handed her a mandarin orange. He was an amusing and probably a kind man, and as he talked he kept raising a plump hand to his mouth. Often his speech would swell up and then break off, suddenly constricted. It turned out that he was from Ekaterinburg himself and had travelled the length and breadth of the Urals and knew them well. And when he took a gold watch from his waistcoat pocket and lifted it right up to his nose before popping it back, Zhenya noticed what kindly fingers he had. Like many stout people, he took things with a gesture of actually giving, and all the time his hand kept sighing as if proffered for someone to kiss, and it bobbed gently as though bouncing a ball on the floor.

"It won't be long now." He squinted, and although he was addressing the boy, he spoke away from him and puffed out his lips.

"You know," Seryozha exclaimed, "there's a post, they say, on the frontier of Asia and Europe, and it has 'Asia' written on it!" He slid off the seat and ran out into the corridor.

Zhenya had understood nothing. But when the fat gentleman explained things to her, she too ran out to look out for the post, fearing she might already have missed it. In her enchanted mind the "frontier of Asia" arose like a phantasmagoric barrier – maybe like those iron bars that marked a strip of terrible, pitch-black, stinking danger between the public and the cage with the pumas. She awaited that post as though it were a curtain rising on the first act of a geographical tragedy of which she had heard many tales from witnesses. And the thought that now she too would shortly see it for herself filled her with solemn excitement.

Meanwhile the thing that forced her to rejoin the adults in the compartment still continued monotonously. There was no foreseeable end to the grey alder trees through which the railroad had started half an hour before. Nature made no preparations for what was shortly in store. Zhenya was annoyed at dull and dusty Europe for sluggishly withholding the miracle. And how put out she was when, as if in answer to Seryozha's furious shriek, something resembling a small tombstone flashed past the window, turned sideways on and rushed away, bearing

169

off the long-awaited fairy-tale name into the alders and away from more alders that came chasing after! At that instant, as if by arrangement, several heads leaned out of the windows of all classes and the train came alive as it raced down the slope in a cloud of dust. Asia had already claimed at least a score of versts, but kerchiefs on flying heads still fluttered, people exchanged glances, there were some clean-shaven and some with beards, and they all flew along through the clouds of swirling sand. On and on they rushed, past the same dusty alders which recently had been European and were now for some time already Asian.

4

Life began afresh. Milk was not brought around to the kitchen by a delivery girl. It was brought each morning by Ulyasha two cans at a time, together with special loaves, quite different from the ones in Perm. The pavements here were made of something like marble or alabaster and had an undulating white gloss. Even in the shade the flagstones dazzled one like icy suns, avidly engulfing the shadows of the elegant trees which flowed away, melting on them and liquefying. Here the way out on to the street was quite different, and the street itself was broad and bright and planted with trees.

"Just like Paris," said Zhenya, echoing her father.

He said that on the very first day of their arrival. Everything was fine and spacious. Father had had a snack before leaving for the station and did not share their dinner. His place at the table stayed clean and bright, like Ekaterinburg, and he merely unfolded his napkin and sat sideways as he told some story. He unbuttoned his waistcoat and his shirt front curved outward, fresh and vigorous. This was a splendid European-style town, he said, and he rang for them to clear away and serve the next course – rang and continued talking. And down unknown passages from rooms still unknown came a silent maid in white, all starched and pleated with neat black hair. She was addressed in a formal manner, and though new, she smiled at the mistress and children as though they were already friends. She was given some instructions regarding Ulyasha who was out there in the unknown and probably exceedingly dark kitchen, where no doubt there was a window with a new view to be seen – some belfry or other, or a road, or birds. And perhaps Ulyasha was there right now, asking this lady questions and putting on her old clothes to begin unpacking their things. She would be asking questions, making herself at home, and looking to see where the stove was – in the same corner as in Perm or somewhere else. . . .

The boy heard from his father that it was not far to the *lycée* – quite near, in fact, they must have seen it as they rode past. Father drank some Narzan water, swallowed and continued. "Didn't I show you? Well, you can't see it from here. Maybe you can from the kitchen (he made a mental estimate). But even then you'll only see the roof."

He drank some more Narzan and rang.

The kitchen turned out to be fresh and bright – exactly, so it seemed to Zhenya a minute later, exactly as she had guessed and imagined back in the dining-room: a tiled range with a whitish-blue lustre, and two windows in just the order she expected. Ulyasha had slipped something on over her bare arms. The room was filled with children's voices. There were people walking on the roof of the *lycée* and the tops of scaffolding poles were showing.

"Yes, it's being repaired," Father said, when they had all filed shouting and jostling down the now discovered but still unexplored passage and made their way back to the dining-room. She would have to visit the passage again tomorrow, when she had laid out her notebooks and hung up her wash-glove by its loop – when she had completed all the thousand and one jobs that had to be done.

"Stupendous butter!" said Mother, sitting down.

The children went through into the classroom which they had first inspected immediately on arriving, still wearing their hats.

"What is it that makes this Asia?" she wondered aloud.

For some reason Seryozha failed to grasp what he would certainly have understood at any other time. Up till now they had always lived as a pair. He turned towards the map that hung there and ran his hand down the crest of the Urals. He glanced at her and she seemed crushed by his argument:

"They agreed on this as the natural frontier, that's all."

But then she recalled the noon of that same day which already seemed so distant. She could not believe that a day with all this packed into it – this actual day, now in Ekaterinburg, and even then not all of it – was still not yet over. The thought that all this had retreated to its proper and appointed distance, still preserving a now lifeless order, filled her with an amazing sense of spiritual fatigue – the sort your body feels towards the evening of a working day. It was as if she herself had helped to shift and remove all that weight of beautiful objects and had overstrained

171

herself. For some reason she was certain that *they*, her Urals, were still *there*. She turned and ran off to the kitchen via the dining-room, where there was now less crockery, although the stupendous iced butter on its perspiring maple leaves still remained together with the angry mineral water.

The *lycée* was being repaired and strident martins ripped the air like seamstresses tearing madapollam with their teeth. As she leaned out she saw down below a carriage gleaming by the open coach-house. Sparks showered from a grinding-wheel, and there was the smell of all the food they had eaten, better and more interesting than when it was served – a persistent, melancholy smell like in a book. She forgot why she had come and failed to notice that her Urals were not there in Ekaterinburg. But she did notice that darkness was descending on Ekaterinburg, gradually, house by house, and that down in the room below they were singing, probably over some light task – they had washed the floor maybe and were now laying out the bast mats with their hot hands. They were teeming water from the washing-up tub. Yet, though the teeming came from below, how silent it was all around! And the tap was gurgling like . . . "Well now, miss . . ." (but she was still avoiding the new maid and would not listen to her). Like. . . . (she tried to finish her thought). Down below them they knew and were probably saying, "That's the new people come to number two today."

Ulyasha came into the kitchen.

The children slept soundly that first night. And they woke, Seryozha in Ekaterinburg and Zhenya in Asia – again that strangely expansive thought occurred to her. The light played freshly on the flaky alabaster of the ceiling.

It began while it was still summer. She was notified that she would be going to the *lycée*. This was entirely pleasant. But she was *notified* of it! She had not invited a private tutor into her classroom where sunlight hues stuck so firmly to the walls with their glue-paint wash that the evening could only rip away the clinging daylight by drawing blood. She had not invited him when he came in accompanied by Mama to make the acquaintance of "my future pupil". Nor had she given him the ridiculous surname Dikikh. And was it her wish that from now on at midday stern soldiers were always drilling, snorting and sweaty like the scarlet convulsions of a tap when the pipes are out of order? Or that their boots were trampled by a violet thundercloud that knew far more about guns and wheels than their white shirts, white tents and their white, white officers? And had she asked for two objects, a basin and a napkin, to be forever combining like carbons in an arc-lamp and evoking a third thing which instantly evaporated: the idea of death – like that sign outside the barber's where it first occurred to her? And was it with her consent that the red turnpikes with "stopping prohibited" became the site of certain illicitly halting urban secrets, or that the Chinamen became something personally dreadful, terrible and peculiar to Zhenya? Of course, not everything settled so heavily on her soul. There was much that was pleasant, like her forthcoming start at the *lycée*. But as in this case, these were all things of which she was notified. Ceasing to be a poetical trifle, life began to ferment as a stern, black story since it had become prose and was transformed into fact. Dull, painful and sombre, as though in a state of eternal sobering, the elements of everyday existence entered her spirit as it took shape. They sank deep into it, real, cold and solid like sleepy spoons of pewter. And there at the bottom the pewter began to melt, congealing into lumps and forming into droplets of obsessive ideas.

5

Belgians often began to appear at the house for tea. That was what they were called. That was what Father called them. "Today the Belgians will be here," he would say. There were four of them. The clean-shaven one came only rarely and was not very talkative. Sometimes he would call in on his own on a weekday – and he always chose nasty rainy weather. The other three were inseparable. Their faces resembled cakes of fresh soap, unstarted and taken straight from the wrapper, fragrant and cold. One of them had a thick, fluffy beard and downy chestnut hair. They always turned up in Father's company from some meeting. Everyone in the house liked them. They talked like spilling water on the tablecloth – noisy, fresh, all at once, and spurting to one side where no one expected. And their jokes and stories, which the children always understood, were always thirst-quenching and clean, and they left trails behind which took a long time to dry out.

There was noise on every side and the light gleamed on the sugar-bowl, the nickel coffeepot, clean, strong teeth and thick linen. They joked amiably and courteously with Mother. As Father's colleagues, they had the subtle ability to restrain him in time whenever he responded to their fleeting hints and mentions of matters and men known only to themselves, the professionals – whenever he started going on in his ponderous, hesitant and very impure French about contractors, *références approuvées* and *férocités*, that is *bestialités, ce que veut dire en russe* embezzlements on the Blagodat.

For some time past, one of them had taken up the study of Russian and he often tested himself in this new pursuit which still eluded him. It was awkward to laugh at their father's French periods, and his *férocités* genuinely irked everyone. But the very situation seemed to sanctify the merry laughter that greeted Negaraat's attempts.

Negaraat was his name. He was a Walloon from the Flemish part of Belgium. They recommended Dikikh to him. He noted the address in Russian, comically tracing out the complicated letters like "ю", "я" and "ѣ".[1] But somehow they come out in two parts, unmatched and sprawling. The children knelt up on the leather cushions of the armchair and put their elbows on the table – everything was permitted. And everything was mixed up. "ю" was not "ю", but a sort of figure ten. There was roaring and laughter all around. Evans banged on the table with his fist. Father shook and went all red as he paced about the room. "No, I can't bear it!" he kept saying and crumpled up his handkerchief.

"Faites de nouveau," said Evans, piling on the agony. "Commencez."

And Negaraat kept opening his mouth, hesitating like someone with a stammer, and wondering how best to deliver himself of this Russian letter "ы"[2] which concealed a mystery as dark as darkest Africa.

"Dites, 'uvý', 'nyevýgodno'," Father suggested moistly and hoarsely, losing his voice.

"Ouvoui, niévoui."

"Entends-tu? – Ouvoui, niévoui – ouvoui, niévoui. Oui, oui – chose inouïe, charmant!" the Belgians exclaimed, bursting out in a fit of laughter.

The summer went by. Examinations were passed successfully – some even excellently. The cold, transparent noise of the corridors streamed as though from a spring. Here everyone knew everyone else. In the garden leaves turned yellow and gold and the classroom windows languished in their dancing, bright reflections. The semi-frosted panes were misty and agitated in their lower portions, while the casements were racked by a blue convulsion and their chill clarity was furrowed by the bronze twigs of maple.

She never knew that all her anxieties would be turned into such a merry joke. Divide so many yards and inches into seven! Was it worth going through all those measures of weight – zolotniks and lots, pounds and poods? And grains, drachmas, scruples and ounces, which always seemed to her like the four ages of a scorpion? Why was the word for "useful" written with an "e" and not a "Ҍ"? She had difficulty answering only because all her powers of reasoning went on an effort to imagine the unfortunate grounds for such a word written with "Ҍ" ever occurring. Spelt like that it seemed so wild and shaggy. She never learned why she was not sent to the *lycée* there and then: she had already been accepted and registered. Her coffee-coloured uniform was already being sewn and later on it was meanly and boringly tried on with pins for hours on end. And in her room new horizons opened up in the form of a bag, a pencil-case, a lunch basket, and a remarkably disgusting eraser.

The Stranger

1

The little girl's head and body were wrapped in a thick woollen shawl that reached down to her knees, and she strutted up and down the yard like a little pullet. Zhenya wanted to go and talk to the little Tatar girl, but that moment the two panels of a small window flew open with a bang. "Kolka!" called Aksinya. Looking like a peasant's bundle with felt boots hastily stuck into the bottom, the child toddled quickly to the janitor's lodge.

To take any schoolwork outside always meant grinding away at the footnote to some rule till it was blunt and had lost all meaning, after which you had to go upstairs and do everything all over again! The rooms inside seized one at the doorstep with their peculiar gloom and chill, and with that peculiar, always unexpected familiarity of furniture that has taken up its allotted position once and for all and stayed put. There was no predicting the future. Yet it could be glimpsed on entering the house from outside, for its scheme was in evidence already – a distribution that would govern it despite its recalcitrance in other respects. And the household's inevitable cheer struck one of a sudden from the threshold of the hall and never failed quickly to dispel any sleepiness induced by the movement of the outdoor air.

This time it was Lermontov. Zhenya creased back the binding of the book. Had Seyozha done that indoors, she herself would have been up in arms about such a disgraceful habit. Out of doors, though, it was quite another matter.

Prokhor put the ice-freezer on the ground and went back into the house. As he opened the door of the Spitsyns' hallway, the devilish, blustering bark of the general's little hairless dogs came billowing forth. The door slammed to with a brief tinkle.

Meanwhile the River Terek, "springing like a lioness with shaggy mane on back",[3] continued to roar as it should, and the only doubt that began to trouble Zhenya was whether it was really on its back rather than its spine that all this was happening. She was too lazy to follow the book, and "golden clouds from southern lands afar" had hardly had time to "accompany the Terek northward" when there they were at the general's doorstep holding a bucket and bast scrubber.

Spitsyn's batman set down the bucket and bent over, and after taking apart the freezer he proceeded to wash it. The August sunlight burst through the tree foliage and came to rest on the soldier's hindquarters. The light glowed red as it settled in the faded cloth of his uniform and greedily impregnated it like turpentine.

The courtyard was broad and oppressive and it had intricate nooks and corners. Paved in the centre, it had not been resurfaced for many a long day. The cobbles were thickly overgrown with short, curly grass which in the afternoon emitted the sort of bitter medicinal smell that hangs around hospitals in hot weather. At one extremity, between the janitor's lodge and the coach-house, the yard bordered on someone else's garden.

And it was here, beyond the woodpile, that Zhenya made for. She propped the ladder from below with a flat billet of wood to prevent it skidding and shook it into place among the shifting logs, and then she found an uncomfortable but interesting perch on the middle rung, as though it were some game. Then she got up and climbed a little higher, and laying her book on the top row of logs which had been partly removed, she prepared to start "The Demon" once again. Then, finding it was better sitting where she was earlier, she climbed down again, leaving her book on top of the woodpile. She forgot about it because she had just noticed beyond the garden something that she had never imagined and she sat there in open-mouthed entrancement.

There were no bushes in the other garden and as the ancient trees' lower branches rose up into the foliage as into a night sky, the garden below was laid bare even though it stood there already, never emerging from its perpetual state of solemn, airy gloom. Fork-trunked, mauve as thundercloud and covered with grey lichen, the trees provided a good view of the little-used deserted alleyway on the far side of the other garden. There was yellow acacia growing there, and the shrubbery was drying, curling up and shedding.

Borne through the gloomy garden from this world to the other, the faraway alley glowed with the light which illuminates events in a dream – very brightly, minutely and noiselessly, as if the sun over there had put on spectacles and was fumbling among the buttercups.

But why was Zhenya gaping so? . . . She was gazing at her discovery, which intrigued her much more than those who had helped her to make it.

Surely there must be a bench over there, beyond the gate in the street? . . . In a street like that – lucky people! She envied those unknown girls. There were three of them.

They showed up black like the word "anchorite" in the song. The napes of three even necks with hair combed up under three round hats leaned as if the one at the end half-hidden by a bush was asleep with her head propped on her elbow, while the other two also slept huddled against her. The hats were a dark grey-blue and kept flashing in the sun then fading, like insects. They were tied about with black crepe. At that moment the three strangers all turned their heads the other way. Doubt-less something had attracted their attention at the far end of the street. For about a minute they looked in that direction – just as in summer an instant is dissolved in light and extended and people have to screw up their eyes and shield them with the palms of their hands. They looked for just about a minute, and then they relapsed into their earlier state of communal dozing.

Zhenya was on the point of returning when suddenly she missed her book and could not recall immediately where she had left it. She turned back to look for it, and on going around the woodpile she saw the strangers had got up and were about to leave. One by one in turn they came through the gate. A short man followed after them, walking with a strange crippled gait. Under his arm he carried an enormous album or atlas. So that was what they had been doing – reading and peering over one another's shoulders! And she had thought they were asleep! Their neighbours went through the garden and disappeared behind the out-buildings. The sun was already sinking. As she retrieved her book Zhenya disturbed the stack of logs. The whole pile awoke and stirred as though alive. A few logs rolled down and fell on to the turf with a gentle thump. That served as a signal, like the night watchman's rattle. Evening was born, and with it a multitude of noises, soft and misty. The air began to whistle an old-time melody from across the river.

The courtyard was empty. Prokhor had completed his work and had gone out through the gate. Low down, just above the grass spread the melancholy twang and strumming of a soldier's balalaika. Above her a fine swarm of quiet midges weaved and danced, plunged and fell, hanging in the air, fell and hung again, then without touching the ground rose up once more. But the strumming of the balalaika was finer and quieter still. It sank earthward lower than the swarm of midges, and without getting dusty soared aloft again more easily and airily than they, shimmering and breaking off, dipping and rising unhurriedly.

Zhenya returned to the house. "Lame . . ." She was thinking of the stranger with the album. "Lame, but one of the gentry – no crutches." She went in through the back entrance. Outside in the yard there was a persistent sickly smell of camomile infusion. "Lately Mama has built up quite a pharmacy – a mass of dark-blue bottles with yellow caps." She slowly mounted the stairs. The iron banister was cold. The steps grated in response to her shuffling. Suddenly something strange occurred to her. She strode up two steps at once and halted on the third. It occurred to her that recently there had been a certain elusive similarity between Mama and the janitor's wife. Something quite indefinable. She stopped. Something like . . . she paused to think. Maybe something like what people mean when they say "We are all human", or "We are all cast in the same mould", or "Fate makes equals of us all . . ." With the tip of her toe she knocked aside a bottle lying there. It flew down and fell without breaking among some dusty bags. Something, in fact, that was very common, common to all people. But then, why not between herself and Aksinya? Or Aksinya, say, and Ulyasha? To Zhenya it seemed all the stranger because it was difficult to find two people more dissimilar. There was something earthy about Aksinya, something of the kitchen garden, something reminiscent of potatoes swelling or the bluish green of wild pumpkins. Whereas Mama. . . . Zhenya smiled wryly at the very idea of comparing the two.

It was Aksinya, though, who set the tone of so compelling a comparison. The association was weighted in her favour. The peasant woman gained nothing from it, but the mistress lost. For a brief moment Zhenya had a crazy notion. She had a vision of Mama imbued with some plebeian element and pictured her mother saying "salmond" instead of "salmon" and "we works" instead of "we work". And, she fancied, what if Mama one day suddenly came billowing in in her new silk negligée without a sash and blurted out: "Thee lean it up agin't door!"?

There was a smell of medicine in the corridor. Zhenya went along to her father.

2

The house was being refurnished. Luxury made its first appearance. The Luvers acquired a carriage and began to keep horses. The coachman was called Davletsha.

At that time rubber tyres were a complete novelty. Whenever they drove out everyone turned around to gaze after their carriage – people, together with fences, churches and cockerels. . . .

They were a long time in opening the door for Madame Luvers, and as the carriage moved off at a walking pace in deference to her, she shouted after them, "Don't go far! Just to the barrier and back! Careful down the hill!"

A whitish sun catching them at the doctor's porch stretched away down the street and reaching Davletsha's tight, freckled, purple neck, heated it and caused it to shrivel.

They drove on to the bridge and heard the chatter of its boards – cunning, round and coherent, composed once to last for all time, reverently incised by the ravine and memorable forever, at noonday and in sleep.

Vykormysh, their homebred horse, climbed the hill and started on the steep, unyielding flint. He strained but it was beyond him. His scrambling suddenly resembled a locust crawling. And like a locust, which by nature flies and leaps, there was a flash of beauty in the humiliation of his unnatural efforts. . . . At any moment it seemed he would lose patience, flash his wings in anger and soar away. And, in fact, he did give a tug, threw out his forelegs and set off across the wasteland in a short gallop. Davletsha began to draw him in and tightened the reins. A dog barked at them with a decrepit, dull and shaggy bark. The dust was like gunpowder. The road turned steeply to the left.

The black street ended blindly in the red fencing of the railway depot. It was in a state of alarm. The sun beat sideways from behind the bushes and watched the crowd of strange figures in women's jackets. It drenched them in pelting white light, which seemed to gush like liquid lime from a pail overturned by someone's boot and surged across the earth in a rolling wave. The street was in alarm.

The horse moved at a walking pace.

"Turn off to the right!" Zhenya ordered.

"There's no way across," Davletsha answered, pointing to the dead end with his whip handle. "It's a blind alley."

"Stop here then. I'll have a look."

"It's our Chinamen."

"So I see."

Realising the young mistress had no wish to talk to him, Davletsha sang out a long drawn "Whoaa!" and the horse's whole body heaved as it came to a halt, rooted to the spot. Davletsha began whistling softly and repetitively, pausing every now and then to make the horse obey.

The Chinese were running across the road holding enormous rye loaves. They were dressed in blue and resembled peasant women in trousers. Their bare heads ended in a knot at the crown and looked as though they were twisted together from handkerchiefs. Some of them lingered and could be properly inspected. Their faces were pale, sallow and smirking. They were swarthy and dirty, like copper with an oxide of poverty.

Davletsha took out his pouch and proceeded to roll a cigarette. At that moment several women came round the corner where the men were heading. No doubt they too were going for bread. The men on the road began to laugh loudly and steal up, twisting about as though their hands were tied behind their backs with rope. Their squirming movements were emphasised by the fact that they were dressed like acrobats in a single garment that covered their whole bodies from the collar down to their ankles. There was nothing frightening about any of this, the women did not run away but stood and laughed.

"Now then, Davletsha, what are you doing?"

"The horse went and jerked! He jerked, I tell you! Just won't keep still!" Every now and then Davletsha gave Vykormysh a flick by tugging and releasing the reins.

"Gently! You'll have us out! Why are you whipping him?"

"I have to."

He drove them out into open country and calmed the horse which had been on the point of breaking into a prance. And only after swiftly transporting his mistress away from that shameful scene did the wily Tatar take the reins in his right hand and put the tobacco pouch he still held in his hand back under the flap of his coat.

They returned by another way. Madame Luvers had probably spied them from the doctor's window. She came out on to the porch at the moment when the bridge had already told them its entire story once and had started to repeat it under the wheels of the water-carrier's cart.

3

It was during one of the examinations that Zhenya met up with Liza Defendova, the little girl who gathered rowan sprigs on the way to school and brought them into class. The sacristan's daughter was retaking an exam in French. "Luvers, Evgeniya" was placed in the first unoccupied seat. And so they became acquainted as they sat, the two of them, over one and the same sentence.

"Est-ce Pierre qui a volé la pomme?"

"Oui. C'est Pierre qui vola . . ." etc.

The fact that Zhenya was left to study at home did not put an end to the two girls' friendship. They began to meet up. But because of Mama's views their encounters were always one-sided. Liza was permitted to visit them, but Zhenya for the time being was forbidden to go to the Defendovs.

Their sporadic meetings did not prevent Zhenya from rapidly becoming attached to her friend. She fell in love with her, which meant that she played the passive role in their relationship and became its pressure gauge, ever watchful, excited and anxious. Any mention by Liza of other classmates aroused in Zhenya a feeling of emptiness and bitterness. Her heart would sink. They were fits of first jealousy. For no other reason than the strength of her own mistrust, Zhenya was convinced that Liza was deceiving her. Though outwardly so direct, she was laughing inwardly at everything about her that was Luvers, and mocking it behind her back, in class and at home. And Zhenya accepted all this as her due, as something in the very nature of affection. Her feeling was as random in its choice of an object as the instinctive demands that evoked it were powerful. It was an instinct that knew no self-love and

181

could only suffer and consume itself in honour of some fetish while its first sense of feeling lasted.

Neither Zhenya nor Liza had the slightest influence on the other, and they met and parted – Zhenya as Zhenya, Liza as Liza – the one with deep feeling, the other without any.

The Akhmedyanovs' father was an iron merchant. In the year between the births of Nuretdin and Smagil he had suddenly grown rich. Smagil then started being called Samoyla, and it was decided to give the sons a Russian upbringing. Their father did not omit a single feature of the free-wheeling nobleman's life-style, and in a ten-year rush through all the points of education things were carried slightly too far. The boys were a splendid success insofar as they followed the prescribed pattern, and they still retained the rapid sweep of father's will and were noisy and destructive as a pair of flywheels set whirling and left to spin under their own impetus. The most true-to-type fourth-formers in the fourth form were the brothers Akhmedyanov. They were all broken chalk, crib sheets, lead shot, banging desks, swear-words, and red-cheeked, snub-nosed self-assurance that peeled in the frost. Seryozha made friends with them in August, and by the end of September he had lost all his own personality. It was quite to be expected. To be a typical schoolboy and anything else besides meant joining up with the Akhmedyanovs. And Seryozha wanted nothing so much as to be a schoolboy.

Mr Luvers did not try to hinder his son's friendship. He saw no change in him, and even if he did notice anything, he ascribed it to the effects of adolescence. Besides, his head was filled with other cares. Some time ago he had begun to suspect he was ill and that the illness was incurable.

4

She was not actually sorry for him, although everyone around could only say how incredibly awkward and annoying it was. Negaraat was too complicated even for their parents, and all that they felt about other people dimly conveyed itself to the children, as it would to spoiled household pets. Zhenya was sad only because nothing would be quite as before. Now there would be only three Belgians, and there would be no more of the laughter that there used to be.

She happened to be at table the evening he announced to Mama that he had to go to Dijon for some sort of muster.

"How young you must be then still!" Mama said and immediately began offering all manner of condolence.

He sat there with his head hanging. The conversation flagged.

"Tomorrow they are coming to seal the windows," Mama said, and asked him whether she should close them now.

He said there was no need, it was a warm evening and back home they didn't even bother sealing the windows in winter.

Soon Father came in too. He too expressed effusive regrets on hearing the news. But before starting to lament on Negaraat's behalf he raised his eyebrows in surprise: "To Dijon? But surely you are Belgian?"

"I am Belgian, but I'm a French subject."

And Negaraat began an account of how his "old folk" had emigrated. The story was so entertaining that he hardly seemed like his own parents' son, and he told it with such warmth that he might well have been reading a book about other people.

"I'm sorry, I'll have to interrupt you," said Mama. "Zhenya, dear, all the same do close the window. Vika, they're coming to seal them tomorrow. Well, do carry on. But that uncle of yours was a real scoundrel! Did he really, literally under oath. . . ?"

"Yes."

Negaraat resumed his interrupted tale. But when he got to the main point – that is, the paper he received yesterday from the consulate – he guessed that Zhenya had grasped nothing of all this despite her efforts to understand. He turned to her and without revealing his intention, so as not to wound her pride, he began explaining what sort of thing this military service was.

"Yes, yes, I understand. Yes, I do understand. I follow you," she repeated with mechanical gratitude. "But why go so far away? Be a soldier here. Do your training here at least, where everyone else does," she corrected herself and vividly pictured the meadows unfolding from the top of Monastery Hill.

"Yes, yes, I understand. Yes, yes," she repeated again. The Luvers parents sat there idly, believing the Belgian was filling the child's head with useless details, and they inserted their own dozy simplifications. But suddenly came a moment when she felt sorry for all those who long ago, or recently, had been Negaraats in various distant places and who had had to say goodbye and out of the blue set off down a road that had brought them here as soldiers to the strange city of Ekaterinburg.

Negaraat explained everything so clearly to her. Nobody had explained things like that before. The veil of soullessness and blinding obviousness suddenly fell away from her picture of those white tents. Companies of men faded and became a collection of individuals in soldier's dress, and she began to pity them just at the point when they became animated, elevated, intimate and drained of colour by their newly acquired significance.

They were saying goodbye.

"I am leaving some of my books with Tsvetkov. He's the friend I've told you so much about. Please continue to use them, Madame. Your son knows where I live. He comes to see the landlord's family. I am handing my room over to Tsvetkov. I'll warn him you're coming."

"Tell him to come and call on us . . . Tsvetkov, did you say?"

"Tsvetkov, that's right."

"Tell him to come. We'll get to know him. I used to know some Tsvetkovs when I was young." She looked at her husband. He stood there in front of Negaraat with his hands tucked in the breast of his jacket and distractedly awaited an opportunity to make final arrangements with the Belgian for tomorrow. "Tell him to come and see us. Only not just now. I'll let him know. Here, take this. It's yours. I haven't finished it. But I wept as I read it. The doctor advised me to leave it – to avoid getting over-excited." She looked again at her husband. Now he had bowed his head and his collar crackled and he puffed as he inspected whether he had boots on both feet and whether they were properly cleaned.

"Well, then. There we are. Don't forget your stick. We'll see each other again, I hope?"

"Oh, certainly. I'm here till Friday. What's today?" He suddenly panicked, as people often do when about to leave.

"Wednesday. Vika, it is Wednesday, isn't it? . . . Vika is it Wednesday?"

"Yes, Wednesday. *Écoutez.*" Father's turn finally came. "*Demain . . .*"

. . . And they both went out on to the stairs.

5

They strode along and talked. Occasionally she had to break into a slight run to avoid lagging behind and to keep in step with Seryozha. They both walked along briskly and her coat jerked to and fro as she kept both hands in her pockets and pumped with her arms to help herself along. It was cold and the thin ice crackled loudly beneath her galoshes. They were going an errand for Mama to buy a present for the man who was leaving. And they talked along the way.

"So they were taking him to the station?"

"Yes."

"But why was he sitting on the hay?"

"How do you mean?"

"Why was he sitting right in the cart, with his legs up? People don't sit like that."

"I've already said: Because he was a criminal."

"Were they taking him to do hard labour?"

"No, to Perm. We don't have our own prison here. Watch where you're going."

Their way lay across the road, past the coppersmith's shop. The doors of the shop had stood wide open the entire summer, and Zhenya was used to seeing the crossroads in a general state of friendly animation dispensed by the hot gaping maw of the workshop. Throughout July, August and September carts kept stopping there, obstructing all departure. Peasants, mainly Tatars, tramped around. Buckets lay about, and pieces of broken, rusty guttering. It was here more often than anywhere else that an awful, viscous sun set amid the dust as they slaughtered chickens beyond the nearby wattle fencing, and as the sun set it turned the crowd of folk into a gypsy camp and painted the Tatars like Romanies. It was here that buffer bars were disengaged from beneath the body of the carriage and their shafts with circles worn on their dragbolt plates plunged into the dust.

The same buckets and bits of iron still lay scattered around and now they were lightly powdered with frost. But because of the cold the doors were tightly shut, as though closed for the holidays. The crossroads were deserted, and only the familiar breath of musty fire-damp came through a circular vent and let out a fulminating scream as it rushed up Zhenya's nose, settling on her palate like cheap pear soda.

"But is there a prison board in Perm?"

"Yes, there's a department. I think it's quicker that way. Perm has one because it's the provincial centre, but Ekaterinburg is only the main town in this district. It's quite small."

The path by the private houses was laid with red brick and framed by bushes. It still bore traces of a dull, feeble sunshine. Seryozha tried stamping as noisily as possible.

185

"If you tickle this barberry with a pin in spring when it's flowering, it flutters all its petals as if it's alive."

"I know."

"Are you afraid of tickling?"

"Yes."

"That means you're nervy. The Akhmedyanovs say that if anyone's afraid of tickling. . . ."

And on they went, Zhenya with her coat swinging as she ran and Seryozha taking his unnatural strides. They caught sight of Dikikh just as their way was barred by a gate that swung like a turnstile on its post in the middle of the path. They saw him from a distance. He had come from the shop where they were heading, half a block away. He was not alone. He was followed out of the shop by a short man who walked as though trying to conceal a limp. Zhenya thought she had seen him once before somewhere. They passed without greeting. The two of them headed off obliquely and Dikikh did not notice the children. He strode along in his high galoshes and kept raising his hands with fingers splayed. He could simply not agree with what was being said and he tried with all ten fingers to prove that his companion. . . . (Where was it she had seen him now? A long time ago. But where? It must have been in Perm when she was a child.)

"Stop!" Something had happened to Seryozha. He had knelt on one knee. "Wait a bit!"

"Have you caught it?"

"Yes, I have. Idiots! Why can't they knock a nail in properly?"

"Well?"

"Wait, I can't find the place. . . . I know that man with the limp. . . . There we are. Thank goodness."

"Is it torn?"

"No, it's all right, thank heavens. There's a hole in the lining, but it's an old one. I didn't do it. Right, let's go. . . . No, wait, I'll just clean my knee. . . . Right, on we go. . . ."

"I know him. He's from the Akhmedyanovs' house. Negaraat's friend. Remember, I told you – he gets a few people together and they drink the whole night, and there's a light burning at the window. Do you remember? You remember when I spent the night at their house? On Samoyla's birthday? Well, he's one of them. Remember?"

She did remember. She realised she was mistaken, and in that case she could not have seen the lame man in Perm. She had imagined it. But she still *seemed* to have seen him. And she still had that feeling, and as she followed her brother with this on her mind she silently went through all her memories of Perm. Meanwhile she moved mechanically, took hold of something, stepped over something else, and looking around, found herself in a half-twilight of counters, small boxes, shelving, fussy greetings and attentions and . . . Seryozha did the talking.

The bookseller, who also traded in all sorts of tobacco, turned out not to have the titles they needed. But he reassured them that Turgenev had been promised. The books had been sent off from Moscow and were already on the way. And just now – only a minute ago – he had been talking about the same thing with Mr Tsvetkov, their tutor. His spry manner and his delusion about Tsvetkov made the children laugh. They said goodbye and left empty-handed.

When they came out, Zhenya asked her brother a question:

"Seryozha, I keep forgetting. Tell me, you know that street you can see from our woodpile?"

"No, I've never been there."

"That's not true. I've seen you there myself."

"On the woodpile? You. . . ."

"No, not on the woodpile, on that street beyond the Cherep-Savvichs' garden."

"Oh, that's what you mean! That's right. You can see it as you go past. Beyond the garden, at the far end. There are some sheds there and logs. Wait. . . . Is that *our* yard?! Do you mean that yard's ours? That's clever! How many times have I been past and thought what fun it would be to climb up on that woodpile, and then climb over from the woodpile into the garret. I've seen a ladder there. So that's our very own yard?"

"Can you show me the way there, Seryozha?"

"What, again? But the yard's ours! Why do I need to show you? You've been there yourself."

"You've not understood again. I'm talking about the street, and you're talking about the yard. I mean the street. Show me the way to the street. Show me how to get there. Will you show me, Seryozha?"

"I still don't understand. We've been past it today already. . . . And we'll soon be going past again."

"What do you mean?"

"Just what I said. You know the coppersmith's on the corner?"

"Oh, that dusty street you mean?"

"Yes, that's the one. And the Cherep-Savvichs are at the end on the right. Don't lag behind. We mustn't be late for dinner. It's crayfish today."

They began talking about other things. The Akhmedyanovs had

promised to show him how to tinplate a samovar. And when she asked what tinplate was, he told her it was a kind of rock – an ore, in fact, dingy-coloured like pewter. They soldered tin cans with it and fired pots, and the Akhmedyanovs knew how to do all that.

They had to run across the road, or else the train of carts would have delayed them. And so they forgot – she about the little-used lane, and Seryozha about his promise to point it out. They passed right by the very door of the coppersmith. And as Zhenya drew a breath of that warm, greasy smoke produced when brass knobs and candlesticks were cleaned, she immediately recalled where she had seen the lame man and the three unknown girls, and what they had been doing. And the next instant she realised the man with the limp was the same Tsvetkov whom the bookseller had mentioned.

6

Negaraat left in the evening. Father went to see him off and came back from the station late at night. His return caused a great disturbance at the janitor's lodge, and it took some time to subside. Someone came out with lights and shouted somebody's name. It was pouring with rain. Someone had let the geese loose and there was the sound of cackling.

Morning rose, overcast and shaky. The wet grey street bounced as though made of rubber. A nasty drizzle hung and spattered mud, carts came galloping, and galoshes splashed as they crossed the roadway.

Zhenya was returning home. Echoes of the night's disturbance could still be heard that morning in the yard. She was not allowed to use the carriage. So she set off for her friend's on foot, having said she was going to the shop to buy some hempseed. But she turned back halfway, realising she would never find her own way to the Defendovs from the merchants' quarter. Then she remembered it was still early, and Liza was at school in any case. She was thoroughly drenched and she shivered. The weather was brightening but had still not cleared. A cold white gleam flitted about the street and stuck to the wet flagstones like a leaf. The murky stormclouds hurried out of town and at the end of the square beyond the three-branched lamp standard they jostled and stirred in a windblown panic.

The person moving house was clearly a disorderly or slovenly man. His meagre office furnishings were not properly loaded but simply placed on the dray as they stood in the room, and at every jolt the armchair casters peeping from under the white covers trundled around the dray as if on a parquet floor. Although they were sodden through and through, the covers were white as snow. They caught the eye so sharply that everything else appeared to be the same colour – weather-worn cobblestones, water shivering under fences, birds flying from the stable-yards, trees flying after them, chunks of lead, and even that ficus in its tub which swayed and bowed awkwardly to everyone as it floated past on the dray.

It was a crazy cartload. It could not help but draw attention. A peasant was walking alongside and the dray listed steeply as it moved along at walking pace, striking against the curb posts. And the soaked and leaden word "town" hovered above everything in a tatter of rook calls, and in Zhenya's mind it evoked a multitude of thoughts, all fleeting as the cold October gleam that flew about the street and collapsed in the water.

She thought about the unknown owner. "When he unpacks his things he's bound to catch a chill," she reflected. And she imagined the man – *any* man in fact, with a shaky and uneven gait – setting out his belongings in various corners of a room. She vividly pictured his mannerisms and movements, and especially how he would take a rag and hobble around the tub as he wiped the drizzle-misted leaves of the ficus. But then he would catch a cold, he would catch a chill and fever. Most certainly he would. Zhenya could picture that quite vividly too. Quite vividly. The cart rumbled as it started downhill towards the River Iset. Zhenya's way led off to the left.

It must have been someone's heavy footsteps outside the door. The tea rose and fell in its glass on the little table by the bed. A slice of lemon in the tea also rose and fell. Strips of sunlight on the wallpaper swayed. They swayed in columns, like the tubes of syrup in those shops that had a signboard with a Turk smoking a pipe. With a Turk . . . smoking . . . a pipe. Smoking . . . a pipe. . . .

It must have been someone's footsteps. The patient fell asleep again.

Zhenya had taken to her bed the day after Negaraat's departure. That same day after her walk she learned that Aksinya had given birth to a boy during the night, and on the same day she had seen the cartload of furniture and decided its owner was in for a bout of rheumatism. She lay in a fever for two weeks. In her sweat she was thickly dusted with distressing red paprika that burned and gummed up her eyelids and the corners of her lips. Perspiration plagued her, and a sense of disgusting obesity combined with one of being stung. It was as though the flame causing her swelling was injected by a summer wasp, and its sting remained in her, fine as a grey hair. And over and over again she kept wanting to pull it out in different ways: from a violet cheekbone, from a shoulder, inflamed and groaning under her nightdress, or from some other place.

But now she was recovering. Her sense of feebleness pervaded everything. And at its own risk and peril it yielded to a strange geometry all its own which made her slightly sick and dizzy. Starting with some episode on the counterpane, for instance, her feeble state began depositing rows of emptiness which soon grew vast beyond belief in the twilight's craving to adopt a form and area to match such a derangement of space. Or else it fell away from the pattern on the wallpaper and chased past her a successive series of latitudes. They went past stripe after stripe, smooth as butter, and like all these sensations they wearied her with their regular, gradual expansion. Or else her feebleness tormented her with endlessly descending depths which betrayed that they were fathomless from the very outset, from their first jerk of the parquet flooring, and young Zhenya together with the bed was gently, gently lowered into the depths. Her head became like a lump of sugar thrown into a gulf of insipid and amazingly empty chaos, and it dissolved and streamed away in it.

This all happened because her aural labyrinth was extra-sensitive. It was all because of someone's footsteps. The lemon fell and rose again. The sun on the wallpaper also rose and fell.

Finally she woke. In came Mama and greeted her on her recovery, producing on her an impression of someone thought-reading. She had heard something similar already as she awoke. It was the congratulations of her own hands and feet and elbows and knees, and she received them as she stretched herself. And now Mama was here. The coincidence was strange.

The household came in and went out, sat down and got up. She asked questions and heard answers. There were some things that had changed while she was ill, and there were others that remained unaltered. She did not bother with the latter, but she could not leave the former in peace. Mama had not changed apparently. Her father – not at all. What had changed was she herself, Seryozha, the distribution of light in the room, the silence of all the others, and something else, many things. . . . Had snow fallen? No – yes – there had been snowfall now and then – it

190

had melted – it had frozen – you could not make out – the ground was bare, there was no snow. . . . She hardly noticed which question she asked of whom. The answers came tumbling in quick succession.

The healthy ones came and went. Liza also came. There was an argument until they remembered measles could not reoccur and they let her in. Dikikh called. She hardly noticed which answers came from whom.

When everyone had gone out for dinner and she was left alone with Ulyasha she recalled how they had all laughed in the kitchen at her stupid question. So she was careful not to ask another one like it. She asked an intelligent and serious question in a grown-up tone of voice. She asked whether Aksinya was pregnant again. The girl jingled the spoon as she removed the glass and turned away.

"Dearie me! Give her a rest. She can't always be at it, Zhenya, love, not all at once. . . ." She dashed out without closing the door properly and the whole kitchen roared as though the crockery shelves had collapsed. Then after the laughter came the sound of wailing. It passed to the cleaning woman and Galim and blazed up under their touch. Then there was a rapid, heated clamouring as though some quarrel was turning into a fight. Then someone remembered the door and came to close it.

She should not have asked that. That was even more stupid.

7

What? Could it be thawing again? Did that mean they would be going out in the carriage today again? And they still could not harness the sleigh? Zhenya stood for hours at her little window with her nose growing chill and hands shivering. Dikikh had left a short while before. This time he was displeased with her. But just you try studying when the cockerels were singing in the yards and the sky was humming with bells – and when the ringing ceased the cockerels started up their song again! The clouds were shabby and dirty like a balding sleigh-rug, and the daylight thrust its snout against the pane like a calf in its steaming stall. It might easily have been spring. But since lunch-time the air was gripped about by a hoop of livid grey frost. The sky was drained and sunken. You could hear the wheezing breath of clouds and passing hours as they strained northward to the winter twilight, breaking a last leaf from the trees, shearing lawns, cleaving fissures and rending the human chest. Gun muzzles of far northern lands loomed black beyond the houses. Loaded with a vast November, they were aimed directly at the courtyard. Yet still it was only October.

But still it was October only. They could not remember such a winter. They said the winter crops had perished and they feared a famine. It was as though someone had waved his wand around all the chimneys, roofs and nesting boxes. Here there would be smoke, here – snow, there – hoarfrost. But as yet there was still neither one nor the other. The desolate, sunken twilight pined for them. It strained its eyes. The earth ached from the early lamplight and the lights in homes, just like a headache from the yearning stare of long waiting. Everything was tense and expectant. Firewood had been brought into the kitchens. For a second week the clouds were full to overflowing with snow and the air was pregnant with darkness. But when would that magician who drew his magic circles around everything the eye could see finally pronounce his incantation and summon up the winter whose spirit was already at the door?

But how they had neglected it! Certainly, they had paid no attention to the calendar in the classroom. They had torn off her own nursery calendar. But still . . . the twenty-ninth of August! "Clever!" Seryozha would have said. A red-letter day: the Beheading of John the Baptist. It was easy to take down from the nail, and with nothing better to do she employed herself tearing off the sheets. Then she got bored with the operation and soon failed to notice what she was doing. From time to time, though, she kept repeating to herself, "The thirtieth. Tomorrow is the thirty-first."

"This is the third day she hasn't been out of the house!" The words from the corridor woke her from her reverie and she saw how far she had got with her work. Even past the Presentation of the Virgin. Mama touched her on the hand.

"Zhenya, come, tell me now . . ." The rest was lost, as though unspoken. She interrupted her mother and as if in a dream she asked Madame Luvers to say the words "Beheading of John the Baptist." Her mother repeated it, puzzled. She did not say "Babtist". That was how Aksinya said it.

But the very next minute Zhenya was filled with amazement at herself. How could she? What had prompted her? Where did it come from? Was it she, Zhenya, who had asked? Or could she have imagined that Mama . . . ? How fantastic and unreal! Whose invention was it?

But Mama just stood there. She could not believe her ears and looked at her with eyes wide open. Zhenya's sudden caprice had nonplussed

her. The question sounded like some mockery, yet there were tears in her daughter's eyes.

Her vague premonitions came true. On their drive she clearly heard the air grow flaccid, clouds fall limp, and the clop of the horseshoes getting softer. They had not yet lit the lamps when small, dry, grey flocks began twirling and meandering in the air. But they had not had time to go beyond the bridge when separate snowflakes ceased, and a solid, fused coagulum came heaving down. Davletsha climbed down from the coach box and erected the hood. Zhenya and Seryozha found it dark and cramped. They wanted to rave like the foul weather that raged about them. They perceived Davletsha was taking them home only because they heard the bridge again beneath Vykormysh's hooves. The streets became unrecognisable. There were simply no streets left. Night fell immediately and the maddened town began to twitch its countless thousands of thick, pallid lips. Seryozha leaned out and propping himself on his knee gave instructions to take them to the artisans' quarter. Zhenya was speechless with ecstasy as she learned all the secrets and splendours of winter from the way that Seryozha's words carried. Davletsha shouted back that they would have to go home so as not to wear out the horse. The master and mistress were going to the theatre, and he would have to harness the sleigh. Zhenya remembered that their parents were going out and they would be left alone. She decided to settle down by the lamp till late at night with that book called *Tales of Purring Puss*,[4] which was not meant for children. She would have to fetch it from Mama's bedroom. And she would read and suck a chocolate and listen to the sound of snow as it covered the streets.

Even now the snow was already heaving down. The heavens quivered and entire white kingdoms and countries came crashing earthwards. They were countless, mysterious and dreadful. It was clear that these lands falling from goodness knows where had never heard of life and of the earth – coming blind from the northern darkness, they covered it over without ever seeing or knowing it was there. And they were ravishingly dreadful, those kingdoms – quite satanically entrancing. Zhenya was breathless as she looked at them. The air staggered and seized at what it could, and far, far away, painfully – oh, so painfully – a plaint was raised by the fields which seemed as if flayed by whiplashes. Everything was confused. The night rushed at them, infuriated by the low-swept grey hair that flogged and blinded it. Everything was scattered,

shrieking, and unable to discern the road. Call and answering cry were lost – they never met, they perished, borne by a whirlwind to different rooftops. Swirling snow upon snow.

For a long time they tramped in the hall, knocking the snow from their swollen white sheepskin coats. And how much water ran from their galoshes on to the chequered linoleum! On the table were many egg-shells, the pepperpot had been taken from the chest and not been replaced, and a lot of pepper was scattered all over the tablecloth, the running egg yolks and half-eaten can of "sardardines". Their parents had already had supper but still sat in the dining-room and hustled the dawdling children. They were not cross with them, they had dined earlier in readiness for the theatre. Mama hesitated, not knowing whether to go or not. She sat there looking sorrowful. At the sight of her Zhenya remembered that actually she too was not at all cheerful. She had finally managed to undo that horrible hook, but she was rather sad and when she came into the dining-room she asked where they had put the nutcake. Father glanced at their mother and said that no one was forcing them to go, so it would be better to stay at home.

"No. Why? Let's go," their mother said. "I need some diversion, and the doctor has allowed it."

"We have to decide."

"Where is the cake?" Zhenya chimed in again and was told that the cake wouldn't run away, there was something else to eat before the cake, you didn't begin with cake, and it was in the cupboard – as if she had only just arrived in the house and didn't know the rules! . . .

. . . That was what her father said, and he turned to mother again and repeated: "We have to decide."

"I *have* decided. We are going." And with a rueful smile at Zhenya, her mother went away to dress.

Seryozha tapped his egg carefully with a spoon so as not to miss, and he warned Father in a businesslike preoccupied voice that the weather had changed. There was a blizzard, he ought to bear that in mind. Then he burst out laughing. Something peculiar was happening to his nose as it thawed out. He began to fidget and took a handkerchief from the pocket in the tight-fitting trousers of his uniform. He blew his nose as father had taught him – "without damaging the eardrums". Then all rosy and washed from the drive, he took his spoon again and glanced straight at Father. "When we were out we saw Negaraat's friend," he said. "Do you know him?"

"Evans?" Father inquired distractedly.

"We don't know *him!*" blurted Zhenya hotly.

"Vika!" a voice came from the bedroom.

Father got up and went out. In the doorway Zhenya collided with Ulyasha who was bringing in a lighted lamp. Soon the next door along banged. That was Seryozha going to his room. He had been splendid today. His sister loved it when the friend of the Akhmedyanovs became a little boy again, and when you were allowed to comment on his nice school uniform.

Doors opened and shut. There was a stamping of overshoes. Then at last the master and mistress left.

Ulyana's letter stated that up to now she had "not ever been one bit stupid," and that they must ask for what ever they wanted, as before. But when "dear sissy" had been sent off festooned with memorised greetings and declarations to be distributed to all her relatives, Ulyasha (who this time referred to herself as Ulyana) thanked the young mistress, turned down the lamp, and went off with the letter and her ink-bottle and remaining sheets of greasy writing paper.

After that Zhenya returned to her task. She did not enclose the figures in brackets, and instead continued the divisions, writing out one recurring set after another. No end seemed in sight. The fraction in the quotient grew and grew. "But what if measles *can* occur again?" The idea flashed through her mind. "Today Dikikh said something about infinity. She was no longer aware what she was doing. She had a feeling that something similar had happened this afternoon and she had felt like sleeping or weeping. But she could not think when it had been and what it was. She had not the energy to think. The noise outside was dying down. The blizzard was gradually abating. Decimal fractions were a complete novelty to her. There was not enough margin on the right. So she decided to begin again and write smaller, checking each stage. It became completely quiet out in the street. She was afraid she would forget what she had borrowed from the next figure and would be unable to retain the product in her head. "The window will wait," she thought, continuing to pour threes and sevens into that bottomless quotient. "I'll hear them in time – it's quiet all around – they won't be up here quickly. They are wearing fur coats and Mama is pregnant. But the point is this: 3773 keeps recurring. Can I simply write it out again or shall I round it off?" Suddenly she recalled that Dikikh had actually told her today that "You shouldn't work them out, but simply throw them away." She got up and went over to the window.

Now it was clear outside. Rare snowflakes came drifting from the blackness. They floated to the streetlight, swam around it, then flipped and disappeared from sight. New flakes drifted down in their place. The street shone, all spread with a snowy sleigh carpet. It was white, glittering and sweet, like gingerbread in fairy tales. Zhenya stood a while at the window, lost in admiration at the loops and figures traced about the lamp by those silvery flakes straight from Hans Andersen. She stood awhile, then went into Mama's room for "Puss". She went in without a light. You could see just the same. The roof of the coach-house bathed the room in a shifting, glistening light. Under the sighs of that enormous roof the beds turned to ice and glinted. Smoky silk lay scattered in disorder. Tiny blouses gave off the stuffy, oppressive odour of armpits and calico. There was a smell of violets and the cupboard was bluish black, like the night outside and like the warm dry darkness in which these freezing sparkles moved. The metallic knob of a bedstead glittered like a lonely bead. The other was extinguished by the nightdress thrown over it. Zhenya screwed up her eyes. The bead detached itself from the floor and floated toward the wardrobe. She remembered why she had come. Carrying the book, she went over to one of the bedroom windows. It was a starry night. Winter had come to Ekaterinburg. She glanced out into the yard and began thinking of Pushkin. She decided to ask the tutor to set her an essay on Onegin.[5]

Seryozha wanted to chat. "Have you been putting perfume on?" he asked. "Let me try it."

He had been very nice all day. Very rosy-cheeked. But she thought there might not be another evening like this. She wanted to be alone.

Zhenya returned to her room and took up the *Tales*. She read one story and with bated breath started on another. She became absorbed and never heard through the wall when her brother turned in. A strange look began to play across her features. She herself was unaware of it. Her face spread in a fishlike expression – her lip hung and her deathly pupils were riveted to the page in terror. She refused to look up, fearing to discover the same thing lurking there behind the chest of drawers. Then she would suddenly start nodding in sympathy at the print, as though she were approving it like someone applauding or rejoicing at the turn of events. She lingered over the descriptions of lakes and rushed headlong into the night scenes holding a scorching chunk of Bengal fire to provide them with light. In one passage a man who was lost kept shouting and listening for an answer, but he heard only his own echo in reply. Zhenya was forced to clear her throat with the soundless straining of her larynx. The un-Russian name of "Mirra"

196

brought her out of her stupor. She laid the book aside and was lost in thought. "So this is what winters are like in Asia! What can the Chinamen be doing on a dark night like this?" Her glance fell on the clock. "How awful it must be to be with those Chinese people in this darkness!" Zhenya looked again at the clock and was horrified. Her parents might appear at any moment. It was already past eleven. She unlaced her bootees and remembered she had to put the book back in its place.

Zhenya jumped up. She sat down on the bed, her eyes staring. It was not a burglar. There were lots of people, and they were stamping and talking as loudly as in daytime. Suddenly a woman screamed with all her force as though she had been knifed. Then chairs were overturned as something was dragged across the floor. Little by little Zhenya recognised them all – all, that is, except the woman. There was an unbelievable scampering to and fro. Doors started banging, and when one of them slammed in the distance it seemed as though they were gagging the woman's mouth. But it opened again and the house was scalded by a burning, flailing scream. Zhenya's hair stood on end. That woman was her mother – she had *guessed*! Ulyasha was wailing, and though she once caught the sound of her father's voice she did not hear it again. Seryozha was thrust into some room and kept on howling. "Don't you dare lock it! . . . We're all part of the family! . . ." Zhenya rushed out into the corridor just as she was, barefoot and in only her nightie. Father almost bowled her over. He was still in his overcoat and as he ran past he shouted something to Ulyasha.

"Papa!"

She saw him rush back from the bathroom with a marble jug.

"Papa!"

"Where's Lipa?" Father ran past shouting in a voice quite unlike his own.

Splashing water on the floor, he disappeared through the door. And when he came out a moment later in his shirt-sleeves and without a jacket, Zhenya found herself in Ulyasha's arms and failed to hear what she said in her despairingly deep, heartrending whisper.

"What's the matter with Mama?"

By way of reply, Ulyasha simply kept repeating. "There, there, you mustn't, Zhenya dear. You mustn't, my dear. Go to sleep, cover yourself up, lie on your side. A-a-ah! Oh Lord! . . . Dearie! There, there, you

197

mustn't . . ." she kept on saying, covering her up like an infant and turning to go.

"You mustn't, you mustn't. . . ." But what exactly she mustn't do Ulyasha never said. Her face was wet and her hair dishevelled. A lock clicked as the third door closed behind her.

Zhenya lit a match to see whether it would soon be dawn. It was only just after midnight. She was very surprised. Had she really slept less than an hour? But the noise in her parents' quarters had not died down. The howls came bursting, hatching forth in salvoes. Then for a short moment there was a broad and age-long silence, and in the midst of it – hurried footsteps and cautious rapid speech. Then there was a ring, and then another. Then the words, discussions and instructions became so many, it seemed as if the rooms were burning with voices – like tables lit with a thousand candelabra. Zhenya fell asleep. She fell asleep in tears, and she dreamed that they had guests. She counted them and kept getting the number wrong. Each time she came out with one too many. And each time she was seized by the same dread at her mistake as at the instant she realised the voice was not someone else's but that of her Mama.

How could one fail to rejoice at that pure, clear morning? Seryozha had a vision of games out there, snowball fights with the children in the yard. Tea was served to them in the classroom. The floor-polishers were in the dining-room, they were told. Father came in. It was immediately apparent that he knew nothing of any floor-polishers. And it was true. He told them the real reason for the rearrangements. Mama had been taken ill. She needed quiet.

Crows flew by above the street's white shroud and their caws resounded broadly. A sleigh ran past, urging on the horse that pulled it. The animal was not yet used to the new harness and kept missing its step.

"You are going to the Defendovs. I have already made arrangement. And you . . ."

"Why?" Zhenya interrupted.

But Seryozha had already guessed why and answered before his father could explain.

"So as not to get infected," he told her.

But something outside prevented him from finishing. He ran to the window as though beckoned there. The Tatar boy in his new rig was elegant and handsome as a cock pheasant. He wore a sheepskin hat and his raw sheepskin coat blazed brighter than morocco leather. He walked with a roll and a swing, probably because the crimson trimming on his white felt boots knew nothing about the structure of the human foot – the patterns roamed so freely, they cared little whether it was feet, teacups or porch roofing that they covered. But most remarkable of all . . . At that moment the feeble moaning from the bedroom grew louder and father went out into the passage, forbidding them to follow. But most remarkable of all were the tracks he had left stretching in a clean, narrow thread across the smoothened field. Thanks to that trail, so sculptured and neat, the snow seemed even whiter – even more like satin.

"Here is a note. You'll give it to Mr Defendov. To him in person. Do you understand? . . . Very well, get dressed. They'll bring your things right away. Go out by the back door . . . And the Akhmedyanovs are expecting you."

"Really, actually *expecting* me?" Seryozha asked mockiingly.

"Yes. You can put your coats on in the kitchen."

He spoke distractedly and went with them unhurriedly to the kitchen, where their sheepskins, hats and mittens lay heaped on a stool. There was a wintry blast of air from the staircase. "Eyeeokh!" – the frozen shrill of passing sleighs stayed hanging in the air. In the rush to dress they could not get their hands into the sleeves. And their coats gave off an odour of trunks and sleepy fur.

"What are you fussing about for?"

"Don't put it at the edge. It'll go and fall. Well?"

"She's still groaning." The maid gathered up her apron, bent over, and threw some logs into the kitchen range with its gasping flame. "Anyway, it's not my business," she said indignantly and went back into the house.

Yellow prescriptions and broken glass were lying there in a battered black bucket. And there were towels impregnated with tousled, crumpled blood. They were ablaze with it – you almost wanted to stamp on them like a puffing, smouldering fire. There was water boiling in saucepans, and all around stood white bowls and mortars of unimagined shape, like in a pharmacy.

Out in the entrance little Galim was cracking ice.

"Is there much left after the summer?" Seryozha inquired.

"There'll be some new ice soon," he said.

"Give it here. There's no point in your crunching it up."

"Why no point? They need it crushed! For these bottles."

"Well, are you ready, Zhenya?"

199

But Zhenya ran back in again. Seryozha came out on to the steps and began drumming with a log against the iron railing as he waited for his sister.

8

They were sitting down for supper at the Defendovs. Grandmother crossed herself and flopped into an armchair. The lamp burned dimly and kept smoking. At one moment it was turned down too far, and the next they turned it too high. Mr Defendov's dry hand kept reaching for the screw. And as he slowly withdrew it from the lamp and settled in his seat, his hand quivered minutely – not like an old man's, but as though he were lifting a glass filled to the brim, and his fingers trembled at the tips.

He spoke in a distinct and even voice. And his speech seemed not to be composed of sounds. It was as if he were setting up each letter and pronouncing everything including every silent "h".

The bulbous neck of the lamp flared, edged about with tendrils of geranium and heliotrope. Cockroaches ran and congregated by the glowing glass, and the clock-hands stretched out cautiously. Time moved at a hibernal crawl. Here it gathered festering. Out in the yard it was numb and malodorous. And just outside the window it scuttled and scurried, doubling and trebling in the gleaming lights.

Mrs Defendova set some liver on the table. The dish was seasoned with onion and it vapoured. Mr Defendov was saying something and kept repeating the words "I recommend. . . ." And Liza chattered without pause. But Zhenya did not hear them. Ever since yesterday she felt like weeping. And now as she sat there in her cardigan, knitted to Mama's instructions, she really longed to burst out in tears.

Defendov realised what was the matter. He tried to amuse her. But at one moment he addressed her as if she were an infant, and at the next he went to the opposite extreme. His joking questions scared and confused her. In the darkness he kept groping the soul of his daughter's friend, as though he were asking her heart how old it was. And when he thought he had caught one of Zhenya's traits *unmistakeably*, he intended to work on it and try to help her forget about home. And by his probings he only reminded her that she was among strangers.

Suddenly she could stand no more. She got up with childish embarrassment and murmured, "Thank you. I've really had sufficient. May I go and look at some pictures?" She blushed deeply as she saw their general puzzlement. "Walter Scott? . . . may I go and look?" she added with a nod toward the next room.

"Off you go, off you go, my dear!" Grandmother mammered, and riveted Liza to her place with her eyebrows.

"Poor child!" she said, addressing her son as Zhenya disappeared and the two halves of the maroon door drape closed behind her.

The bookcase was bowed down by a forbidding set of *The Northern Magazine* and below it was the dingy gold of Karamzin's complete works.[6] A rose-coloured lamp hung from the ceiling, leaving a couple of frayed armchairs unlighted. And the rug was lost in total darkness and came as a surprise to her feet.

Zhenya had imagined she would go in and sit down and burst into sobs. But the tears welled in her eyes and still could not break the resistance of her sorrow. How could she ever throw off that anguish which had pressed upon her like a beam ever since yesterday? No tears came to console it. They were powerless to breach the dam. In order to try and assist them she began thinking of her mother, and for the first time in her life, as she prepared to spend the night in a strange house she was able to measure the depth of her attachment to that dear, that most precious person in the world.

Suddenly she heard Liza's loud laughter behind the door drape.

"Oooh, what a fidget! What a little imp you are!" quavered Grandma with a cough.

Zhenya was amazed that at one time she imagined she was fond of that girl whose remote, unwelcome laughter rang out next to her. Then something inside her turned over and the tears were released. And at the same instant in her memories Mama reappeared – she seemed to be suffering and left standing in the chain of yesterday's events like one of a crowd seeing her off, and she was left spinning back there by the train of time that bore Zhenya away. But utterly, utterly unbearable was the penetrating glance Madame Luvers had fixed on her yesterday in the classroom. It was carved deep in her memory and would not go. Everything that Zhenya now felt was bound up with it, as though it were something that should have been taken up and treasured but instead had been forgotten and ignored.

The sensation was enough to drive her mad – its drunken, crazy, inescapable bitterness spun her giddily. She stood by the window and wept silently. The tears flowed and she did not bother to wipe them away. Her hands and arms were occupied, although she was not holding anything. Something caused them to straighten with a vehement, impulsive obstinacy.

A sudden thought dawned on her. She suddenly felt that she was *terribly* like Mama. And this feeling combined with a sense of vivid certainty which would have turned conjecture into fact (if the latter were not yet established) and would have made her like her mother by mere dint of the astonishing, sweet condition she found herself in. The sensation was a piercing one, sharp enough to make her groan. *It was the inner sensation of a woman perceiving from within her own outward appearance and her charm.* Zhenya could not appreciate what it was. She was experiencing it for the first time. But in one thing she was not mistaken. This was just how Madame Luvers had been that time when she stood by the window and turned away in agitation from both her daughter and the governess, biting her lip and tapping her lorgnette against a kid-gloved palm.

Zhenya went back to rejoin the Defendovs, drunk with tears and with a bright serenity. And she entered the room walking not as before but changed in some way, with a bearing that was broad and new and dreamily uncoordinated. As he saw her come in, Mr Defendov sensed that the impression he had formed of the girl in her absence was totally mistaken. And had it not been for the samovar, he would have set about trying to form a different impression.

Mrs Defendova went into the kitchen for the tray she had left on the floor. Everybody's gaze fixed on the panting copper, as though it were a live thing whose mischievous tricks had ended only when it was transferred to the table. Zhenya resumed her seat. She decided to talk to everyone, and she was vaguely aware that the choice of conversation was hers. Otherwise they would only reinforce her loneliness without realising that Mama was actually there both beside her and in her. And such shortsightedness would have caused pain both to her and, more important, to her Mama. And as though encouraged by *her*, she turned to Madame Defendova who had set the samovar down heavily on the end of the tray. "Vassa Vasilyevna," she began. . . .

"Can you have babies too?"

Liza did not answer Zhenya immediately.

"Shhh! Quiet, don't shout! Of course I can. All girls can." She spoke in a whispered burst.

Zhenya could not see her friend's face. Liza was groping round the table trying to find the matches.

She knew much more than Zhenya about such things. She knew *everything*, in the way that children do who hear it from other people. But in such cases all human nature admired of its Creator rises in revolt and is outraged. It cannot survive that ordeal without some pathological excess. It would be unnatural if it were not so, and childish manias at such times are merely a sign that deep down all is well.

Liza had once had a lot of horrors and filth whispered to her in a corner. She did not choke on what she heard and in her mind she carried it away along the street and brought it home. She dropped nothing of what she had heard on the way and she kept all that rubbish preserved. She had found out everything. And her organism did not blaze up, her heart sounded no alarm, and her soul inflicted no blows on her mind for having dared to find out something without permission, and for discovering something on the side instead of from her soul's own lips.

"I know." ("You know nothing," Liza thought) "I know," said Zhenya again. "That's not what I'm asking about. What I mean is do you ever feel that you might suddenly go and have a baby, like . . ."

"Come in here!" said Liza hoarsely and stifling her laughter. "A fine place you've picked to yell! They can hear you from the doorway!"

The conversation took place in Liza's room. Liza was speaking so quietly one could even hear water dripping in the washbowl. She had found the matches now. But she delayed lighting one and was still unable to put on a serious face. She did not wish to offend her chum. And she spared her ignorance because she never suspected one could tell her about it without using expressions that could never be spoken here at home in front of someone who did not go to school. She lit the lamp. Luckily the pail was full to the brim and Liza hurried to wipe the floor and conceal a fresh fit of laughter in her apron and the slopping floorcloth. Finally, though, she burst out laughing openly. She had found an excuse: her comb had fallen into the bucket.

All those days she was aware only of thinking about her family and waiting for them to send for her. Meanwhile in the afternoons, when Liza went off to the *lycée* and only grandmother was left at home, Zhenya also dressed up and went out for a walk alone.

Life in the suburb was very unlike where the Luvers lived. Most of the day it was bare and dull. There was nowhere for the eye to disport itself. Whatever it lighted on was good for nothing except perhaps a birch rod

203

or a broom. There was coal lying around, and blackened slops were poured out into the street and immediately turned white as they froze. At certain hours the street was filled with common folk. Factory workers swarmed like cockroaches across the snow. The swing doors of tearooms opened and shut and soapy steam came billowing out as from a laundry. Strangely, it seemed to be getting warmer in the street with spring coming round again as laundered shirts ran along stooping and glimpses of felt boots were seen worn over flimsy footcloths. The pigeons were not afraid of these crowds. They flew out into the road when food was to be had. Millet, oats and droppings were scattered on the snow in plenty. . . . The pie-woman's stall was shiny with warmth and fat, and the gloss and glow disappeared into mouths rinsed with raw brandy. The fat hotted up their throats and farther along the way it escaped from rapidly panting chests. Was it perhaps this which had warmed up the street?

And just as suddenly the street emptied. Twilight descended. Empty sleds ran past, and low, wide sleighs with bearded men engulfed in fur coats that mischievously rolled them on their backs and clasped them in a bear hug. In the road behind them nostalgic wisps of hay remained together with the slow, sweet melting of receding sleigh bells. The merchants disappeared around the turn, behind the birches which from here resembled a rickety stockade. It was here that the crows gathered which cawed expansively as they passed above the house. Only here there was no cawing. Here they only raised a shout and drew up their wings as they hopped and perched along the fences. Then suddenly, as though on a signal, they rushed in a cloud towards the trees and jostled as they spread themselves about the empty branches. One could sense how very, very late it was across the whole wide earth. So late, so very late, that no clock could ever register.

And so one week went by, and toward the end of the second, on the Thursday at dawn, she saw him again. Liza's bed was empty. As Zhenya woke, she heard the wicket gate close behind her with a clatter. She got up and without lighting the lamp went over to the window. It was still completely dark. But in the sky, in tree-branches and the movement of dogs one could sense the same heaviness as yesterday. It was the third day of this sullen weather and it could no more be dragged from the crumbling street than a cast-iron kettle from some knotted floorboard.

In a small window across the way a lamp was burning. Two bright stripes fell beneath a horse and settled on its shaggy pasterns. Shadows moved across the snow. The sleeves of a phantom moved as it wrapped a fur coat around itself. The light moved in the curtained window. But the little horse stood motionless and dreaming.

Then she saw him. She recognised him immediately by his silhouette. The lame man lifted his lamp and began to walk away with it. The two bright stripes moved after him, distending and elongating, and behind the stripes a sleigh flashed quickly into view and plunged back into the gloom even faster as it went slowly round the house towards the porch.

It was strange for Tsvetkov to keep appearing before her even here in the suburbs. But it did not surprise Zhenya. She hardly gave him a thought. Soon the lamp appeared again. It passed steadily across all the curtains and was on the point of retreating when it suddenly turned up again behind the same curtain on the windowsill from which it had been taken.

That was on Thursday. And on Friday they finally sent for her.

9

On the tenth day after returning home, when lessons were resumed after a break of more than three weeks, Zhenya learned the rest of the story from her tutor. After dinner the doctor packed up and departed, and she told him to give greetings to the house where he had examined her in spring, and to all the streets, and to the River Kama. He expressed a hope that it might no longer be necessary to summon him all the way from Perm. She went out to the gate with the man who had made her shudder so on her first morning back from the Defendovs, while Mama was still asleep and could not be visited. When she had asked what Mama's trouble was, he began by reminding her that her parents had been at the theatre that night. And at the end of the show, as people started coming out, their horse . . .

"Vykormysh?!"

"Yes, if that's his name. . . . Well, Vykormysh started struggling. He reared up and knocked down a man who happened to be passing and trampled him and . . ."

"What? To death?"

"Alas!"

"And Mama?"

"Mama had a nervous upset." He smiled and just had time to adapt his Latin *partus praematurus* for Zhenya's benefit.

"And then my little brother was born dead?!"

"Who told you? . . . That's right."

"But when? Were they there? Or was he already lifeless when they found him? No, don't tell me. Oh, how dreadful! Now I understand. He was dead already. Otherwise I would have heard him anyway. You see, I was reading till late in the night. I would have heard. But when was he alive? Doctor, do things like that really happen? I even went to the bedroom! He was dead. He must have been!"

How fortunate that what she observed from the Defendovs was only yesterday at dawn, whereas that horror at the theatre was the week before last! How fortunate that she had recognised him! She vaguely imagined that if she had not caught sight of him all that time, now, after the doctor's story, she would certainly have decided he was the cripple who was crushed to death at the theatre.

And now, after such a long visit, during which he had become quite one of the household, the doctor departed. And in the evening the tutor came. They had been laundering that afternoon and now they were mangling linen in the kitchen. The hoarfrost had melted from the frames and the garden pressed up against the windows, got entangled in the lace curtains and came right up to the table. Short bursts of rumbling from the mangle kept breaking into the conversation. Like everyone else, Dikikh also found she had changed. And she noticed a change in him.

"Why are you so sad?" she asked.

"Am I really? It may well be. I have lost a friend."

"So you have some sorrow too? So many deaths – and all so sudden!" she sighed.

But he was just about to tell her his story when something quite inexplicable occurred. She suddenly changed her ideas about how many deaths there had been. Clearly forgetting the evidence she had seen by lamplight that morning, she said anxiously, "Wait. One time you were at the tobacconist's – when Negaraat was leaving – I saw you with someone. Was that him?" She was afraid to say "Tsvetkov".

Dikikh was dumbfounded. He reflected on what she had said, and he remembered that indeed they had both gone for some paper and had asked for a complete Turgenev for Madame Luvers – and, yes, that was the dead man. She shuddered and tears came to her eyes. But the most important thing was yet to come.

With pauses in which the goffered rumbling of the mangle could be heard, Dikikh told her what sort of young man he had been and what a good family he came from. Then he lit a cigarette and Zhenya realised with horror that only this pause to inhale was delaying a repetition of the doctor's story. And when he made the attempt and uttered a few words that included the word "theatre", Zhenya screamed in a voice quite unlike her own and rushed out of the room.

Dikikh listened. Apart from the noise of the mangling there was not a sound in the house. He stood up and looked like a stork as he stretched his neck and raised one foot, ready to fly to her aid. Deciding nobody was at home and that she must have fainted, he rushed to look for her. But all the time he was bumping in the dark into puzzling things made of wood, wool and metal, Zhenya was sitting in a corner weeping. But he continued to rummage and grope and in his thoughts was already picking her up from the carpet in a dead faint. He shuddered when a voice sounded loudly at his elbow. "I'm here," she said amid whimpers. "Be careful, there's the cabinet. Wait for me in the classroom. I'll come in a moment."

The curtains reached down to the floor. And outside the window a starry night also hung down to the ground and low down, waist-deep in snow drifts, two thick dark trees rambled into the clear light of the window, trailing the glittering chains of their branches through the deep snow. And somewhere through the wall, tightly constricted by sheets, the firm rumbling of the mangle still went up and down. "What is the cause of this excessive sensitivity?" the tutor wondered. Evidently the dead man meant something special to the girl. She had changed greatly. He had been explaining recurring decimals to a child. But the person who had just sent him back into the classroom. . . . And all in the space of one month! Obviously at some time the dead man must have made a specially deep, indelible impression on this little woman. There was a name for impressions of that sort. How strange! There he was, giving her lessons every other day, and he had noticed nothing. She was an awfully nice girl and he was fearfully sorry for her. But when was she going to stop weeping and reappear? Everyone else must be out. With all his heart he was sorry for her. But what a wonderful night!

He was mistaken. The impression he imagined did not at all fit the facts. But he was right in that the basic underlying impression was an indelible one. And its depth was greater even than he imagined. It lay beyond the girl's own control, because it was vitally important and significant. And its significance lay in the fact that this was the first time

207

another human being had entered her life – a third person, totally indifferent, with no name (or only a fortuitous one) and arousing neither love nor hate. It was the person the Commandments have in mind, addressing men with names and consciousness, when they say "Thou shalt not kill", "Thou shalt not steal", et cetera. . . . "As a living human individual," they say, "you must not do to this featureless generalised man what you would not wish for yourself as a living individual." Dikikh's greatest error lay in thinking there was a name for such impressions. They have no name.

And Zhenya wept because she believed she was to blame for everything. It was *she* who had brought him into the life of the family that day when she noticed him on the far side of someone else's garden. And having noticed him quite gratuitously without rhyme or reason, she had then begun meeting him at every step – constantly, directly or indirectly, and even, as on the last occasion, quite against all possibility.

When she saw which book Dikikh was taking from the shelf, she frowned and said, "No, I can't answer on that today. Put it back. . . . I'm sorry. Put it back, *please*."

And without another word Lermontov was returned by the same hand and replaced in the little slanting row of classics.

LETTERS FROM TULA

1

The skylarks in the open freely poured forth their song, and a suffocating sun was borne along on many striped bench seats in the train from Moscow. The sun was setting. A bridge with the inscription "Upa" sailed across a hundred carriage windows. At that same instant the stoker racing along in the tender at the head of the train discovered the town away to one side of the track, and through the roar of his own hair and the fresh excitement of the evening he saw it speeding to meet them.

Meanwhile people there greeted one another in the street.

"Good evening," they said. To which some added, "Have you just been there?"

"Just on our way," the others replied.

"You're too late," they were told. "It's all over."

"Tula, the 10th.

"So you changed then, as we agreed with the conductor. Just now the general who gave up his seat went over to the bar counter, and on his way he bowed to me, as he might to an old acquaintance. The next train to Moscow goes at three o'clock in the morning. He was saying goodbye as he left just now. The porter is opening the door for him. Out there the cabmen's clamour sounds like the sparrows from a distance. My love, that leave-taking was madness. Now the separation is ten times more painful. Now imagination has something real to work on. It will gnaw me away. Out there a horse-tram is drawing up, and they are changing the team. I shall go and look around the town. What anguish I am suffering! But I shall choke it back, this raging anguish. I shall blunt it down with verses."

"Tula.

"Alas, there is no middle road. One must leave at the second bell, or else set off together on a journey to the end, to the grave. Look, it will be dawn already when I make this entire journey in reverse – and in every detail too, in every trivial detail. And now it will all have the subtlety of some exquisite torture.

"What misery to be born a poet! What torment is imagination! The sun glints in the beer – sunk to the very bottom of the bottle. Across the table sits an agriculturist, or something of the sort. He has a ruddy face. And he stirs his coffee with a green hand. Ah, my dear, they are all strangers around me. There was one person who witnessed it all (the general), but he has gone. And there is still one more, the magistrate – but they do not recognise him. Nonentities! Why, they think it is *their* sun that they sip with milk from the saucer. They don't realise it is your sun, or ours, that their flies stick in. The kitchen boys' saucepans clash, seltzer water spatters, and roubles clatter noisily like clicking tongues on the marble tabletop. I shall go and look around the town. It has remained so far remote. There is the horse tram, but it isn't worth it. They say it is about forty minutes on foot. I have found the receipt. You were quite right: I will hardly have time tomorrow. I must catch up on my sleep. The day after tomorrow. Don't worry. It's a pawnshop. It isn't urgent. Oh, writing is mere self-torment! But I have not the strength to break off."

Five hours passed. There was a quite extraordinary stillness. It became impossible to tell where the grass ended and where the coal began. A star twinkled. Not a living soul remained by the pumphouse. Water showed black through a mouldering cavity in the moss-covered swamp. The reflection of a birch tree trembled there. It quivered feverishly. But all this was far away. Far, far away. Apart from the birch tree there was not a soul on the road.

There was a quite extraordinary stillness. Lifeless boilers and coaches lay on the flat earth like piles of low storm cloud on a windless night. Had it not been April, summer lightning might have played. But the sky was troubled. Stricken with transparency, as though with some illness, and sapped from within by spring, it was a troubled sky. The final horse-drawn coach of the Tula tramline came up from town. The reversible backrests of the seating banged. The last to alight was a man bearing letters which jutted from the broad pockets of his overcoat. And while the rest made their way into the waiting-room and headed towards a group of extremely strange young folk noisily dining at the end of the room, the man remained outside at the front of the building, searching for the green letterbox. But there was no telling where the grass ended and where the coal began. And when a tired pair of horses dragged the towing shaft across the turf, harrowing the path with its iron tip, still no dust could be seen, and only a lantern by the stables gave a dim impression of events. The night uttered a long-drawn guttural sound – then everything was silent. It was all far, far away, beyond the horizon.

"Tula, the 10th [crossed out], the 11th, one o'clock in the morning. Look it up in a textbook, my love. You have Klyuchevsky with you. I put it in the case myself. I don't know how to begin. I still understand nothing. So strange it is, so terrible. As I write to you, everything pursues its course up at the far end of the table. They behave as if they were geniuses, declaiming and hurling phrases at one another, and theatrically flinging their napkins on the table when they have wiped their clean-shaven lips. I have not said yet who they are. They are the worst of bohemians [carefully crossed out] – a cinema troupe from Moscow. They have been shooting *The Time of Troubles* in the Kremlin and in places where the ramparts were.

"Read Klyuchevsky's account.[1] I have not read it myself, but I think there must be some episode with Pyotr Bolotnikov.[2] This is what brought them to the River Upa. I find they have set the scene at the exact spot and have filmed it from the far bank. And now they have the seventeenth century stowed away in their suitcases, while the remnants linger on over the dirty table. The Polish women are horrible, and the boyars' children are even more dreadful. My dear, it sickens me! This is a display of the ideals of our age. The vapours that they give off are my own – vapours common to us all. It is the burning smell of woeful insolence and ignorance. It is my own self. My love, I have posted two letters to you. I can't recall them. But this is the vocabulary of these [deleted and nothing substituted]. This is the vocabulary they use: genius, poet, ennui, verses, mediocrity, philistinism, tragedy, woman, I and she. How dreadful to see one's own qualities in others! It is a caricature of [left incomplete].

"Two o'clock. My heart's faith is greater than ever. I swear to you, the time will come . . . no, let me tell you something first. Night, come and savage me, savage me! Everything is not over yet. Scorch me to a cinder! One word that bursts through all accumulated dross, burn, burn bright and clear – the forgotten, angry, fiery word 'Conscience'! [heavily underscored with a line that tears through the paper in places] Blaze, you furious oil-bearing tongue that lights up the darkness!

211

"A fashion has established itself in life, such that there is no place left in the world where a man can warm his soul at the fire of shame. Everywhere shame has gone damp and refuses to burn. Confusion, dissipation, falsehood everywhere. For thirty years now men of singularity both young and old have lived like this, damping down their own shame. And now it has spread to the world at large, to men obscure and unknown. Now for the first, the very first time since those distant years of childhood I am consumed with fire [all crossed out]."

Another fresh attempt. The letter remains unposted.

"How can I describe it to you? I shall have to start from the end. Otherwise nothing will come of it. And let me also tell it in the third person. I surely wrote about the man who was strolling past the luggage office counter? Well, in the disgusting behaviour of the actors and in the outrageous spectacle that exposes his fellow men and his age for what they are the poet (henceforth he is going to use this word in inverted commas, until it is purged in the fire) – the 'poet' observes himself. Perhaps he is only adopting a pose? – No, for they confirm that his identity is no illusion. They rise to their feet and approach him. 'Colleague, have you got change for three roubles?' He dispels their illusion. Actors are not the only ones who shave. There are three roubles' worth of twenty-kopeck pieces. He gets rid of the actor. But it is not a question of shaving one's moustache. 'Colleague,' the scum said. Yes indeed! And he was right! Here was a witness for the prosecution. But at this point something new occurs – a mere trifle, but one which in its way sends a shiver through all the events and all he has experienced in the waiting-room up until this moment.

"The 'poet' at last recognises the person strolling by the luggage office. He has seen that face before. Somewhere locally. He has seen it on several occasions in the course of a single day, at different times, and in different places. It was when they were assembling the special train at Astapovo,[3] with a goods waggon as hearse. Crowds of strangers had left the station in different trains, which then wheeled and crossed all day long around the unexpected turns of that tangled junction where four railroads converged and parted, returned and split again.

"In an instant, realisation dawns, weighing in on all that has so far happened to the 'poet' in the waiting-room. Acting like a lever, it sets the entire revolving stage in motion. Why? Because this is Tula! This is a night in Tula, in a place bound up with the life of Tolstoy! Is it any wonder that compass needles start to dance here? Such things are in the very nature of the place. This is an occurrence *on the territory of conscience*, in its gravitational, ore-bearing sector. Now there will be no more of the 'poet'. When he sees *The Time of Troubles* on the screen (it will be shown eventually, one imagines), he swears to you that the sequence on the River Upa will find him utterly alone – that is unless actors have reformed by then, and if all manner of dreamers can stamp around for a whole day on the mine-sown territory of the spirit and still survive with their braggadocio and ignorance intact.''

While these lines were being written, the trackmen's lamps emerged from their huts and, creeping low, moved away down the tracks. Whistles began to sound. Iron was awakening and bruised chains screamed. Coaches slipped ever so gently down the platform. They had long been sliding past and were already countless. Behind them – the swelling approach of something breathing heavily, something unknown and coming from the night. Down the jointed tracks behind the locomotive there came that sudden sweeping clear of rails, the unexpected appearance of night in the deserted platform's vision, the emergence of silence across a whole expanse of stars and signals, and the advent of a rural peace. And this moment came snoring in the rear of the freight train. Bending low beneath the covered overhang, it made its gliding approach.

While these lines were being penned, they began to couple up the passenger-freight train for Elets.

The man who had been writing went out on to the platform. Night lay spread down the whole extent of the dampened Russian conscience. It was illuminated by lanterns and crossed by rails that flexed beneath the slowly moving freight cars with their tarpaulin-covered cargo of winnowing machines. It was trampled by shadows and deafened by flocks of steam that screeched like cockerels from beneath the valves. The writer went around the station. He walked out to the front of the building.

While these lines were being written, nothing had changed in the entire space of conscience. From it rose the smells of putrefaction and of clay. Far, far away, from its farthest extremity, a birch tree gleamed and a cavity in the swamp showed up like a fallen earring. Strips of light broke from within the waiting-room and fell outside beneath the seats

213

on the floor of the horse tram. The strips of light skirmished together. The rattle of beer, stench, and madness followed them and fell in turn beneath the seats. And still, whenever the station windows faded, a crunching and snoring could be heard somewhere nearby. The man who had been writing strolled up and down. He thought of many things. He thought of his art and of how to find the right path. He forgot who he had been travelling with, who he had seen off, and who he was writing to. He supposed that everything would begin when he ceased to hear himself, and when there was a complete physical silence within his soul. Not a silence as in Ibsen, but one in the acoustic sense.

Those were his thoughts. A shiver ran through his body. The east was turning grey, and a perplexed and rapid dew settled on the face of all conscience, which was still plunged in deepest night. It was time to think about his ticket. It was cock-crow, and the ticket office was coming to life.

2

It was only then that down in the town a highly eccentric old man finally settled down to sleep in his apartment on Posolskaya Street. While those letters were being written up at the station, this apartment had quivered with soft footfalls and the candle at the window had caught a whisper broken by frequent silences. It was not the voice of the old man, although apart from him there was not a soul in the room. It was all amazingly peculiar.

The old man had spent an unusual day. He had left the meadow, saddened when he realised that this was not a play at all, and that for the moment it was merely a flight of fantasy that would only turn into a play when shown at the "Chary" Cinema. When he first saw the boyars and governors milling on the far shore, and the commoners leading in bound men and knocking off their hats into the nettles – when he saw the Poles clinging to laburnum bushes on the scarp, and their battle-axes that gave no bright ring and no response to the sunlight, the old man began to rummage through his own repertoire. But he could find no such chronicle there. He decided it must be from something before his period, Ozerov or Sumarokov.[4] It was then that they pointed out the cameraman to him, they mentioned the "Chary" – an institution he detested wholeheartedly – and they reminded him that he was old and lonely, and that times had changed. He went away, dejected.

He walked along in his old nankeens and reflected that now there was no one left in the world to call him "Savva, old boy". It was a holiday today, and it basked in the warmth of scattered sunflower seeds.

They spat their raw novelty at him through their deep chesty speech. High above, the moon crumbled like a round loaf and melted. The sky appeared cold and amazed at its own remoteness. Voices were greased by food and drink. Even the echo that mellowed across the river was steeped in saffron mushroom, rye loaf, fat, and vodka. Some of the streets were thronged. Crude flounces gave the skirts and the women-folk a special patchwork appearance.

The steppe grasses kept pace with the strollers. Dust flew up, causing eyes to squint and obscuring the burdocks that beat in whirls against the wattle fences and clung to people's dress. The walking-stick felt like a fragment of senile sclerosis, and he leaned on this extension of his knotted veins, clutching it with a cramped and gouty grip.

All day he felt as if he had been at some inordinately noisy rag fair. It was the result of that spectacle he had witnessed. It had left the old man's need for the human speech of tragedy unsatisfied, and this silent lacuna now rang in his ears.

All day he was sick at having heard not a single line of pentameter from the far bank of the river.

And when night fell, he sat down at the table, propped his head on his hand, and immersed himself in thought. He decided that this must be his death. This mental turmoil was so unlike his recent years of steady bitterness. He decided to take his decorations from the cupboard and warn someone – the janitor, at least – no matter whom – yet he still just sat, expecting that maybe it would simply pass off.

A horse tram jingled as it trotted by outside. It was the last tram to the station.

Half an hour passed. A star gleamed brightly. There was not another soul around. It was late already. The candle flamed, shivered, trembled. The softened silhouette of the bookcase stirred its four undulating strips of blackness. The night uttered a long-drawn guttural sound. Far, far away. A door banged in the street below. People started talking in low, excited tones – as befitted such a night in spring with not a soul about and only one light still burning in the open window of an upper apartment.

The old man rose. He was transformed. At last! Found! Both himself and her! They had helped him to it, and he hurried to assist their promptings. He hastened to avoid missing both of them, and to fasten

215

on and sink in them and prevent their slipping away. In a few steps he reached the door, half-closing his eyes, flourishing a hand and covering his chin with the other. He was remembering. Suddenly he stood erect and walked back briskly with a gait not his own but that of a stranger. He appeared to be acting some part.

"Well, there's a snowstorm, there's really quite a snowstorm blowing, Lyubov Petrovna," he said, and he cleared his throat and spat into his handkerchief. He began again. "Well, there's a snowstorm, there's really quite a snowstorm blowing, Lyubov Petrovna," he said, this time without coughing. Now it was more real.

He began to shake and flail his arms, as if coming in from the weather, unwrapping himself and throwing off his fur coat. He paused for some reply to come from beyond the partition. Then, as if unable to wait, he asked, "Are you at home, Lyubov Petrovna?" still in the same stranger's voice. And he gave a start when after five-and-twenty years he heard – just as he was supposed to, from behind that other partition – the beloved gay reply: "Yes, I am at home!" Then he continued again, this time most authentically and with a mastery of illusion that any colleague in such circumstances would have been proud of. As if fumbling with his tobacco and breaking his speech with sidelong glances at the partition, he drawled, "M-mm-er, sorry, Lyubov Petrovna – I don't suppose that Savva Ignatyevich is, er, here?"

It was altogether too much. He could see both of them. Her and himself. The old man was stifled with silent sobs. The time ticked by. He kept weeping and whispering. There was an extraordinary stillness. and while the old man shuddered and feebly dabbed his eyes and face with a handkerchief, trembled and crumpled it, shook his head and made dismissive waves of the hand like a person who giggles and chokes and is amazed that, God forgive him, he is still there and hasn't actually burst . . . while this was going on, on the railway track they began assembling the passenger-freight train for Elets.

For a whole hour he kept his youth preserved in tears, as though in spirits. Then, when he had no tears left, everything collapsed, everything fled and disappeared. He faded immediately and seemed to gather dust. Then, sighing, as if guilty of some wrong, and yawning, he began to get ready for bed.

Like everyone else in the story, he too shaved his moustache. And like the main character, he too was in search of physical silence. But in the

216

story he was the only one to find it, having caused another to speak through his own lips.

The train headed for Moscow, and an enormous crimson sun was borne along on the bodies of many sleeping passengers. It had just appeared from behind a hill, and it was rising.

WITHOUT LOVE

A Chapter from a Tale

He had a brother, and it was the brother who walked around the house, his feet crunching in the snow and on the frozen steps as he went up them, to knock on the door, to knock as one does on the door of a blizzard-swept house when the wind turns your fingers to ice, and, whistling and howling, roars into your ears that you should knock even louder, if you know what's good for you . . . and all the time the same wind hammers on the shutters to drown your knocking and confuse the people inside.

They heard him and opened. The house stood on a hill. The door was torn from his grasp together with one of his gloves, and, as the door flew to and fro and they tried to catch it, the grey snow-swept countryside rushed into the hall and breathed on the lamps, bringing with it the distant tinkle of a sleigh bell. The sound sank in the vast snow field and, gasping for breath, called to the rescue. It was carried to the house by the overwhelming onrush of the blizzard, which had gripped the door in its clutches, and by the dips in the sleigh track, which had been caught up in some demoniac movement and was slithering under the runners, throwing up swirling columns of choking snow for all to see for miles around.

When the door had been caught and shut, they all got up to meet the spectre in the hall; in his high boots of reindeer skin he was like a wild animal standing on its hind legs.

"Is it coming?" Kovalevsky asked.

"Yes, they're on the way. You must get ready." He licked his lips and wiped his nose. There was pandemonium as bundles and baskets were brought out; the children had sulked since nightfall (till then, for want of something better to do and on learning that everything was packed, and that there would still be a long wait and nothing to talk about, they had pointlessly weighed out raisins on the bare table) and now they set up a great wail, putting the blame on each other ("It's not me; it's Petya who's howling because Papa's going away.") and, seeking fair play and a refuge from the night, the raisins, the blizzard, the chaos, their papas about to depart, the travelling baskets, the oil lamps, and the fur coats, they tried to bury their heads in their mothers' aprons.

But instead they were snatched up, as though on a signal, by their nurses and mothers and carried with a sudden gust of feeling into the passage, and in the hall, which echoed the voices of the coachmen through the folding door, they were held up to their fathers. They all stood bareheaded and, crossing themselves with emotion, exchanged hurried kisses and said it was time to go.

Meanwhile the Tatar coachmen (they were three in number, but there seemed to be ten), carrying lights that splashed the snow without spilling into it altogether, dashed up to the horses harnessed in file and, ducking down to look at the girths and fetlocks, jumped up again at once and began to race around like madmen, brandishing their flares and lighting up in turn the trunks standing around the sleigh, the snow, the underbellies and flanks of the horses, and their muzzles, which together formed a slender garland, borne aloft, as it seemed, by the wind. The moment of departure depended on the Tatars. Round about the snow sang in the forest and raved in the open country, and it seemed as though the surging sound of the night knew Tatar and was arguing with Mininbay, who had climbed onto the roof of the sleigh, and, clutching at his hands, was telling him to fasten down the trunks not in the way Gimazetdin was shouting, nor in the way suggested by Galliula, who was hardly able to keep his feet because of the storm and had gone quite hoarse. . . . The moment of departure depended on the Tatars. They could hardly wait to take up their whips, whistle at the horses, and abandon themselves to the final devil-may-care *ayda!*[1] After this no power on earth would hold the horses back. Like drunkards to the bottle, the Tatars were drawn irresistibly, more and more eagerly with each passing minute, to the mournful whoops and cajolery of their trade. Hence the feverish movements of their frenzied alcoholic hands as they rushed to help their masters into their heavy fur coats.

And now the flares sent a last farewell kiss to those who were being left behind. Goltsev had already stumbled into the depths of the sleigh, and Kovalevsky, floundering in the tails of his three coats, climbed after him under the heavy travelling rug. Unable to feel the floor through their broad felt boots, they nestled down in the straw, the cushions, and the sheepskins. A flare appeared on the far side of the sleigh but suddenly bobbed down out of sight.

The sleigh shuddered and heaved. It slithered forward, lurched over, and began to turn on its side. A low whistle came from the depths of an

220

Asian soul, and after righting the sleigh with their shoulders, Mininbay and Gimazetdin leaped into their seats. The sleigh shot forward as though borne on wings and plunged into the nearby forest. The open country, dishevelled and moaning, rose up behind it. It was glad to see the end of the sleigh, which disappeared without a trace among the trees with branches like carpet slippers, at the junction with the main road to Chistopol and Kazan. Mininbay got off here and, wishing his master a good journey, vanished in the storm like a flurry of powdered snow. They sped on and on over the arrow-straight highway.

"I asked her to come here with me," one of them thought, breathing in the dampness of thawing fur. "I remember how it was." A lot of streetcars had got stuck in front of the theatre, and an anxious crowd was milling around the first one . . . "The performance has begun," the usher said in a confidential whisper and, grey in his cloth uniform, he drew back the cloth curtain separating the stalls from the lighted cloakroom with its benches, galoshes, and posters. In the intermission (it went on longer than usual), they walked around the foyer, peering sideways at the mirrors, and neither of them knew what to do with their hands, which were hot and red. "So there now; thinking it all over," she took a sip of seltzer water, "I just don't know what to do or how I should decide. So please don't be surprised if you hear that I've gone to the front as a nurse. I shall enrol in a few days' time . . ." – "Why don't you come with me to the Kama River?" he said. She laughed.

The intermission had gone on so long because of the musical item at the beginning of the second act. It could not be played without an oboe, and the oboist was the unfortunate cause of the street car stoppage in front of the theatre. "He's badly hurt," people whispered to each other, taking their places when the painted hem of the curtain began to glow.

"He was unconscious when the pulled him from under the wheels," their friends told them as they padded over the cloth-covered carpet in heavy galoshes, trailing the ends of kerchiefs and shawls.

"And now they'll be surprised," he thought, trying to synchronise the flow of his thoughts with the movement of the sleigh and lull himself to sleep.

The other man was thinking about the purpose of their sudden departure, about the reception awaiting them at their destination, and about what should be done first. He also thought that Goltsev was asleep, not suspecting that Goltsev was wide awake and that it was he himself who was asleep, plunging in his dreams from pothole to pothole together with his thoughts about revolution, which now, as once before, meant more to him than his fur coat and his other belongings, more than his wife and child, more than his own life, and more than other people's lives, and with which he would not part for anything in the world – even in his sleep – once he had laid hold of them and kindled them within himself.

Their eyes opened languidly, of their own accord. They could not help their surprise. A village lay in a deep otherworldly trance. The snow glittered. The three horses had broken file, they had left the road and stood huddled together. The night was bright and still. The lead horse, its head raised, was gazing over a snowdrift at something left far behind. The moon shone black and mysterious behind a house tightly swathed in frosty air. After the solemnity of the forest and the blizzard-swept loneliness of the open country, a human dwelling was like an apparition in a fairy tale. The house seemed conscious of its awesome magic and was in no hurry to answer the coachman's knock. It stood silent, unwilling to break its own oppressive spell. The snow glittered. But soon two voices, unseen to each other, spoke loudly through the gate. They divided the whole world between them, these two, as they talked to each other through the timbers, in the midst of infinite still-ness. The man who was opening the gate took the half that looked north, unfolding beyond the roof of the house, and the other man, who was waiting for him, took the half the horse could see over the edge of the snowdrift.

At the previous station, Gimazetdin had wakened only Kovalevsky, and the coachman who had driven them to this point was a stranger to Goltsev. But now he immediately recognised Dementii Mekhanoshin, to whom he had once issued a certificate in his office – a good sixty miles from here – to the effect that, being the owner of a troika and plying the last stage between Bilyar and Syuginsk, he was working for defence.

It was odd to think that he had certified this house and its coach yard and that, knowing nothing at all of them, he had underwritten this magic village and the starry night above it. Later, while the horses were being reharnessed and the sleepy wife of the coachman gave them tea; while the clock ticked and they tried to make conversation, and bugs crawled sultrily over calendars and portraits of crowned persons; while bodies sleeping on the benches snored and wheezed fitfully like clock-work devices of different systems, Dementii kept going out and return-ing, and each time his appearance changed, depending on what he had taken down from a nail or dragged from under his bed. When he came in the first time to tell his wife to give the gentlemen sugar and to get out the white bread for them, he was wearing a smock and looked like a hospitable peasant; the second time, coming for the reins, he was a labourer dressed in a short Siberian jacket; and finally he appeared as a coachman in a heavy fur coat. Without coming in, he leaned through the doorway and said that the horses were ready, that it was past three in the morning and time for them to leave. Then, pushing open the door with the stock of his whip, he went into the dark world outside, which reverberated loudly at his first steps.

The rest of the journey left no trace in their memories. It was getting light when Goltsev woke and the countryside was covered in a haze. An endless, straggling convoy of sleighs was lumbering by in a cloud of steam. They were overtaking it, and it looked therefore as though the timber-loaded sleighs were creaking and swaying without moving forward and that the drivers were just marking time, stomping their feet on the ground to keep warm. The broad cart road ran to one side of the track over which they were racing, and it was on a much higher level. Legs rose and fell, trampling the still lit stars, and there was a movement of hands, horses' muzzles, cowled heads, and sleighs. It seemed as though the grey and weary suburban morning was itself drifting over the clear sky in great damp patches towards the place where it sensed the railroad, the brick walls of factory buildings, heaps of damp coal, and the drudgery of fumes and smoke. The sleigh raced on, flying over ruts and potholes, its bell jingling frantically. There was still no end to the convoy, and it was high time for the sun to rise, but the sun was still far away.

The sun was still far away. They would see it only after another five versts, after a short stop at the inn, after the message from the factory manager and the long, restless wait in his anteroom.

Then it appeared. It entered the manager's office with them, flooded rapidly over the carpet, settled behind the flowerpots, and smiled at the caged chaffinches by the window, at the fir trees outside, at the stove, and at all forty-four volumes of the leather-bound Brockhaus Encyclopedia.

After this, during Kovalevsky's conversation with the manager, the yard outside was alive and at play, tirelessly scattering turquoise and amber, wafts of pungent resin from the sweating pines and beads of molten hoarfrost.

The manager glanced towards Goltsev. "He's my friend," said Kovalevsky quickly. "Don't worry, you can talk freely. . . . So you knew Breshkovskaya?"[2]

Suddenly Kovalevsky got up and, turning to Goltsev, shouted in panic, "And what about my papers? Just as I said! Kostya, now what shall I do?"

Goltsev didn't at first understand: "I've got our passports . . ."

"That bundle of papers!" Kovalevsky interrupted him angrily. "I asked you to remind me."

"Oh, I'm sorry, Yura. We left them behind. It really is too bad of me. I can't think how I . . ."

Their host, a short, thickset man who had difficulty with his breathing, attended in the meantime to his managerial business. He kept looking at his watch and, puffing and blowing, stirred the logs in the stove with a poker. Sometimes, as though changing his mind about something, he would suddenly stop in his tracks halfway across the room, swivel around, and dart over to the desk at which Kovalevsky was writing to his brother, ". . . in other words, all is well. I only hope it goes on like this. Now for the most important thing. Do exactly as I tell you. Kostya says that we left a bundle with all my illegal stuff lying on Masha's suitcase in the hall. Open it up, and if there are any manuscripts among the pamphlets (memoirs, notes on the scope of the organization, letters in code relating to the secret rendezvous in our house, to the period of Kulisher's escape, etc.), wrap it all up, seal it, and send it to me in Moscow at the office in Teploryadnaya with the first reliable person – depending of course on how things work out. But you know what to do as well as I do, and if there is a change of . . ."

"Do come and have some coffee," whispered the manager with a shuffle and a click of the heels. "I mean you, young man," he explained to Goltsev with even greater care, and he paused respectfully at the sight of Kovalevsky's cuff, which was poised over the paper, waiting to pounce on the needed word.

Three Austrian prisoners of war went past the window, talking and blowing their noses. They carefully walked around the puddles that had formed.

". . . if there is a change of climate," Kovalevsky found the word he needed, "don't send the papers to Moscow, but hide them in a safe place. I'm counting on you for this and all other things we agreed on. We have to catch the train soon. I'm dead tired. We hope to have a good sleep in the train. I'm writing to Masha separately. Well, all the best. . . . P.S.: Just imagine, it turns out that R., the manager, is an old Socialist Revolutionary. What do you make of that?"

At this moment Goltsev looked into the office with a slice of buttered bread in his hand. Swallowing the half-chewed piece he had just bitten off, he said, "You're writing to Misha, are you? Tell him to send," he took another bite at his bread and butter and continued chewing and swallowing, "my papers as well. I've changed my mind. Don't forget, Yura. And come and have some coffee."

Translated by
Max Hayward

THREE DRAMATIC FRAGMENTS

1

Paris. The apartment of Lebas.[1] The windows are wide open. It is a summer's day, and thunder can be heard in the distance. The action takes place some time between the 10th and 20th messidor (29th June and 8th July) in the year 1794.

SAINT-JUST:[2] Before us Paris lies, a changing city . . .
    What of its past and future? This broad day
    Which lights the world around, like dungeon steps
    That form the threshold of my soul, will not
    Forever be a stormy lantern flame
    That shivers worlds into a fevered order.
    This age will pass; the scorching beam will cool,
    Turn charcoal-black, and curiosity
    One day will pore by candlelight in archives
    For works which thrill and dazzle men today.
    What passes now for clarity and wisdom
    Our grandsons will regard as raving. Gloom and
    Obscurity await. Insanity
    Will claim our day, our God, all light and reason.
    The ages rush and fear to look around.
    And why? – That they might see themselves! They don
    Night's shroud, while other write their epoch's chronicle –
    Snuff out their years to read it in the gloom.
    But who has fame as guest within his soul,
    Fate guides his eye: he draws the shroud across
    His days, himself to write his age's book and
    Inscribe therein his own renown and glory.

[He now addresses Henriette, who sits sewing, and speaks more simply and animatedly]

    Then why should men consider that mere birth
    Is warranty for living? Who can prove
    This world is like some inn wherein we pay

To rest a while in freedom, comfort, warmth? . . .
When will they understand that man is nothing
Save the Creator's Sword of Damocles –
Man's soul has no abode but in a world
That he himself has snared and recreated?
But in our towns, Lyon, Bordeaux and Paris
Men crawl like crabs about the ocean bed,
Like hunted tigers louring in the reeds.
Yet reason still can shatter life's dark pane,
Tear idleness in shreds, and by its actions. . . .

HENRIETTE: You say. . . .

SAINT-JUST: I mean that action is a flash
Of ecstasy unleashed upon the years.

HENRIETTE: You go. . . .

SAINT-JUST: To lance the abscess of desires.

HENRIETTE: But when. . . .

SAINT-JUST: To bleed away impurity.

HENRIETTE: I do not understand.

SAINT-JUST: Is it so often
That Paris's linden trees applaud the thunder,
That clouds are wroth and heaven's eyes unsealed
To blink with lightning glare in showers? Yet
Here storms are rare, here silence reigns and slumber.
You are not always with me here.

HENRIETTE: Not always?
But there? . . .

SAINT-JUST: Out there? Attacks at every moment. . . .

HENRIETTE: Out there there is. . . .

SAINT-JUST: No Henriette?

HENRIETTE: None.

SAINT-JUST: Not so! Out there you're with me constantly!
Believe me, whether you are mine or no,
No matter were your love no match for mine,
But you are there! The towns, the air of battles
All breathe of Henriette and invade
My inmost heart, so none can stand between us,
'Tween you, cloud-wrapped, and my dilated breast,
Between the heavens and my troubled dreaming.
The guardian of the spirit's cause out there
Is Saint-Just – Saint George who holds at bay the dragon

Of mediocrity; in here with you
His strength's a hundredfold reduced, in here
That dragon is a hundredfold more dread.
HENRIETTE: What lance out there can probe such ulcers?
SAINT-JUST: Duty,
The soul, the urgency of my commands!
Used as I am to the consuming fire,
Accustomed as I am to leave on men
The brand-mark of my own self-immolations!
Like dark mulled wine, I love the smokeless flame
Of men intoxicated by the glow
Of flaring nerves, of men immersed in thought
Who burn like candle-wicks when dipped in oil.
At night there is no rest for me. I lie here
Dressed.
HENRIETTE: Dressed for burial!
SAINT-JUST: No rest for me
At night! There are no nights! Only the daylight
Glows dimmer now and drearer than before,
As if the sun were breathing on a window
And tracing out the hours across the pane
And staggering in the dizzy heat. For each
New day's still sicker than the last, each night
Still more bewitched; a heat-haze dusts the stubble;
The sunbeams gleam taut-stretched like skins on drums
Of military bands..................................
HENRIETTE: How close to me and how familiar
These thoughts! It's true, it's true! Yet still I sleep,
Yet still I eat and drink; I have my senses,
My sanity; the nights do not seem white;
No violet tarnish overcasts the sun.
SAINT-JUST: How can one sleep when a new world is born, when
The silent storm of one's own thoughts is raging?
For then one hears the converse of the peoples
Who use one's head to play some game or sport.
How can one sleep when one's own silent thoughts
Have set the grasses and the stars aquiver,
Disturbed the rest of birds, that all night long
Their din still rises from the sleepless thickets?
There is no night. The light still lies uncleared,

229

Forgotten, cooling; yet no sundown comes
To end this painful, long, eternal day.

2

Part of a scene on the night of the 9th to 10th thermidor, 1794.[3]
*The interior of the Hotel de Ville, Paris. Off-stage one hears the sound of
preparations for the siege, the rumble of guns being wheeled into position, people
shouting, etc. Coffinhal has just read the decree of the Convention, addressing
the audience seated in the boxes as he proclaimed the list of outlaws. The hall of
the Hotel de Ville is vacated for a moment and it echoes emptily. The first signs of
dawn are glowing on the capitals of the pillars, while the rest of the scene is
plunged in gloom. In the centre of the tiled floor stands a large office desk with a
candle burning on it. Hanriot*[4] *is lying on one of the benches in the vestibule.
Upstage Coffinhal, Lebas, Couthon,*[5] *Augustin de Robespierre*[6] *and others walk
about talking among themselves and come up to Hanriot. During the opening
scene none of their speech can be heard. Downstage Maximilien de Robespierre*[7]
*sits at the desk while Saint-Just paces up and down. Both are silent. There is an
atmosphere of alarm and stupefaction.*

ROBESPIERRE: Don't pace so restlessly, Saint-Just! I had
    A thought just then!
SAINT-JUST: Oh! I'm disturbing you?

[*Long silence*]

ROBESPIERRE: Tell me, Saint-Just, where did it all take place? –
    Versailles, October, August, the Bastille?

[*Saint-Just stops in surprise and looks at Robespierre*]

ROBESPIERRE: Well, are they there?
SAINT-JUST: I cannot hear.
ROBESPIERRE: Saint-Just,
    I asked you! I am trying to recall. –
    Did Augustin give warning to Duplay?
SAINT-JUST: I do not know.
ROBESPIERRE: You do not know.
    Then ask no questions. I cannot collect
    My thoughts. – But hark! The chimes! What hour is it? –
    I have a plan. – Why are you here? – Away!

Begone! Your presence gnaws me like a dormouse,
And I forget to think. – But still, perhaps
The hour is not too late. – Yes, wait. Please stay.
I'll find some way. – Just now I had the answer! –
Please do not go. I need you. – Curse upon it!
What torment! Who remembers? Who can tell me
What I was thinking of? – I must recall!

[*Silence. Saint-Just walks to and fro*]

ROBESPIERRE: Tread softer, lest they hear. Give me your kerchief.
SAINT-JUST: My kerchief?
ROBESPIERRE: Yes. I need you. Curse upon it!
  No, leave me! We are lost! I cannot think!
  No thoughts, a whirlwind rushes through my head!

[*Robespierre beats his forehead with his hand and hoarsely addresses the
following words to his head*]

The final hour – this foolish head refuses
To save itself! This wonder-working mind
Shies like a stubborn mare. Bring women, wine! –
What mockery! The so-called "incorrupt"
Robespierre pledged to the cause a head which now
Betrays its master to his murderers!
I dedicated time to it that others
Devote so willingly to hours of passion.
That simpleton Danton could never grasp
My schemes! He never dreamt what barricades
Of concepts I erected, fortresses
Of intellect and reason; mutiny
Of dreams he never knew, nor ecstasy
Of lofty, pure ideas in revolt!
Suppose he was a criminal – what matter?
Danton was sacrificed for me, Robespierre,
And for the honour of this brain, this mind,
The one false god I deigned to recognise.
SAINT-JUST: Robespierre, what troubles you?
ROBESPIERRE: The traitorous
  Confusion of this mind enrages me!
  I try, yet cannot think. Cold perspiration,
  Dry fog and mist are all it will produce.

My throat runs dry. My skull's an aching void,
An emptiness unvisited by thought.
No, thoughts there are! But how can I convey
Their rapid scuttling and their rat-like patter?
There goes a thought! – I chase it. – Gone! – Again
A thought! – But no! – I pounce once more – in vain!
Oh, for a second head! I'd sacrifice
The first together with its wanton thoughts!

SAINT-JUST: Do not torment yourself. Allow your thoughts
To wander. Let them roam unhindered, freed
For one last time.

ROBESPIERRE: No. For the first time! Hence
My anger. What a time to choose! Enough!
No more! My sole recourse is now to yield,
To curse this mind's betrayal and surrender.

SAINT-JUST: Permit your mind just once to roam. You asked
Where did it all occur: October, August,
And June the second. . . .

ROBESPIERRE: [interrupting, and absorbed in his own thoughts]
I remember!

SAINT-JUST: Useless!
I thought of that myself.

ROBESPIERRE: [still absorbed] For one brief instant
I had it!

SAINT-JUST: Useless! I myself have meanwhile
Explored that question – how it all occurred. . . .

ROBESPIERRE: [bitter] I beg of you! While we have been discussing. . . .
So must it be! . . .

[There is a pause in which Coffinhal, Lebas and the others leave, and the
upper stage empties except for Hanriot who still lies sleeping]

ROBESPIERRE: [hoarsely and in despair] If only. . . . Never mind,
Please do continue. You were telling me. . . .
Now all is lost. I said I would surrender.
Please finish. Pardon me. I'm overwrought. . . .

SAINT-JUST: Such words are natural: – when you compare
Me to a mouse, and your own thoughts to rats,
It's true. Your thoughts are scurrying like rats
Trapped in a blazing house. They sense the fire
And raise their snouts before the flames and sniff

The heated air; and yet, not just your brain
Is seething, but the kingdoms of the world
Within throb to the scuttling of those rats,
Those hordes of loathsome thoughts which swarm in frenzy,
Each tainted by the horrid fumes of death.
Not we alone, no, all have known the dread
Realisation. All men have endured
The numbness of their final day and hour.
Yet some, who overcame the infernal din
And brazen uproar, smiled and laid their heads
Triumphantly beneath the guillotine.
And those brief days preceding their demise
Compose the history of our republic.
For no man's end perhaps comes unexpected;
No one is visited unwarned by death.

ROBESPIERRE: [*distractedly*] Where's Augustin?

SAINT-JUST: He's with Couthon.

ROBESPIERRE: With whom?

SAINT-JUST: Couthon.

ROBESPIERRE: But that's no answer. Where's Couthon?

SAINT-JUST: Upstairs. They've gathered in the upper hall.
Now Frenchmen will no longer rack their brains
And question what the morrow holds in store.
All secrets are uncovered. All who passed
Across that square, where mysteries lay revealed
And deaths exhibited, could witness there
The course and outcome of their fates enacted.

ROBESPIERRE: Why such remorse?

SAINT-JUST: No, these are no regrets. But,
The very chronicle of the republic
Recounts the greatness of our dying days.
It seemed the very country kept some journal
Of lives beyond the grave. France was unlit by
The flickering of changing nights and days;
For worlds in revolution, the universe's
Last twilight, death's black occident were France's
Grim sentinels. They stalked our every move. . . .

June–July 1917

233

3

Dialogue

DRAMATIS PERSONAE: A CHARACTER
A POLICE OFFICIAL
LEFÈVRE

POLICE OFFICIAL: That's what we call theft.

CHARACTER: I know.

POLICE OFFICIAL: The law punishes theft.

CHARACTER: Here? Now?

POLICE OFFICIAL: Everywhere. Always.

CHARACTER: [*rushes to the window*] Where? I can't see.

POLICE OFFICIAL: [*calmly*] Stop fooling around.

CHARACTER: Property? – I've read about it. I know. I know my geography. It's not my ignorance that is to blame. It's absent-mindedness that caused it all. And habit.

POLICE OFFICIAL: Precisely. [*meaningly*] A pernicious habit.

CHARACTER: [*coolly*] You're misunderstanding me again. I had forgotten that I was abroad. [*Pause*] It was in the country. They were transporting some convicts. Actually, it all started later. You know, there's a slope that goes down to the boats. A slanting black shadow. Pitch-painted fences, canvas. . . . A crowd had collected. . . . [*sighs deeply*] I can't tell you. [*Sighs again. Pause*] You see . . . [*crumples a scrap of paper in his hand, hangs his head and examines the paper*] I expect you are puzzled by the secret of my success with your masses?

POLICE OFFICIAL: [*busy writing; absent-mindedly, and with no apparent relevance*] Yes. One can tell you're a foreigner straight away, the moment you open your mouth.

CHARACTER: I am just as puzzled as you. But the peculiarities of my pronunciation are nothing to the peculiarities . . . [*rises*]

POLICE OFFICIAL: Lefèvre, hold him!

CHARACTER: What are you shouting for?

POLICE OFFICIAL: What do you mean? . . . [*calmly*] That's my wife.

CHARACTER: Here we are, shouting. Admittedly we're at the end of the corridor; but all the same. She never turned round once. Is she deaf?

POLICE OFFICIAL: [*irritated*] She's cooking. She's standing by the stove, do you hear? [*calmer*] What an expert you are at confusing the issue. Do you admit your guilt or not?

CHARACTER: Of course. Absent-mindedness is a vice. A natural vice in someone in a strange country.

POLICE OFFICIAL: What has absent-mindedness to do with it?

CHARACTER: There's a slope there. The crowd stretched right down to the boats. I noticed the stern of a boat with "Dugong" painted on it.

POLICE OFFICIAL: Fabre's boat. Fine. Go on. [*Both listen*]

CHARACTER: When I finished they all started asking questions. Everybody was thrilled. They guessed straight away where I came from. They got interested. They asked me "What's your profession?" – I couldn't answer. "How much do you earn?" – I answered that with a gesture. I pointed at them, at myself, at the sea . . .

POLICE OFFICIAL: [*interrupting*] What rubbish! What did you mean by that?

CHARACTER: The situation. Relationships. Their position around me, mine – among them, the position of each one of them among . . .

POLICE OFFICIAL: [*flourishes his pen*] So you're a preacher? [*prepares to cross out a line of his questionnaire*]

CHARACTER: Stop, what are you doing? You've got it down right. I am what I said I was. [*Walks round behind the Police Official's back*]

POLICE OFFICIAL: [*turning round*] Go away, please. That's your place, there.

CHARACTER: Well then. After that . . . [*both listen*]

POLICE OFFICIAL: [*irritably*] Well? What are you waiting for? After that . . . Keep to the point. [*A pause, then, quite calmly*] That's our friend.

CHARACTER: [*slowly and meaningly*] We don't have that sort of thing where I come from.

POLICE OFFICIAL: [*indignantly*] That's no concern of yours. Nothing to do with you. [*Both listen*] One minute. [*Slams the bureau shut, gets up*] Lefèvre, look after him. [*Exit. He can be heard walking away down the corridor.*]

[*Character and Lefèvre remain silent. Character reads a local newspaper. Smiles condescendingly.*]

LEFÈVRE: [*overcoming his embarrassment*] I've always wanted to know – what sort of language is . . . Sacred Slavonic?

CHARACTER: [*correcting him*] Church Slavonic.

LEFÈVRE: Yes. Church Slavonic. Is it like Latin? Is it your kind of Latin?

CHARACTER: It's the ancient form of our language. How much did you pay for that bicycle?

LEFÈVRE: That was given to me. I'm a fighter.

CHARACTER: I'm bored with waiting for that official. Where is he?

LEFÈVRE: He'll come. It's Saturday today, he's going to Leclusot to see his son.

CHARACTER: Delighted to hear it.

LEFÈVRE: No, don't laugh – I mean it. He won't keep you long, because he's in a hurry to get to the country. Well, I mean, you'll have to stay here, of course. No question about it. It's the law. [*Silence*] It's good to be in the country just now. I always send my family somewhere for the summer. With my savings. It's so stifling and dusty here. . . . Of course, there's the sea . . . but it's so far away! And so polluted. And the town. . . .

CHARACTER: Leave the fly alone. What harm has it done you?

LEFÈVRE: True. [*mechanically*] When I start talking about the country-side, my hands get irresistibly attracted to the window-panes. . . . I start squashing flies. . . . Look at this great fat green one. . . . Spreading disease. . . . Here he comes. What are you doing?

CHARACTER: I've got a blister. [*Removing his boot and tapping the toe on the edge of the chair to shake out the sand.*]

POLICE OFFICIAL: [*Enters, watch in hand*] What are you doing?

CHARACTER: It's full of sand from the shore. Where I was just now.

POLICE OFFICIAL: Well – I'm in a hurry. Go on telling me about it. [*Sits down*]

CHARACTER: They thought I was going to pass the hat round. Got their purses out. This was after lunch, and I was wearing clean clothes – I'd just come back from bathing.

POLICE OFFICIAL: So what? I don't understand.

CHARACTER: At that moment, I did not have any needs. Except one.

POLICE OFFICIAL: What need?

CHARACTER: The need to produce.

POLICE OFFICIAL: Well? Why have you stopped?

CHARACTER: [*does not understand.*]

POLICE OFFICIAL: To produce what?

CHARACTER: [*getting the point*] Oh, I see. That's not important. To produce – well, an effect, say. That's my speciality.

POLICE OFFICIAL: [*shrugs his shoulders and looks at Lefèvre who turns away, snorts into a checked handkerchief and goes over to the window*]

POLICE OFFICIAL: [*chewing his moustache, irritably*] Fine. Fine. So . . . Pardon me. That's not what we're interested in. We're interested in something else. We're . . .

CHARACTER: [*taking a deep breath, so that he can get everything out at once. Animatedly*] Look. I forgot that I was abroad. This is what we do at home. Everyone unburdens his soul in his work. How can I put it. . . . Look. You have got your telegraph, water, gas – and we have got work. It's laid on everywhere. Stations, machinery. People live as if it were a game. They produce – in passing, now here, now there – wherever the day finds them. When they are in an inflammable state – whenever they encounter a spark. . . . Good. Nobody pays them anything. That would be absurd. It's an absurdity which fixes one to a particular place. Your man, here, is a mere place in the space of humankind. A point. With us, a man is . . .

POLICE OFFICIAL: A man is . . .

CHARACTER: With us, he is a state. A state of humankind. A degree. A boiling-point.

POLICE OFFICIAL: Well, go on. Lefèvre, my holdall, please. And then call a cab. Go on. I know all this. That's not what we're interested in. We're interested . . .

CHARACTER: I know. It was in the evening. At the other end of the town. I liked the way the market was laid out. Before that, I'd been with my French publisher.

POLICE OFFICIAL: What are you laughing at?

CHARACTER: I had just remembered that ceremonious reception. Of course, we had never met before. Only written.

POLICE OFFICIAL: Go on.

CHARACTER: I declined the dinner. Didn't feel like eating. And how hard it was to convince him! But I managed. So we began to clear up. We cleared away the draperies and the carpets. There was no one else to do it. The concierge had left, and the servants too. While we were doing it I explained to him the system of suspended cultures and fractured . . .

POLICE OFFICIAL: [*rapidly*] I've read about it! You're marvellous at it! Yes. All right, you can put it down, Lefèvre. Down here. Where are you off to? No, wait. Don't bother. You can go. I'll call one myself. It's too early. – Well, go on. Listen. For clearing up, you might have got three francs; while if you'd read a paper on refracted cultures of barley, you could have made a round three hundred. A thousand, if you did it in winter. Honestly. I mean, it's frightfully interesting. But just now there isn't a soul in town. Everyone rushes off in the evening. Yes. And then you'd have no need [*pauses, then, in a soft, velvety voice*] to steal.

CHARACTER: When I got to the market on the way home, I suddenly felt hungry. It's a beautiful square. It's good that it has blank walls – windows would have spoiled everything. As it is – have you ever noticed? – you have the impression that the clouds are dizzy, they are afraid to look down. Have you ever noticed? They avoid it. And you only have to look, for everything to go dark before your eyes. The buckets and the market-women's kerchiefs start to fade. . . . Sorry, I'm off the point. Anyway, I felt hungry. I forgot that I was abroad. I picked out a melon – over to one side from the baker's stall. They were starting to light the lamps. Well, people started shouting. The rest you know yourself. Our country is a living bank – nothing could be simpler. My body and soul vouched that somewhere – never mind where – they had paid in what they could, that day. Otherwise they would have been grumbling. And I would not have felt hungry. I would have ended up in hospital.

POLICE OFFICIAL: [*excitedly*] Go on, go on. I'm listening. [*enthusiastically*] Do you see, Lefèvre – I've always admired your system. Only here we are all subject to the same laws. What do you say, Lefèvre?

LEFÈVRE: It would never catch on here.

POLICE OFFICIAL: [*absently*] Yes. [*Suddenly, to the Character*] Well, go on. It's like a stock exchange, you say?

CHARACTER: The important thing was that some deposits had been paid in. Where? – On this planet, under this sky. And so – under this same sky I could make a withdrawal. Need is your best accountant. We have developed a feeling for nature to a fantastic degree. We have a moral shivering fit if we find humanity's temperature lower than it becomes when we add our own to it. Every day you wake up burning, full of reserves of heat; and it's impossible not to give it out. So you get colder. And you go to get new reserves of heat. Anywhere. It's like a Bourse for heat exchange. You would call it a sense of duty. Without it, we'd suffocate. You call it the duty to work, social justice. That's a moral plaster on a painful spot: raw flesh. With us, these raw patches have regenerated. Look: [*shows him*] these nails have not turned into claws – or these into hooves. You were afraid that everyone would pounce on the good things of life. Instead of which – you know what. Here. [*Nods at the newspaper*]

POLICE OFFICIAL: Yes, yes. Well, time will tell.

CHARACTER: Some people like variety; they go from one workshop to another. Those are the people of yesterday – they are dying out. Getting rare. Other people are slaves of their own talents – they are the race of the future. Each new generation widens the gap. Today, they are different tribes. Tomorrow they will be different races. One day they will be different varieties of higher animals. Later still, different worlds. Have no fear. We know. We have guarantees. – I see you are in a hurry.

POLICE OFFICIAL: Yes. Lefèvre, the cab, please. [*Lefèvre goes out.*] Listen. Why did you leave a country like that? It must be the best place in the world. I can't understand anyone coming from your country to ours. I don't understand your countrymen who travel. . . .

CHARACTER: I do. Let me explain. I love my country like. . . . O, I love it madly, sometimes! Everyone does. How they love it! I mean, it's the future of the universe – you can feel the wind of the future blowing through it everywhere. Everyone is a genius, because everyone gives himself up to it, like flax, gives up the last fibre of himself to make its web. Could you find a mediocre cat? An untalented skylark? And in order to give, in order to be able to give, we take all that we can. It turns out that in a state of genius humanity restores the balance that life has lost. Your own life is not unsteady only because it has already fallen, it is lying there and has not yet risen up.

POLICE OFFICIAL: Yes – that makes it all the more incomprehensible to me. How could you go away from there – with all your . . . [*cannot find the right word*] – patriotism?

CHARACTER: My country. O, how I love it! And – what that means! Your lovers – look. Look here. That house and that fence. Come on, come and look.

POLICE OFFICIAL: [*grins*] Why? I know them. I don't need to look. *Dix parcelles*, and down below – *En vente. Courtois, V.L. 63807.* I could repeat it in my sleep.

CHARACTER: You see. As long as they are whole, they stand side by side. They have been standing a long time, and they will stand there for a long time to come.

POLICE OFFICIAL: Yes. They are not selling well.

CHARACTER: There you are. With you, love is a matter of disposition. I'm sorry, that's ambiguous – a matter of position, I meant. The

239

position of two among a multitude. The settling of a soul that was already immobile. With us, a man finds himself wherever he is carried by the power that ferments within him. Wherever the storm has tossed him. Sometimes it rushes into his arms, his legs, his breast. And sometimes – into his head. Then he will seek solitude. There are many things you do not know. We have seen men's brows burning with the love of woman. The storm tossed them up to Mars. That is how the love of our country sometimes carries us abroad.

POLICE OFFICIAL: Still, I don't understand your people. Look, N has arrived too.

CHARACTER: I know. He's at Dieppe.

POLICE OFFICIAL: No, he's here.

CHARACTER: What? Here?

POLICE OFFICIAL: Yes, give me that paper. I'll find it in a second. There you are. Look.

CHARACTER: Well, well! . . . Yes. . . . True. . . . The man who wrote this knew what he was talking about.

LEFÈVRE: I've been round the whole district.

POLICE OFFICIAL: O, yes! Of course, they're on strike today. Well, nothing to be done. I'll walk. And you'll have to stay inside a day or two. Nothing I can do about that.

CHARACTER: Here?

POLICE OFFICIAL: No, in gaol. You'll be taken there.

LEFÈVRE: I'll take you.

POLICE OFFICIAL: Well, I'm off. Goodbye. I'm sorry. It's not up to me.

CHARACTER: All the best.

[*Exit Police Official*]

LEFÈVRE: Come along, young man.

Translated by
Nicolas Pasternak-Slater

THE QUINTESSENCE
(To Ryurik Ivnev, poet and friend)

Historical note: The history of this word is as follows. To the four "basic elements" of water, earth, air and fire, the Italian Humanists added the new, fifth, element of Man. The expression "quinta essentia" (fifth essence) for a time became a synonym for the concept of "Man" as a basic alchemical element of the universe. Later it acquired a different meaning.

A Concern

1

Whenever I talk about mysticism, painting, or the theatre, I can speak with all the amiable lack of constraint that a liberal-minded reader brings to any discussion. But when the subject is literature, I recall some book and lose all capacity to reason. I need to be shaken and brought around by force as though from a faint, from a state of actual dreaming about that book. And only then, and very unwillingly, can I overcome my slight revulsion and join in a conversation on some other literary topic, where the subject is anything else but that book – the stage, let us say, or poets, movements, new writing, etc. But never of my own volition and unforced, never at any price will I abandon the world of my real concern and move to this other realm of amateur solicitude.

My embarrassment is understandable. A close relation of mine has been clumsily referred to in my presence. Instead of simply saying "book", they should have named my sister – my younger sister. My older one is Life.[1]

241

A Modern Perversion

2

Contemporary movements have imagined that art is like a fountain, whereas in fact it is a sponge. They have decided that art ought to spout and gush, whereas it should absorb and saturate itself. They consider it can be resolved into means of representation, whereas it is composed of organs of perception. It should always be one of the audience and have the clearest, truest, most perceptive view of all. But in our day it has seen make-up powder and the dressing room, and it is exhibited on stage. It is as if there were two forms of art in the world, and one of them had enough in reserve to indulge in a luxury of self-perversion tantamount to suicide. It is put on show, whereas it should be hiding up in the gallery, unrecognised, hardly aware that it cannot fail to give itself away, and that when it hides in a corner it is stricken with translucency and phosphorescence as though with some disease. And lo and behold, as it bites its nails and conceals itself, it sparkles and blinds us, X-rayed from behind by the Lord God.

The Book

3

The book is a cube-shaped chunk of blazing, smoking conscience – nothing more.

The mating call is a sign of nature's concern for the preservation of all feathered fowl. A book is like a capercaillie giving its mating call. The book hears nothing and no one, deafened and enraptured by its own music. Without it there could be no continuation of spiritual kind, and it would have been transferred elsewhere. Apes have never possessed the book.

The book was written. It grew, increased in intelligence, became worldly wise – and there it was, full-fledged and ready. It is not the book's fault that we see right through it. Such is the way of the spiritual universe. Not long ago men thought that the scenes in a book were just a series of dramatisations. This is a misconception; why should a book need them? People have forgotten that the only thing in our power is knowing how not to distort the voice of life that sounds within us.

Inability to discover and state the truth is a fault that no skill in lying can cover up. A book is a living being. It is in full possession of its memory and faculties. Its scenes and pictures are the things it has preserved from the past and recorded, and which it refuses to forget.

For it seems to me that the artist observes *through* colour, rather than looking *at* colour, the composer listens *through* harmony, rather than listening *to* harmony, not to mention the writer who – if he *is* a writer – is told by the word itself of the purpose for which it is granted to him.

The Noise of Eternity

4

Life has not just begun. Art had no beginning. It was forever present till the very moment when it ceased to be.

Art is endless. And such it is, both behind me and within me here at this moment, and its fresh and urgent ubiquity and eternity come blowing over me as from a suddenly opened assembly hall – as though I was immediately summoned to take some oath.

No genuine book has a first page. Like the sighing of a forest, it is born goodness knows where, and it grows and rolls along, arousing forbidden backwoods, and suddenly, at its darkest, thunderstruck and panic moment, it reaches its goal and speaks out all at once from every treetop.

The Law of the Miraculous

5

Wherein lies the miracle? It rests in the fact that once there lived on earth a seventeen-year-old girl called Mary Stuart, and one October, with Puritans whooping outside her window, she wrote a poem in French that ended with the words:

> Car mon pis et mon mieux
> Sont les plus déserts lieux.

It rests secondly in the fact that once in his youth, with October revelling and raging outside his window, the English poet Algernon Charles Swinburne completed *Chastelard*,[2] in which the quiet plaint of Mary's five stanzas was conceived as the fearful roar of five tragic acts.

It rests thirdly and finally in the fact that once, about five years ago, when the translator glanced through his window he did not know which was more surprising – the fact that the Elabuga blizzard knew Scots and was still perturbed as of yore for that seventeen-year-old girl, or that the girl and the English poet who sorrowed for her were able to tell him so well and sincerely, in Russian, what still disturbed them both as before and had never ceased to haunt them.

"What can this mean?" the translator asked himself. What is going on there? Why is it so quiet there today (yet at the same time so snow-blown)? It might seem that because we send our messages out there they should be shedding blood. Meanwhile, in fact, they smile.

This is the miracle: In the unity and identity of the lives of these three people, and of many others (eyewitnesses and spectators of three epochs, characters, biographies, readers) – in the real-life October of some year unknown that howls itself hoarse and goes blind out there, outside the window, below the hill, in . . . in art.

That is what it is.

Leave Me Be

6

There are misunderstandings. They have to be avoided. This leaves room for boredom. They claim it is the writer, the poet . . .

Aesthetics does not exist. It seems to me that aesthetics does not exist, as a punishment for its lying, its pardoning, conniving, and condescension – for knowing nothing about man, yet bandying gossip about specialities. Portraitist, landscape artist, genre painter, still-life specialist? Symbolist, Acmeist, Futurist? What murderous jargon!

It is quite clear that this is science, classifying air balloons by the position and distribution of the holes in them that prevent their flying.

Definitions

7

Poetry and prose are two polarities, indivisible one from another.

Through its inborn hearing, poetry seeks out the melody of nature amid the noise of the lexicon, and picking it up like some motif, it proceeds to improvise on that theme. By its feeling, through its spirituality, prose seeks and finds man in the category of speech. And when man is found lacking in an age, then it recreates him from memory and sets him there and pretends for the good of mankind to have found him in the present. Nature and man – they are the central axis. They are the fountain-springs and the final goals.

As it improvises, poetry strikes up against nature. The vital world of reality – this is imagination's sole scheme, successful once and forever more. It continues at every moment, never failing. It is still always effective, profound and endlessly absorbing. It serves much more as the poet's example than as a subject or a model.

Pure Poetry

8

It is madness to trust in common sense. It is madness to doubt it. Madness to look ahead. Madness to live without looking. But to roll up one's eyes occasionally and with rapidly rising blood heat hear the reflected fresco of some unearthly, transient, yet forever vernal thunderstorm begin to spread and roar through the consciousness stroke by stroke, like convulsions of lightning on dusty ceilings and plaster – this is pure. . . . This, at any rate, is purest madness!

It is natural to strive for purity.

Thus we come close to the pure essence of poetry. And it disturbs us like the sinister turning of ten windmills by the edge of some bare field in a black and hungry year.

Gaudeamus. Rhythm.
That Without Which It Is Unthinkable.

9

Eternal Memory is a lugubrious affair. Eternal rest is frightful. The eternal Jew is an equally striking phantom. But perhaps they are not dangerous. Nobody has ever seen them.

Plainly visible and truly eternal, though, is the Eternal Student whom everyone knows by the name of Rhythm and who is alive in positively all poets by the grace of God.

He is grey-haired and unhappy, and in his comical and august excitement he has lost count of eternities and faculties. But as in the days of the stagecoach, he even bows the knee before his beloved, flings his hat under the piano and bares his heart to her. For her it beats and will never cease to beat. Glory to her! There will be centuries to come, and faculties, and still it will not cease to beat. Glory to the heart!

A Further Concern[3]

10

"Vers libre" is the spittle which you notice only when it is *rabid*. Only such spittle can infect me. Then for a short time I fall sick with hydrophobia. But after being cured, a healthy phobia of water compels me to shun vers libre, – altogether this time. Only keep clear of the spittle! One must look after one's health. How much longer has the heart to beat! How many centuries lie ahead! How many faculties! Keep away from waters and from essences. Cleave closer to the *fifth* of them!

I shall finish as I started: with concern.

NOTES

SAFE CONDUCT

1 Author Lev Tolstoy's wife (1844–1919).
2 I.e. Count Lev Nikolayevich (Tolstoy), the Russian author (1828–1910).
3 I.e. by Leonid Osipovich Pasternak (1862–1945), the celebrated artist and illustrator.
4 The well-known realist and genre artist Ilya Efimovich Repin (1844–1930).
5 Artist friend of the Pasternaks (1831–94).
6 The Acmeist poet Nikolai Stepanovich Gumilyov (1886–1921) composed a poem with this title, in which it is suggested that through evolution man is developing a further, sixth, sense which is only vaguely adumbrated by his present inarticulate response to beauty.
7 I.e. the family of composer Aleksandr Nikolayevich Scriabin (1872–1915).
8 Scriabin's *Poème de l'Extase* for orchestra.
9 The Russian dish *tyurya* is made of bread pulped in kvass (a type of Russian beer), milk or water.
10 Reinhold Moritsevich Glière (1875–1956).
11 Yulian Pavlovich Anisimov (1889–1940), translator, poet and painter, host and founder of the "Serdarda" group.
12 One of Rilke's early verse collections.
13 The name of a square and of the surrounding area in Moscow.
14 Andrei Bely was the *nom de plume* of the celebrated Symbolist poet and prose writer Boris Nikolayevich Bugayev (1880–1934).
15 The Symbolist poet Aleksandr Aleksandrovich Blok (1880–1921).
16 A well-known Symbolist-orientated publishing house.
17 Hermann Cohen (1842–1918), professor at Marburg University in Germany and doyen of the Marburg Neo-Kantian school of philosophy.
18 Paul Natorp (1854–1924), German Neo-Kantian philosopher and professor at Marburg.
19 Prince Trubetskoi (1862–1905) was a Russian idealist philosopher and had been professor at Moscow University from 1900 to 1905.
20 I.e. Moscow University.
21 Hero of Tolstoy's novel *Resurrection* (and also a character in two of his earlier works, *A Landowner's Morning* and *Childhood, Boyhood, Youth*).
22 Pasternak's university friend Konstantin Grigoryevich Loks.
23 The title of a story by Gogol.
24 Mikhail Vasilyevich Lomonosov (1711–65), the Russian scientist, scholar and writer. After studying in Moscow, he was sent to Marburg, where from 1736 to 1741 he studied philosophy, physics and chemistry under Christian Wolff.
25 German dramatist and poet (1494–1576).
26 The German words mean literally "poverty" and "care".

27 Mitrofan Petrovich Gorbunkov, with whom Pasternak for many years afterwards maintained a sporadic friendship.

28 Genrikh Ernestovich Lanz (1886–1945), philosopher in Moscow and after the Revolution in the USA (where he was known and published as Henry Lanz).

29 Nicolai Hartmann (1882–1950), German philosopher, lecturer and eventually professor at Marburg University.

30 A major work by philosopher Immanuel Kant.

31 The two elder daughters of the rich Moscow tea merchant David Vysotsky. It was with the older of the two, Ida, that Pasternak was in love, later also dedicating some verse to her.

32 A variant of the Russian children's game *palochka-vyruchalochka*, which is a form of hide-and-seek. When the searcher discovers someone, the two of them must race to grasp the "tig-stick" which has been left in a prearranged place; whoever loses this race becomes the next person to search for the other players.

33 Tolstoy is here referred to as author of "The Kreutzer Sonata", in which the hero kills his wife in jealousy and rage against her as a sex object; all sex, he maintains, is bad, and in the interests of morality self-control should be exercised even in marriage, even though it led to extinction of the human race. Frank Wedekind (1864–1918), the German playwright, is referred to as author of the play *Frühlingserwachen* (*Spring Awakening*), which deals with young people whose lives are blighted by prevailing repressive attitudes to sex and pleads for greater naturalness and freedom.

34 Pasternak contrasts the two Russian verbs *lgat'* and *vrat'*. The former means plainly to tell lies; the latter, while having this meaning, also implies to "invent stories", "spin yarns", "talk nonsense".

35 Joachim Nettelbeck (1738–1824), the Prussian patriot who in 1807 helped defend Kolberg against the French.

36 The various bolshevik Commissariats were moved to Moscow in 1918 with the transfer of the capital from Petrograd.

37 Italian for warehouse.

38 Vera Fyodorovna Kommissarzhevskaya (1864–1910), celebrated Russian actress and director of her own theatre company.

39 I.e. the year of social and political revolution in Russia.

40 At Khodynka Field, just outside Moscow, in 1896 a celebration in connection with Nicholas II's coronation got out of hand; when an enthusiastic crowd stampeded, the injured and dead numbered several thousand.

41 One of the worst outbreaks of anti-Jewish violence under Nicholas II in 1903.

42 January 22nd of 1905, when a large but peaceful demonstration of workers was fired on by police in the square before the Winter Palace in St Petersburg; the massacre caused a burst of indignation throughout the country and helped fuel the revolutionary movement.

43 I.e. named after Emperor Alexander I, who reigned at the time of the victory over Napoleon.

44 Valentin Aleksandrovich Serov (1865–1911), artist, colleague and close friend of Leonid Pasternak.

45 The princely family of Yusupov were well known as patrons of the arts.

46 N. I. Kutepov, designer of a luxurious four-volume edition with pictures by major Russian artists on the theme of the imperial hunt; the volumes appeared over the period 1896–1911.

47 Artist Nikolai Alekseyevich Kasatkin (1859–1930). The incident alluded to was the arrest and imprisonment of Kasatkin's son for sedition in 1905.

48 Vladimir Vladimirovich Mayakovsky (1893–1930), the most outstanding member of the Russian Futurist artistic movement. His suicide in 1930 as a result of personal, political and artistic disappointments prompted Pasternak to write the third part of *Safe Conduct* as a form of obituary memoir.

49 *Sadok sudei*, a literary almanac produced in 1910 as one of the first manifestations of Russian Futurism.

50 Pasternak's début was in 1913 under the imprint of the Symbolist-orientated "Lirika" group; in early 1914, however, he followed Sergei Bobrov in a break-away venture which had an innovatory and moderately Futurist tendency; entitled "Tsentrifuga", it was intended as a rival to the more extreme Cubo-Futurist avantgarde.

51 Vadim Gabrielevich Shershenevich (1893–1942), a posturing, second-rate talent among the Cubo-Futurists.

52 Konstantin Aristarkhovich Bolshakov (1895–1940), Futurist poet whose work was admired by Pasternak.

53 Sergei Pavlovich Bobrov (1889–1971), Russian poet, literary critic and entrepreneur, founder of "Tsentrifuga".

54 A regular feature of Mayakovsky's Futurist dress, designed partly to outrage conventional bourgeois taste.

55 A Russian folktale in verse by Pushkin, which also served as the basis of an opera by Rimsky-Korsakov.

56 Vladislav Felitsianovich Khodasevich (1886–1939), poet.

57 Mayakovsky's revolutionary work celebrating the aspirations of Russia's 150 million population.

58 Mayakovsky's last major poetic work was entitled *At the Top of My Voice*; it recaptured some of the spirit of his earlier works, much admired by Pasternak and lost during Mayakovsky's more "committed", political years.

59 An allusion to a phrase in *At the Top of My Voice*.

60 Nikolai Nikolayevich Aseyev (1889–1963), Futurist poet and member of "Tsentrifuga", who also shared Pasternak's enthusiasm for Mayakovsky.

61 The Sinyakov sisters. One of them, Kseniya (Oksana), married Aseyev; Pasternak had a brief affair in the mid-1910s with Nadezhda, another of the sisters.

62 Viktor (pseudonym Velemir) Vladimirovich Khlebnikov (1885–1922), one of the most talented and original members of the Cubo-Futurist movement.

63 Jurgis Baltrušajtis (1873–1945), Lithuanian born poet, most of whose output was in Russian; he was an important member of the Russian Symbolist movement; after the Revolution he was Lithuanian diplomatic emissary to Moscow.

64 Vyacheslav Ivanovich Ivanov (1866–1949), prominent Symbolist poet and philosopher.

65 The traditional Russian peasant offering to a guest on arrival, a token of hospitality.

66 Zinaida Mikhailovna Mamonova was the eldest of the Sinyakov sisters.

67 Isai Aleksandrovich Dobrovein (1891–1953), pianist and composer friend of Pasternak, whom he met through Glière and the young people of the Conservatoire; he later emigrated and had a distinguished conducting career; in the West his name was spelt Issay Dobrowen.

68 Igor Vasilyevich Lotarev (1887–1941), a poet of the so-called Ego-Futurist movement, wrote under the name of Igor Severyanin.

69 Mikhail Yuryevich Lermontov (1814–41), Russian Romantic poet of Byronic mould.

70 Sergei Aleksandrovich Esenin (1895–1925), peasant poet famed for his evocations of rural scenes; his later verse records a gradual disenchantment with life in bolshevik Russia and a disintegration of personality; his death was by suicide.

71 Ilya Lvovich Selvinsky (1899–1968), poet who achieved prominence during the 1920s as leader of the so-called Constructivists.

72 Marina Ivanovna Tsvetaeva (1892–1941), poetess whom Pasternak regarded as one of the greatest of the age; after her emigration to Western Europe in 1922, Pasternak and she corresponded; she returned to Russia in 1939, but committed suicide two years later.

73 Nikolai Semyonovich Tikhonov (1896–1979), poet and friend of Pasternak's during the 1920s, when he was noted especially for his romantic balladic verse; subsequently a prominent figure in the Soviet literary establishment.

74 Lili Yuryevna Brik (1891–1978), wife of Formalist critic Osip Brik, for many years beloved and close friend of Mayakovsky, who spent a long period living "à trois" in their home.

75 A poem and two novels, by Pushkin, Dostoevsky and Andrei Bely respectively, all three in various ways contributing to the urban "myth" of St Petersburg.

76 Anna Andreyevna Gorenko, or Akhmatova (1889–1966), poetess, one-time wife of Gumilyov, and associated with the Acmeist poetic movement of Petersburg.

77 Sergei Listopad, the natural son of the philosopher and literary critic Lev Shestov (*nom de plume* of Lev Isaakovich Shvartsman, 1866–1938).

78 Maksim Gorky, *nom de plume* of Aleksei Maksimovich Peshkov (1868–1936), the prominent left-wing publicist and author.

79 The title of a short novel by Pushkin which is set during the peasant uprising led by the Cossack Emelyan Ivanovich Pugachev (1742?–75).

80 A volume of verse by Pasternak, published in 1917; a revised version appeared again in 1929.

81 The volume of verse written mainly in 1917 which first brought Pasternak celebrity; it was published in 1922.

82 In September 1917 General Kornilov marched on Petrograd in an unsuccessful attempt to take power from the insecure Provisional Government.

83 Konstantin Abramovich Lipskerov (1889–1954), poet and translator.

84 I.e. Vladimir Goltsshmit. Advertised as the "Futurist of life", he was not a poet but combined the functions of performing "strong man" and of "bouncer" at the Futurist "Poets' Café" in winter 1917–18.

85 "Amari", pen name of the amateur poet and patron Mikhail Osipovich Tseitlin; the period of his resplendent artistic gatherings was shortlived under the bolsheviks and he eventually emigrated.

86 Konstantin Dmitrievich Balmont (1867–1943), distinguished poet and elder Symbolist.

87 Ilya Grigoryevich Ehrenburg (1891–1967), Russian Jewish writer and journalist, also wrote a certain amount of verse.

88 Vera Mikhailovna Inber (1890–1972), poetess.

89 Pavel Grigoryevich Antokolsky (1896–1978), poet.

90 Vasilii Vasilyevich Kamensky (1884–1961), Futurist poet.

91 David Davidovich Burlyuk (1882–1967), one of three brothers, and himself an artist and poet and energetic organiser of Futurist activities.

92 Tsvetaeva's *Versty*, a volume of verse forming a sort of poetic diary for 1916 when it was written; the book was published in 1922.

93 Meaning "The Contemporary", an important literary journal in the nineteenth century, founded in 1836 by Pushkin, the year before his death. This and the plans for a peasant journal refer to Pushkin's last year; the twenty years' work exhibition and attempts to obtain a foreign travel visa refer to Mayakovsky. Both Mayakovsky and Pushkin (1799–1837) died violently (Pushkin in a duel) at the height of their creative careers.

94 An allusion to a volume of poems published by Aleksandr Blok in 1916. The foregoing paragraph also contains reminiscences of Blok's Petersburg and urban mystique some of which, according to Pasternak, Mayakovsky inherited.

95 Olga Grigoryevna Petrovskaya, widow of Vladimir Aleksandrovich Sillov, the Proletkult literary theorist who was arrested and executed shortly before Mayakovsky's suicide.

96 Yakov Zakharovich Chernyak (1898–1955), critic, editor and scholar.

97 Nikolai Mikhailovich Romadin (b.1903), artist and fellow art-student of Pasternak's first wife.

98 Pasternak's first wife, Evgeniya Vladimirovna (née Lurye, 1899–1965).

99 An episode in Mayakovsky's poem "Cloud in Trousers"; the passage concerned is quoted by Mayakovsky's sister later in this section of "Safe Conduct".

100 Semyon Isaakovich Kirsanov (1906–72), poet and translator.

101 Lev Aleksandrovich Grinkrug (b.1889), art critic and close friend of Mayakovsky.

102 Lili Brik and her husband were visiting London at the time of Mayakovsky's suicide.

103 Mayakovsky's play *The Bath-house* had been performed in March and April of 1930; it was damned by the critics, and this may have been one of the several factors prompting his suicide.

SUBOCTAVE STORY

1 The town described here is evidently a fictional one rather than the actual German town of Ansbach in Franconia. Probably several details of Pasternak's Ansbach are based on his impression and memories of Marburg (see Part II of "Safe Conduct"), including the names of the Schützenpfuhl Hotel and the Elisabethkirche.

ZHENYA LUVERS' CHILDHOOD

1 The Russian letters "Yu", "ya" and "yat'" (pronounced "e").

2 The letter has no precise equivalent in French or in English; it roughly corresponds to the sound of "i" in the word "pill".

3 This and the quotations following are taken from Lermontov's poem "The Demon". This particular line is notorious for the author's zoological error, since a lioness has no mane.

4 A popular collection of tales (*Skazki Kota-Murlyki*) by Nikolai Petrovich Vagner (1829–1907).

5 Hero of Pushkin's famous novel in verse *Eugene Onegin*.

6 Nikolai Mikhailovich Karamzin (1766–1826), celebrated Russian author and historian.

LETTERS FROM TULA

1 Vasilii Osipovich Klyuchevsky (1841–1911), celebrated historian and author of a standard history of Russia.
2 Presumably *Ivan* Bolotnikov (?–1608), leader of a peasant revolt during the Time of Troubles, a period of upheaval and dynastic uncertainty in Russia in the late sixteenth and early seventeenth centuries.
3 The name of the railway station where Tolstoy died.
4 Vladislav Aleksandrovich Ozerov (1769–1816) and Aleksandr Petrovich Sumarokov (1718–77), well-known Russian dramatists.

WITHOUT LOVE

1 A Tatar word with the approximate meaning: "Let's go!"
2 Ekaterina Konstantinovna Breshko-Breshkovskaya (1844–1934), a founder member of the Socialist Revolutionary Party, nicknamed "Grandmother of the Russian Revolution". After the Bolshevik uprising of October 1917, she emigrated to Prague.

DRAMATIC FRAGMENTS

1 Philippe Lebas (or Le Bas) (1765–94), friend and ally of Robespierre; arrested along with him, he committed suicide in the Hôtel de Ville.
2 Louis Antoine Léon Saint-Just (1767–94), theoretician and promoter of the revolutionary government and apologist for the Terror. He was brought to his death on 9th thermidor (27th July) 1794 along with Robespierre.
3 I.e. 27–28th July.
4 François Hanriot (1761–94), leader of the sans-culottes during the Terror, executed along with Robespierre.
5 Georges Couthon (1755–94), member of the Convention and one of the revolutionary "triumvirate" together with Saint-Just and Robespierre; he was arrested and guillotined on 10th thermidor.
6 Augustin de Robespierre (1763–94), younger brother of the more notorious Maximilien, whom he followed to the scaffold.
7 Maximilien de Robespierre (1758–94), chief inspirer of the revolutionary Terror and for a time virtual dictator until overthrown by the Convention. After a failed suicide attempt, he was guillotined on 10th thermidor.

THE QUINTESSENCE

1 Pasternak here alludes to his volume of poetry *My Sister Life*, written mainly in 1917 and published in 1922, and which best incorporates all the ideas about the aim of creativity set out in *The Quintessence*.

2 In his late twenties Pasternak translated this part of Swinburne's dramatic trilogy; "the translator" referred to in the next paragraph is himself, and the work was carried out partly in the Elabuga region where Pasternak spent part of the First World War. The translation never actually appeared, and it seems to have been lost in one of Moscow's publishing houses. Later on Pasternak returned to the theme of Mary Queen of Scots, and in 1957 translated Schiller's *Maria Stuart*; his version of Polish dramatist Juliusz Slowacki's play of the same title was published in Russian in 1960.

3 Before he properly discovered his own poetic voice in *My Sister Life*, Pasternak had experimented with long impressionistic poetic fantasies in "vers libre". The abandonment of this genre and metre in 1917 was one of the reasons for eliminating this section of "The Quintessence" in the version which he finally published in 1922. See below note on Sources, p. 257.

SOURCES

"Safe Conduct" (Okhrannaya gramota) was begun in the late 1920s and first published in separate parts – Part I in the journal *Zvezda* (*The Star*), No. 8, 1929, Part II in *Krasnaya nov* (*Red Virgin Soil*), No. 4, 1931, and Part III in the same journal, Nos. 5–6, 1931. The work appeared in 1931 also as a separate book with certain textual alterations. The version translated in this volume uses this latter version and also restores certain passages excised by the censorship.

"The Apelles Mark" (Apellesova cherta) was written in 1915 and appeared first in *Vremennik "Znameni truda"* (*The "Banner of Labour" Chronicle*) in 1918. It was later republished by Pasternak under an Italian title, "Il Tratto di Apelle".

"Suboctave Story" (Istoriya odnoi kontroktavy) was written in the winter of 1916–17. The manuscript was never quite completed, and certain gaps are footnoted in the translated text. A complete Russian scholarly edition of the extant text appeared in *Slavica Hierosolymitana*, No. 1, 1977, and the present translation is based on this.

"Zhenya Luvers' Childhood" (Detstvo Lyuvers) was written in 1918, and its original publication was in the almanac *Nashi dni* (*The Present Day*), No. 1, 1922. Some manuscript extracts which were omitted from the published text have been printed in the appendix of Lazar Fleishman, *Stat'i o Pasternake*, K-Presse, Bremen, 1977; they have not been incorporated in the present translation.

"Letters from Tula" (Pis'ma iz Tuly), written in 1918, was first printed in the almanac *Shipovnik* (*The Wild Rose*), 1922.

"Without Love" (Bezlyub'e), written in 1918, was published the same year, on November 20th, in a shortlived Socialist Revolutionary paper entitled *Volya truda* (*Liberty of Labour*).

The "Dramatic Fragments" in verse were composed in 1917 and published in the Socialist Revolutionary *Znamya truda* (*Banner of Labour*) in the issues for 1st May and 16th June; the dramatic prose "Dialogue" appeared in the same paper on 17th May. None of these three items was republished by Pasternak during his lifetime.

"The Quintessence" printed here is a translation of Pasternak's original manuscript text, which was first published in L. Fleishman, "Neizvestnyi avtograf B. Pasternaka", *Materialy XXVI nauchnoi studencheskoi konferentsii. Literaturovedenie. Lingvistika*, Tartu 1971. What Pasternak himself published in the almanac *Sovremennik* (*The Contemporary*), No. 1, 1922, was a revised and shortened version: the original title "The Quintessence" was changed to "Some Propositions"; the dedication and historical note were cut out, as also were the titles for each section and the final two sections, 9 and 10; there were also one or two very minor textual amendments.

With the exception of "Suboctave Story" and the "Dramatic Fragments", the items in this book have all been anthologised in two posthumous Russian collections of Pasternak's prose: *Sochineniya*, vol. II, University of Michigan Press, Ann Arbor, 1961, and *Vozdushnye puti*, Moscow, 1982. A certain number of items have appeared in other versions in earlier translations of Pasternak's prose work; "Suboctave Story" and the "Dramatic Fragments" have not previously been included in any translated anthology.